The Ascension Lightworker Guide

A Handbook for Weary Souls

Vidya Frazier

First Edition Design Publishing
Sarasota, Florida USA

The Ascension Lightworker Guide
A Handbook for Weary Souls

Copyright ©2020 Vidya Frazier

ISBN 978-1506-909-36-3 PBK
ISBN 978-1506-909-27-1 EBK

LCCN 2020909309

June 2020

Published and Distributed by
First Edition Design Publishing, Inc.
P.O. Box 17646, Sarasota, FL 34276-3217
www.firsteditiondesignpublishing.com

Table of Contents

Recognizing the Dimension You're In

Remembering Yourself as a Soul

PREFACE

My hope in writing this book is to assist the reader through the intense and complex times currently playing out in which unprecedented change, loss and uncertainty are happening on both the global stage and in everyone's personal lives. I wish to offer not only assistance in meeting the challenges during these times, but also a great deal of hope and optimism.

As in my previous books, I use the spiritual paradigm known as *Ascension* to explain the tumultuous events occurring, believing its explanation is not only a very hopeful one, it's also one that makes sense of all that is happening. The paradigm is based on prophesies over the centuries in countless traditions across the world that have described how, during these times now, humanity would be experiencing a period of great chaos and darkness. They've predicted great hardship for many and foretold that global structures based in greed, corruption and domination would finally be collapsing.

Fortunately, the prophesies have further described how these times would eventually lead to a "Golden Age" that would last for at least a thousand years. As improbable as this may seem, the prophesies are based on ancient wisdom within many different cultures around the world, describing how all that is playing out now in the world – although new and unique in certain ways – is part of a long cycle that has occurred over and over again in a similar way throughout the history of the planet.

Reflecting these prophesies, the Ascension paradigm indicates that, despite the chaos and disruption currently happening worldwide, a process of ascension – a profound leap of consciousness into what's been called the *Fifth Dimension* – is occurring within humanity. And that, ironically, it is the very chaos that is creating the opportunity for humanity to make this shift into a more highly-evolved consciousness.

Using my many years' experience as a transpersonal therapist and energy healer, and also my long-time experience on a spiritual path, I offer in this book numerous keys and tools for navigating this tumultuous, yet exciting, shift in as peaceful, empowered and harmonious way as possible.

It's important to note, however, that this is not just another new age book offering healing help or advice on how to become more "spiritual". It's written specifically for these times we're living in, indicating that the healing and spiritual awakening process we're experiencing now is unique, in that it is extremely rapid in order to create the profound transformation that is being demanded of us due to the Earth's immanent shift into the Fifth Dimension. Thus, some of the old ideas and techniques found in both traditional and new age teachings are no longer effective or relevant.

Although I have written the book to be helpful to *anyone* who is needing this assistance, I have especially addressed it to those I call "Ascension Lightworkers" – those who feel strongly called to assist others on an energetic and spiritual level through these inordinately stressful times.

If you are one of these people, you are likely finding that your experience during these days of great change and disruption are perhaps even more challenging and confusing than that of people you know who do not feel the same kind of call. It's helpful to understand that you are here as a pioneer to help forge the path for others following behind you through the uncharted territory we're now encountering. For this reason, you may well require greater courage, fortitude and wisdom than others to walk this path.

To give the book some context, in my first chapter I have attempted to present information about current events occurring at the time of writing the book (toward the middle of 2020) in a full and yet succinct way. This has been challenging, in that much of the information pertains to events happening behind the scenes; and it is therefore likely to be unknown to readers who only listen to mainstream news sources, and it is also probably somewhat frightening. Yet I believe it is necessary for this information to be known, so that a fuller, more informed awareness can happen for the reader.

This book has also been difficult to finish, due to the fact that so much in the world at this point is changing so quickly. From day to day, monumental shifts seem to be occurring and new information is being revealed. But, at some point, I just finally had to declare the book completed, despite the likelihood that a week after it is published, certain things I've stated in my first chapter may either be outdated or even incorrect. I am hopeful you will be understanding and gracious about these possible errors you may find.

The rest of the book will likely not be outdated for a long time, as humanity will probably be making the emotional, mental and spiritual shift into a higher dimension of consciousness for some time yet. And during these tumultuous "transitional times" until then, many will be needing guidance, support and hope. The major part of this book therefore addresses the many challenges people are facing as they are being compelled to heal and awaken on many levels more rapidly than ever before.

My conviction is that, within the next decade or so, humanity *will* be making the great leap of consciousness that numerous prophesies throughout the ages have predicted. And this gives me a joy that only tears can express.

Vidya Frazier, May, 2020

Introduction

Chapter 1

World on the Edge

There's no doubt about it – life is getting progressively strange these days. It's next to impossible to keep up with all the rapid change occurring both in the world and in people's lives. Any sense of a reliable, predictable future is essentially gone, leaving us wondering where we all may be headed.

This is particularly notable on the world stage, especially since the beginning of 2020 with the outbreak of the Covid 19 virus, as we began experiencing an escalation of a breakdown that had already been occurring in many political, social, and health structures across the world – along with a global financial collapse on a scale never before seen.

Indeed, in all of known history, the world has never experienced this kind of tumultuous chaos affecting humanity across the entire planet. We are living through times that feel shaky at best, and catastrophic at worst. Certainly, no matter what occurs, there will be no going back to "normal". It is unknown as to what continued disasters and disruptions may still be in store for us as time goes on, but they seem likely to happen.

Are We in the "End Times"?

In fact, even before the events of early 2020, in many ways, humanity was already coming to the brink of disaster worldwide. We saw multiple conflicts spanning the globe, polluted rain forests, rising unemployment, peak oil, global food shortages, severe climate changes, and ongoing escalation of division between races, genders, and political parties. We also saw more and more clearly the huge inequities in wealth and power across the world. At the point of this writing in May, 2020, all of these issues have simply been magnified.

On the personal level, many of us seem to be living through a microcosm of what is occurring in the world at this time: Change, loss and uncertainty are key experiences for many. There is no returning to "normal" in our personal lives, either. Relationships are shifting, financial concerns are increasing, careers hang in the balance, health issues have escalated, and the future is unknown. In addition, many are experiencing deep, unsettling journeys into an inner world of turmoil, as unresolved core issues and past woundings arise amidst all the outer concerns.

It begs the question: Are we now in the "End Times"? Is humanity finally on a trajectory leading toward total extinction?

Prophesies and Predictions for a Golden Age

According to a great variety of spiritual texts, and also to the words of numerous prophets, sages, and indigenous elders in the world, this is not the case. We are *not* headed toward extinction. In fact, their prophesies have told us over and over that, in the not-too-distant future now, we will actually be entering into a long period of peace that could be called a "Golden Age".

However, the prophesies have further explained that, before that will occur, we will be passing through times of unprecedented chaos, confusion and darkness in the world. There will be a great dismantling of global structures that have been operating in greed, corruption and domination; and that as individuals, we will also be experiencing a dismantling of our personal structures of belief, our sense of identity, and our entire understanding of reality.

In the prophesies, these times have sometimes been referred to as the *Transitional Times* or the *In-Between Times* – times which will precede a quantum leap of consciousness for all of humanity and will eventually lead to a Golden Age.

There have been similar predictions from an entirely different source, that of certain developmental biologists. According to this biological perspective, humanity can be seen as a species that has reached a state of crisis in which extinction is immanent, and that it will probably follow the pattern other species on Earth have followed when similarly threatened: the experience of a sudden and profound leap in evolution. It is explained that crisis or extreme pressure tends to naturally spawn a higher order of life. For this reason, certain biologists are predicting that humanity is about to do just this.

Events Occurring Behind the Scenes

It's understandable if you doubt that a Golden Age or a leap in consciousness could possibly come about from the mess we find happening on the planet now. It may seem an impossible utopian dream, a complete fantasy. And yet, it can begin to make sense if you look at all that is happening through a different lens, one that is informed by a knowledge of what is taking place beyond what most people are aware of. Among other things, it involves being aware of world events that are generally not covered in the mainstream news – or are distorted by these news sources.

It's important also to put aside any ideas you may have about "conspiracy theories" – and realize that many of the claims about conspiracies involving a small elite group of people controlling the world are actually based on facts; they are not theories. Understanding this, an ever-expanding group of "truthers" around the world has evolved, eagerly ingesting the many forms of "disclosure" that are appearing on the internet.

Numbering now in the millions, the truthers have gleaned information from documents, records and emails that have now been leaked to the public. The information has come also from alternative journalists featuring interviews with numerous whistle-blowers and insiders from within secret space programs, intelligence agencies, military forces, multi-national tech corporations, the entertainment industry, and from concerned members within the elite families, themselves.

If you're wondering why almost none of this information about actual conspiracies has ever been reported by the mainstream news stations or papers, it's important to understand that 90% of these news outlets are owned by only six mega-corporations – all of them run by a very small group of powerful people who have essentially been involved in controlling both the events in the world and the narrative about them for a number of decades.

With just a little research online and in libraries (starting with the sources I've listed at the end of this chapter), you can discover that these people, known as the *Cabal,* the *Global Elite,* the *Deep State* or the *Illuminati*, have managed over time to infiltrate pretty much every political, financial, social, religious and health structure in the world. They have started wars, and then financed both sides. They were responsible for 9/11 and Fukushima. They have exercised mind control on various parts of the population, arranged numerous assassinations, and committed egregious crimes, especially to children. They have had thriving businesses of human and drug trafficking.

Living in a Controlled and Toxic World

Indeed, it becomes clear in researching this information about actual conspiracies that just about everything we believe to be true in our modern culture has been shaped and controlled by the Cabal. It started with what we learned in school. Textbooks written with the distorted and inaccurate history the Cabal has wished us to learn and curriculums based on these books shaped our minds from a very early age.

The entertainment available to us through TV, movies, music and video games has also greatly manipulated us, telling us a story over and over again of the violence, cruelty, weakness and corruption of humanity. As has become very clear in recent years, Hollywood has been ruled by some of the most inhumane forces on the planet, clearly managing to manipulate, blackmail and mind-control many people in the entertainment industry, as well as an unsuspecting worldwide audience. They have also, in devious ways, inserted dark illuminati images and subliminal messages into movies and music videos – even those for children – that most people are totally ignorant about.

The appalling dramas and messages we've been subjected to in these forms of entertainment have been especially able to penetrate deeply into our minds, due to the Cabal's contribution to religious dogma through the centuries that many of us learned in religious institutions, such as describing a wrathful God, a place called "hell" and asserting that humans are "born in sin"; and further, that suffering is the way through which we can redeem ourselves.

In all of these ways, including what we are bombarded with through advertising – most of which is also controlled by the Cabal – we have unconsciously taken in ideas that hinder all possibility of sovereign thought; our beliefs and choices we make are often not really our own. This has been further exacerbated lately by the extreme censorship that has been escalating on the internet in the last year.

As if all of this were not enough, you can also easily find other credible research online about how we have been intentionally subjected to toxic chemicals in our food, our water, our air, our soil. All these chemicals have been proven by scientists to undermine intelligence and to make people sick and overweight. Then there is evidence that the electromagnetic fields from cell towers have created serious illness for many over the last couple of decades – and that the addition of 5G to many areas in the world now is creating serious immune system problems for people in those areas.

In addition, the Deep State has invaded our medical systems, pushing chemicals through Big Pharma, including vaccinations that have been proven not only toxic, but deadly to shocking numbers of children who have received them. But perhaps most stunning is the fact now known that they have created and patented deadly viruses, including AIDs, Ebola and the Covid 19 virus, in an attempt to kill off millions of people. It is now known that members of the Illuminati have met with an agenda to do just this.

Many of these Illuminati members are known to worship Satan and practice rituals involving human sacrifice, believing they belong to a superior race here to rule humanity. Their plan has been to create what's been called the "New World Order", wherein they would eventually be in complete control of all systems in the world, having eliminated much of the human race through disease and global disasters, and then essentially enslaving the rest.

Extra-Terrestrial Races on Earth

According to yet other numerous credible sources that can be easily researched, this story of a controlled humanity actually goes back many thousands of years. It's been documented that a number of different extra-terrestrial races came to Earth in the days of humanity's early development. Most of them were spiritually more evolved and had highly-advanced technology which they used to assist in the evolution of humanity.

However, there were a few races who also arrived with advanced interdimen-sional AI technology, but they were hostile and aggressive toward humanity. Once establishing themselves here, they then proceeded to set up ways to control the then-evolving human race. One way was to mate with certain humans, thus creating the bloodlines that still exist today within the illuminati families, which include royal families around the world, many in the global banking industry and corporate structures, and many of the top political figures in governments.

Again, if this information is new to you, it may well sound outrageous, stuff of science fiction or conspiracy theories. But, with just a little research, you will find a plethora of information about it all in many sources online and in libraries.

It initially demands a great deal of courage to take in the kind of information discussed here. It can shake your entire belief system about what is true about humanity's plight in the world – indeed, about anything you've learned about the reality we live in. It can leave you feeling shaky and vulnerable. But if you are yearning for full awakening, it is necessary to take in the information and allow it to do the necessary clean-out work of old, false beliefs and mind-control programs you've been subjected to your entire life.

Final Battle for Control

In any case, all this is important to understand if you are to grasp the significance of what is happening on the planetary level today – for what is occurring is the final stage of a global battle for control of humanity. For many, it is considered the third world war.

Fortunately, for many decades, there have been positive forces within the US and a number of other countries that have joined to fight the Deep State, which have become known as the *Alliance*. Consisting mainly of military forces dedicated to wresting power from the Deep State and returning it to the people of the world, these individuals have dedicated their lives to creating a plan for how to do this.

During this same period of time, it is reported that a great number of benevolent Galactic forces have joined the Alliance as the "sky crew" in this battle. And individual members of these races have also been conferring with certain military leaders and government heads for a number of years now, concerned about the possible destruction of the planet and the effect this would have on other civilizations in the galaxy. In order to help prevent this destruction, forces from the Pleiades, in particular, have evidently succeeded numerous times in melting nuclear warheads and modulating other destructive efforts of the Cabal.

But the process of liberation has been a long and arduous one, including actual battles behind the scenes, as well as those in space that most people know nothing about. It has been challenging for the Alliance. One of the main reasons is that, since the 1950s, the Deep State has developed secret space programs through factions in both the Navy and the Air Force. In these programs, they have back-engineered extremely advanced technology they've gathered from crashed UFOs, and they have been using this powerful technology to control activities on earth – as well as on the moon, and on other planets.

All this information has been coming out gradually in the last few years, much of it available now – some even on official sites – showing documents that have been recently de-classified. This has been part of a "soft, controlled disclosure" effort to slowly inform the public about what has been going on.

The important thing at this point, however, is that the Alliance has finally been winning battles against the Deep State, both on earth and in the skies. This can be seen, in part, by the fact that there are many thousands of sealed indictments in the US that are slowly being unsealed, indictments against many of the Deep State players.

Although few of the identities of people named in the indictments are yet available to the public, the existence of these indictments *is* available online for anyone to see. Through them, and through evidence shared by whistleblowers within the system, it is now possible to learn that numerous arrests over the last few years have already been made of many involved in pedophilia and child trafficking.

These arrests, along with others that are even more key in the process of clean-up, will likely continue. Recently, thousands of children have been rescued from deep underground bases that span the planet, where they had been held by the Illuminati for their dark rituals. These bases are being blown up by the Alliance, where life-destroying technologies have also been developed and stored, such as those for creating dangerous clones, poisoning large populations, and conducting mind-control. People living above on the surface of these areas are noting strange earthquakes and inexplicable noises and events due to the explosions.

Another sign that the Alliance is making progress is the great number of CEOs of large corporations and institutions in the world that have been suddenly resigning since late 2019. It is speculated that many of them have been given the option by the Alliance to either resign or go to prison.

But the battle is not yet over. Further disasters and battles may still occur throughout the remainder of 2020, and into the next few years, as the Deep State players continue to make further last-ditch efforts to wreak more havoc and destroy whatever they can before they are fully taken down.

New Earth Emerging

If this is the first you've read about this information, it can be overwhelming and frightening. And yet, there is much optimism within the Alliance and many other people across the globe at this point about the final outcome of this momentous battle. There is great confidence that the Deep State will be brought to justice and all their nefarious activities will at long last cease. Ironically, the Alliance was able to take advantage of the virus lockdown situation to keep people relatively safe during certain of their operations to arrest some of the most dangerous members of the Deep State.

The Alliance was also able to begin the revival of the global economy during this time by providing stimulus monies directly to individuals and businesses, beginning what some are predicting to be a global "debt jubilee". Involved in this shift has been a move to put in place an entirely new financial system that lies outside the realm of the Cabal's age-old system that has dominated the world and kept 90% of the population struggling, if not actually in poverty.

In looking at everything that has been changing since the virus first hit, it's as if Mother Earth had finally decided that enough was enough: Humanity had caused such havoc and destruction through greed, corruption, conflict and control that the entire human civilization had to finally be "flattened" in order for an entire energetic reset of humanity to take place.

In any case, the balance of power does seem to be slowly shifting in a positive direction. Indeed, the predictions made in prophesies down through the ages seem to be coming true, slowly but surely. We are witnessing the collapse of an old age and the beginning of a new one. Humanity is being liberated, and we will likely begin to truly see a new Earth emerging soon.

Actually, if we look closely, we can already see many signs of this new age blossoming on the planet. We can especially see it if we remember the ways in which many thousands of people worldwide responded to the lockdown situation during the days of the Covid 19 virus outbreak.

Indeed, huge numbers of people appeared to be waking up out of fear and despair, even amidst the tumultuous events they were experiencing and witnessing. Thanks to being compelled to stay at home, they were discovering there was a whole lot more to life than they'd realized: more than working simply to create as comfortable a life as possible for themselves and their families; more than just waking up in the morning, going to work, buying stuff, watching TV, then going to bed.

They also began questioning themselves about how they'd lived their lives simply believing what they'd been taught by their parents, teachers and the media. They began realizing they had been simply accepting, without question, life in a world that was totally unjust, controlled by a small elite group of people. In essence, the lockdown situation, despite all its inherent hardships, inspired people to see the many gifts and opportunities for deep reflection it was presenting to them.

In fact, many people were coming alive like never before. There was an outpouring of love and compassion for others, a flood of people helping people. Medical teams on the front lines across the planet were especially proving themselves heroic with their tireless work in treating and stemming the spread of the virus. It brought tears too many to witness this.

There was also a call within people to ignore traditional governmental prejudices and sanctions, as individuals made their own decisions to help people in need, no matter where they lived in the world – such as when Cuban medical teams responded to the need of their help in numerous other countries, and individuals in China did as well.

There were even a number of CEOs of large corporations who voluntarily slashed their huge salaries to show solidarity with the workers. Others donated their entire salaries to charity. This kind of compassion on the corporate level has rarely, if ever, been seen before.

And then there were the people who were responding in over-the-top creative ways that could not have been predicted beforehand. We all saw the reports of people offering an outpouring of gifts through free online courses, musical performances, trips through museums. Compassionate people everywhere were offering to buy and deliver groceries for elderly and sick neighbors – or actually to provide and prepare food for them.

And then there were the mass meditations that took place across the world, especially the one on April 4-5, 2020, in which over a million people participated. This truly affirmed the sense that unity in humanity was occurring on a phenomenal level, along with a collective awakening on the mental, emotional, spiritual and social levels.

The Great Awakening

Indeed, by the beginning of April 2020, we were seeing what was being described as "The Great Awakening". We saw people taking their power back. They were beginning to question the mainstream news, realizing it was perennially negative, inciting fear, despair and anger in people. They saw how the system was rigged to make them believe that humans are weak and helpless in the throes of a desperate fall into chaos and needed external political protection and guidance. And they realized that, if they believed this, they could more easily be controlled.

In addition, with this new sense of empowerment, individuals also seemed to be having profound spiritual awakenings. Many of the responses of people on social networks could be described as a shift into the heart, into caring and compassion. And a realization that, far from being weak and helpless humans caught in a hopeless situation, we humans will make it through any adversity that is thrown our way.

Rare and Profound Astrological Picture

As another sign that we are in dramatically-eventful times, the current astrological picture also tells us this story. I am not an astrology expert, but from what I understand about what's currently happening with the planets, none of what is occurring on the planet is surprising. There is evidently a rare constellation of planets, which, when it has happened in the past, has also coincided with major upheavals and systemic planetary events.

The dramatic constellation involves four outer planets: a triple conjunction of Pluto, Saturn and Jupiter – with all of these planets squaring Uranus. Astrologers tell us that this constellation is providing volcanically-intense evolutionary pressures, creating an opportunity for a radical reconfiguration of all life structures to take place.

If you're not familiar with astrology, briefly, here's the picture: When Saturn and Pluto are conjunct, this can influence revolutionary changes to happen on the planet. In particular, it can create profound emancipatory movements, bringing about radical reform. Pluto is about destruction and regeneration, death and rebirth. To add to this planet's current influence in this constellation, the US is also currently going through its Pluto return; as one astrologer put it: "The jaws of Hades are opened up and we're pulled into the underworld".

Bring in Jupiter, and all this energy is greatly enhanced. Jupiter expands whatever energies are being emitted by the planets it is conjunct with. The conjunction between Jupiter and Pluto, in particular, tends to bring in geo-political high drama; justice issues and moral principles are brought to the surface, highlighting vast social inequities. On the other hand, Jupiter also fortunately provides for elements of benevolence, generosity, and faith in positive outcome to come present.

Then, if we add these energies to those of Uranus – sudden unpredictability, liberation, reform, and opening to new horizons – we see all of these things happening in a sudden and transformational way, likely creating a lot of chaos and disruption and an experience of profound uncertainty about outcome. Yet, at the same time, we also get an explosive opportunity for transformation on a planetary scale.

Sound familiar? This constellation in the sky is obviously both influencing and reflecting what is happening here on Earth. It's evidently at its peak now at the time of this writing, in mid-2020. Jupiter will be leaving the configuration by the end of the year, but the Pluto/Saturn/Uranus constellation will be continuing for a few years.

However, a few of these planets will soon be moving into Aquarius; some say the beginning of 2021 heralds the beginning of the Age of Aquarius – also known as the Golden Age.

All in all, we are in a time of powerful opportunity for us to make a profound transformational shift, to usher our world and ourselves into a dramatically new place. Seeing how humanity has responded thus far to the challenges, it does seem reasonable to expect that a huge transformation will be occurring on the planet during the next decade or so on many levels, that a new and more awake humanity will have evolved.

We are now simply experiencing what could be called a "planetary dark night of the soul" – the state of being that generally precedes enlightenment.

Resource List for Further Research

Ascension and the Fifth Dimension:

- Beckow, Steve: https://goldenageofgaia.com/
- Benedicte, Meg: https://newearthcentral.com/
- Cannon, Dolores: https://ozarkmt.com/product-category/dolores-cannon/
- Day, Christine: *Pleiadian Principles for Living*
  http://www.christinedayonline.com/
- Elkins, Don, et al.: *The Law of One* (series)
- Frazier, Vidya: *Ascension: Awakening to the Fifth Dimension; Embracing the Transformation,* http://vidyafrazier.com/ ;
  https://www.youtube.com/results?search_query=vidya+frazier
- Hamilton, Craig: http://integralenlightenment.com/home.php
- Kahn, Matt: http://www.truedivinenature.com/
- Kenyon, Tom: http://tomkenyon.com/
- Lipton, Bruce: *Spontaneous Evolution*
- Marx-Hubbard, Barbara: http://barbaramarxhubbard.com/
- Melkizedek, Drunvalo: *Serpent of Light,* http://www.drunvalo.net/
- Self, Jim: *What Do You Mean the Third Dimension is Going Away?* ;
- https://masteringalchemy.com/

Disclosure – Videos giving Full Picture of Cabal and Deep State Activities

- Lopez, Gabriel: Out of Shadows:
  https://www.youtube.com/watch?v=GOsgIi8xeG4
- Ossebaard, Janet: Cabal, Deep State , QAnon:
  https://www.youtube.com/watch?v=GA5HcfVUYlo&feature=youtu.be

General Disclosure

- Chasteen, Ben and Counts, Rob - Edge of Wonder:
  https://www.youtube.com/results?search_query=edge+of+
- Cobra: https://2012portal.blogspot.com/
- Goode, Corey: https://www.youtube.com/results?search_query=corey+goode
- https://www.youtube.com/watch?v=AeP8dY7S4SQ
- Frazier, Vidya: *Triumph of the Light: Story of Humanity's Enslavement and Impending Liberation;* https://www.youtube.com/watch?v=bvtJfMbxSJc&t=1s
- Fulford, Ben: https://benjaminfulford.net/
- Gilliland, James: http://www.eceti.org/
- Martino, Joe: https://www.collective-evolution.com/author/joe/
- Munder, James:
  https://www.youtube.com/watch?time_continue=1607&v=l5cUsNTr4Yw&feature=emb_logo
- Parkes, Simon:
  https://www.youtube.com/results?search_query=simon+parkes
- Pixie, Magenta:
  https://www.youtube.com/results?search_query=magenta+pixie+this+week
- Sealed Indictments:
  https://pbs.twimg.com/media/EU3Yh7rX0AAjWFy?format=jpg&name=medium

- Stone, Sacha: https://www.youtube.com/watch?v=9jbrlcl-DgQ&feature=em-uploademail ; https://newearthnation.org/member/sacha-stone/
- Wilcock, David: *Ascension Mysteries*; https://www.youtube.com/results?search_query=david+wilcock

Disclosure about Extraterrestrials

- Goode, Corey and Wilcock David: The Cosmic Secret: *https://www.thecosmicsecret.com/*
- Greer, Steven: Close Encounters of the Fifth Kind: https://www.youtube.com/user/SDisclosure
- Ray, Aurora: Wake Up Call for the Family of Light: https://www.youtube.com/watch?time_continue=11&v=JAkCoJ8Ivps&feature=emb_logo

Chapter 2

Ascension into the Fifth Dimension

As we can see, there is a great paradox occurring on the Earth at this time. A profound darkness, producing chaos and destruction, is still reigning on certain levels – and yet, huge amounts of light within humanity are simultaneously flooding the planet, showing hopeful signs of a civilization awakening into love, joy and empowerment.

The best way I've found to describe this phenomenon is through using the paradigm known as *Ascension,* which makes reference to a shift that the Earth and humanity are making into the *Fifth Dimension.* This paradigm presents an explanation of current times that is not only extremely positive; it also makes sense of the puzzling, contradictory events taking place.

There is a great variety of teachings and channelings I've come across about ascension and the Fifth Dimension. I present here a distillation of them, along with my own intuitive downloads and my direct experience of ascension and this higher dimension. In general, ascension teachings describe how the planet Earth is in the process of rapidly shifting into a much higher frequency. And that we, both as individuals and as a collective human consciousness, are therefore being compelled to quickly awaken as well into this higher frequency.

In essence, ascension is a natural evolutionary step we are taking, but it is a very rapid one at this time. It is a spiritual awakening – but a sped-up version of it, required for the current times when the Earth is rising so quickly in vibration. And it's the speed of this awakening that is causing a great deal of the turmoil, chaos and confusion that are occurring.

The Dimensions

The ascension teachings describe the evolutionary stages of consciousness in terms of "dimensions". They state that there are many dimensions of consciousness in the universe in which all of creation lives, and that these dimensions create structures of reality – structures that inherently have certain rules, possibilities, and limitations for those living within them.

They refer to the higher dimension the Earth is in the process of shifting into as the *Fifth Dimension,* and the one we have been living in for thousands of years as the *Third Dimension.* This lower dimension, as we know, is one that has been filled with experiences of war, injustice, poverty, and varying degrees of emotional and physical suffering. It's a reality we have all believed to be the only one available to us; we've simply assumed that this is just how life is.

However, according to the ascension context, the Earth did not always live in this dark and challenging third-dimensional reality. At one time, it existed in the Fifth Dimension, in which all Beings on it lived in a much higher consciousness. The Third Dimension came into being many thousands of years ago due to a number of factors, when what's known as the *Fall of Consciousness* occurred. At that time, everything physical and nonphysical began dropping energetically into greater density, first into the Fourth Dimension, and then finally into the Third Dimension.

But it is not the first time this dimensional shift downward, and then upward again into the Fifth Dimension, has happened. We are told that these shifts have occurred cyclically throughout time, about every 26,000 years or so. And it's when the Earth has passed through the area of the Milky Way it's now traversing that the upward shift into the Fifth Dimension has occurred.

The cause of the upward shift in frequency is due to powerful high-frequency waves of light existing in this part of the Milky Way. These waves, which carry a vibration of unity conscious with them, are currently streaming onto the Earth and all other celestial bodies in our solar system, impacting the vibration of everything existing here. Essentially, the waves have been preparing us to make the rapid leap in consciousness from the Third Dimension, through the Fourth Dimension, and into the Fifth Dimension, in order for us to follow the same path of the Earth in its planetary ascension.

The teachings explain that as of December, 2012, we entered the Fourth Dimension, a short transitional "bridge" we'll be on for just a matter of years. At some point, in the not-too-distant future, we will be shifting, along with the Earth, into the much higher frequency of the Fifth Dimension.

This recent shift into the Fourth Dimension back in 2012 may be surprising, because it was not noted by most people. This is because the Fourth Dimension is a dimension of *thought*; it was not a shift that changed anything physically. And therefore, most people have been unaware of this dimensional shift and have attempted to continue living with all their 3D habits of operating intact; and this has caused a lot of the discomfort and confusion many are experiencing.

However, what *is* different now in the Fourth Dimension is there is a lot that is now available to us on the level of *consciousness.* We now have much greater capability for manifestation, as well as ways in which we can wake up to deeper levels of reality much more quickly. Becoming aware of these newly-available aspects of consciousness, and using them, will greatly prepare us for shifting into the Fifth Dimension.

The Fifth Dimension

But what exactly *is* the Fifth Dimension? First of all, it's important to understand that it's not a place; we're not going anywhere. We will still be on Earth – but our experience of it and of ourselves will be very different. Like all dimensions, the Fifth Dimension is a structure of reality created by the consciousness in which we are living.

The Fifth Dimension has often been described as the dimension of love, of living totally from the Heart. It's where we will finally awaken into full consciousness of who we are – truly powerful multidimensional beings – and we will live in the true knowing of the oneness of all that exists.

In this dimension, we will merge and reintegrate with our Soul. We will live from a state of unconditional love, inner peace, joy, harmony, kindness and reverence. We will enjoy an on-going freedom from fear, shame, judgment and separation. Cooperation, co-creation, and collaboration will come naturally to us as we work and create together.

The Fifth Dimension is a reality without limitations; all possibilities are available. As we progress through the several levels of this dimension, our full DNA will gradually be activated, and the 90% of our brain that's been dormant for thousands of years will be turned on again. Physical density as we know it now will be gone. Form will be fluid and physical bodies will have morphed into a crystalline structure.

As fully-conscious beings, we will be able to access within ourselves information and wisdom that reside in many of the higher dimensions. We will think from our Hearts and make soul-guided choices. We will experience psychic abilities we had long ago, such as telepathy and clairvoyance. Much of what we will experience will pour forth wordlessly from our Hearts, rather than from our minds. Speaking out loud will be optional.

The Fifth Dimension is a state of being that will feel like "Home". In finally making the shift into this reality, it will truly feel as if we are returning Home after eons of existing elsewhere, times in which we only had a sense of longing and dreams of this Home to sustain us.

"The Event"

Again, this description of the Fifth Dimension may sound much too idealistic, a utopian dream impossible to imagine happening any time in the near future. However, there are many sources, including certain informed astronomers, who report about a phenomenon that is due to occur sometime in the next few years, one that will quite probably make this phenomenal shift in consciousness possible. It has been called "the Event".

There are varying descriptions of the Event, ranging from rather frightening to incredibly blissful. In truth, it will probably be both, depending on the individual. But, either way, it is something that will be signaling the beginning of the actual shift of the planet into the Fifth Dimension.

In general, the Event has been described as an intensely powerful "solar-flash" event that will originate from Source (or the "cosmic sun"), and make its way to our sun; and, from there, it will stream out to the Earth and all other planets in the solar system. It will be a blast of extremely high-frequency light which will greatly raise the vibration of everyone and everything it impacts.

In this way, the Event will begin the process of ascension of the planet and its inhabitants into the Fifth Dimension. It is predicted that many people who have generally been living in a positive consciousness will be lost in bliss for a few days following it. However, it will also probably cause a breakdown of all technology and social, financial and political structures still existing that are of a low-frequency; and the energies will initially be very difficult for individuals who are living at a low vibration.

Some sources tell us that the solar event may also bring powerful earth changes with it, depending on how much the Earth needs to cleanse itself at the time. Others state that it will not happen just once; that several less powerful solar events may happen more gradually. There are evidently different timelines it may come in on which will determine exactly how it will occur.

But, at any rate, when the Event does happen, it will give a great boost in consciousness to everyone in the world. However, it will not create a sudden and complete shift for everyone into the Fifth Dimension. Ascension into this higher level of consciousness is a gradual experience, one that demands the attention and inner work of each individual.

Many of us have already been experiencing this ascension process over a number of years now, as we dip in and out of fifth-dimensional consciousness. However, at some point after the Event, it is said that all people still living on the planet at the time will have the experience of making a permanent shift into the Fifth Dimension. This process will evidently be occurring in several waves over a period of a few years, after the Event occurs.

Already, the high-frequency waves of light that have been streaming onto the planet for a number of years have been helping to prepare us for the Event. They contain powerful photonic light codes that are both disruptive and supportive in nature: they are causing the breakdown of old patterns and structures that do not resonate with the higher frequencies in the waves, and they also offer us support and ease to shift into a higher vibration to match them. Although mainstream scientists tend not to speculate on the spiritual ramifications of these new frequencies flooding the planet, many do acknowledge they exist and that they have never been seen before in our known history.

So, in summary, we are now in the process of leaving the Third Dimension behind, passing relatively quickly through the Fourth Dimension, and shifting gradually into the Fifth. There is no exact date known either for the Event or for the actual shift into the Fifth Dimension. However, it is generally predicted, even by certain scientists looking at past planetary cycles, that they will likely occur sometime within the 2020s.

Journey through the Fourth Dimension

It's clear there is much that must change during this period of time as we find our way through the Fourth Dimension, not only in the world at large, but also within everyone's personal consciousness. If you are fully engaged in your ascension process, you are likely experiencing the dismantling of all old third-dimensional patterns in yourself that do not resonate with the frequencies that exist in the Fifth Dimension.

Just as all darkness that is occurring in the world at large is simply a revelation of what has always been there – just unseen – the same is happening on an individual level within you. The darkness, often hidden in the unconscious, must be revealed in order for it to be rooted out, healed, and returned to the Light. And although this process can be deeply liberating, it can also be both painful and scary.

In fact, in realizing how difficult the ascension process may be for you as someone already on a conscious spiritual path, you may wonder how other less-awake individuals could possibly make the leap into 5D consciousness at this point or even in the near future. There are too many who are so steeped in negativity and spiritual ignorance – even aside from those involved in the dark agenda of the Cabal – it seems it couldn't be possible.

And the truth is, not every Soul incarnated today on earth will be making the shift into the Fifth Dimension. Many will have decided that it would be too difficult to make it in this lifetime and will choose to leave the planet beforehand in one way or another. When the Shift occurs, these Souls will be taken to other places in the universe in which the Third and Fourth Dimensions are still available for further evolution in those vibrations.

If you look closely, you will see there are currently two different groups of people on the planet who appear to be moving in very different directions. The first group consists of those Souls who have chosen at this time to make the journey into the Fifth Dimension. They are currently traveling through the *Higher* Fourth Dimension, rapidly waking up and are often focused on healing, service to others, and wanting to help create the "New Earth". There are other Souls, currently less awake, but nonetheless also planning on ascending. They are also finding their way into the higher levels of the Fourth Dimension, just more gradually.

The group of people going in the other direction includes those Souls who have decided not to ascend, and they remain in the process of continuing to learn from their third-dimensional experiences. These people are moving more and more into the *Lower* Fourth Dimension, into a world that will increasingly be reflecting this lower consciousness of division, separation and conflict. As strange as it may seem, although operating very differently from each other, both groups will be co-existing in the world until the planetary shift occurs.

So, this is the basic outline of what the ascension teachings describe about the journey of the Earth and the collective of humanity during these times we're currently traveling through. In the next chapter, we'll take a look at what is occurring for the increasing numbers of people who are waking up to the knowing that they have an important role to play in this global drama.

Chapter 3

Ascension Lightworkers

If you are reading this book, you are likely part of a particular group of awakening Souls who, as well as finding their own way into the Fifth Dimension, are also here to assist others in some way to do the same. For this reason, you could be called an "Ascension Lightworker", a spiritual pioneer with a mission to help transform the planet with your love, light and wisdom.

In essence, you are helping to forge a path through the unknown territory of the higher Fourth Dimension and into the Fifth, so you can then turn around to assist those who will be coming behind you. Because of this, your journey is likely going to be somewhat more rapid and challenging than that of those who follow later. In fact, you may be finding that your task requires a great deal of courage, fortitude, and conviction.

Starseeds

As an Ascension Lightworker, it's probable you are also someone who could be called a "Starseed" – an ancient Soul who lived in other star systems in the universe before arriving on Earth. And you likely came here in answer to a call from the Earth to assist humanity through the darkness this race was struggling through in the Third Dimension.

When the call first went out many thousands of years ago, a large number of highly-evolved Souls began to stream into Earth, answering the plea for help in several different waves. Some came thousands of years ago, committing themselves to a great many lifetimes in the Third Dimension before the time of ascension could occur. Others arrived somewhat later. And some have more recently arrived – in some cases, for the first time ever on Earth.

If you are a Starseed, the description of the Fifth Dimension probably feels very familiar to you; you are likely remembering it. Maybe you've also felt somewhat different from other people your entire life. You've perhaps been confused and appalled by the existence of war and hatred and by how cruel certain people can be to others.

Maybe you've also had strange abilities since childhood that others lack, or psychic experiences you initially assumed everyone had, only to find out later that wasn't the case. You may even have memories of lifetimes on planets in other star systems. Perhaps you've had visitations from celestial or extra-terrestrial Beings during your life – or wish you could have. Or maybe, in some other way, you've just felt you have never quite fit in here on Earth, as if you've somehow been separated from your "real" family. To some degree or another, you've simply felt like a stranger in a strange land.

Starseeds come from a number of different star systems, and often those from the same general area of the universe have similar qualities and missions to accomplish. Certain Souls tend to be extraordinarily sensitive and have had a particularly rough time adapting to the density of consciousness on Earth; they have sometimes been named the "Crystals".

Other starseeds are also sensitive, but have a certain tougher warrior-like ability to be outspoken in their beliefs and convictions. These Souls could perhaps more aptly be called "Ascension Lightwarriors" and have sometimes been named the "Indigos". And then there are Starseeds who, prior to arriving on Earth, had lived in many different star systems, and they have a mixture of both qualities, as well as other particular ones.

Some of the children being born in recent years are extremely high Beings who have already been through the full cycle of ascension to the 12th Dimension and higher. They are here to walk the path created by the Starseeds who have come here before them and will be leading humanity fully into the Golden Age.

The exciting news for all Starseeds is that, after the Event occurs, and people are generally in a high enough vibration, our galactic friends will be landing here to assist us further in our ascension process. Many of these Galactic Beings are ancestors of all of humanity, having contributed strands of their DNA in the formation of the human race, and have therefore been eagerly waiting to introduce themselves to us when the time is right.

If you are a Starseed, you will likely find that some of them are part of your particular star family. You will especially resonate with them; and because of this, it may be a very emotional time for you when you first begin meeting and reuniting with them.

Ancient Earth Souls, Angels, and Devas

However, not all Ascension Lightworkers are Starseeds. Some are Souls who originally came into being on Earth itself in very ancient times. Yet, even then, they often feel like strangers on the planet as it is now, remembering deep within themselves what the Earth was once like in one of its earlier periods in the Fifth Dimension.

Another group of Ascension Lightworkers include those from the angelic kingdom. Initially a species that was not a part of the human drama on Earth, certain Angels came out of curiosity to see what it was like to be incarnated in human form. Unfortunately, some of them got caught in the darkness of the matrix that had been formed on the planet and were unable to return back to their home realm.

As a result, angelic loved ones made the sacrifice of coming here to assist them – as well as devoting themselves to the ascension of the human race, as well. They exist among us today, adding their light and wisdom to all other Ascension Lightworker groups.

And lastly, there are certain Ascension Lightworkers who are from the Devic Kingdom (e.g., fairies) incarnated in human form. These are often people who are very concerned about the Earth itself, wishing to rescue their beloved planet from the destruction humanity has brought about.

As interesting as it initially may be to discover which kind of Ascension Lightworker you are, the important thing to realize is you are an ancient, highly-evolved Soul who has likely had experiences in many different dimensions and assisted civilizations in other star systems, and you have wisdom and abilities beyond your comprehension at this point.

In fact, you have likely worked side by side with the Ascended Masters, the Archangels, the Lords of Light, and the Elohim, as well as many races of Galactics. You are powerful. Your waking up during these times is simply a *re*-awakening, a *remembering* of who you are.

Resolving Personal Karma

Your essential task as an Ascension Lightworker is to bring the living presence of Light onto the planet. As part of this task, you are here to help transmute the dark energies that humanity's sojourn through the Third Dimension has created into Light.

This entails, of course, initially clearing all mutations and distortions of Light from within your own being by keeping a steady focus on your own healing from past traumas and woundings. This is no small undertaking. In particular, it means learning to love yourself unconditionally, something most people have a difficult time achieving. And yet, it's a condition essential for your ascension into the Fifth Dimension.

As you've probably discovered, a major part of this personal healing work includes exploring your shadow self in all its aspects – all those rejected parts of your personality that have been kept hidden due to trauma and deep survival issues. It's important to learn how to meet this hidden self with understanding and compassion for yourself, so you can then release the negative mental and emotional energies attached to it. Section Three of this book is designed to assist you in this process.

Another important aspect of personal healing at this time has to do with discovering and nurturing the balance of the Divine Feminine and Divine Masculine energies within yourself. For most people, this involves healing wounds they've inherited from the culture they're born into and from society at large, and also those they've personally received in this lifetime.

As we all know, this imbalance between masculine and feminine energies has existed in the world for thousands of years. In many ways, women have been dominated, persecuted, diminished, and controlled by the rule of the patriarchy. And this imbalance, among many others, is what is now being highlighted by some in the world, often through a focus on bringing the energies of the Divine Feminine forward to help guide us into greater awakening as a species. This is what is needed for now, until a true balance between the two energies can be achieved.

However, this balance between the Divine Masculine and Feminine energies can only happen in the outer world when each one of us begins to balance them inside ourselves. We need to recognize we have both types of energy within us and they both need to be embraced and expressed in a natural and balanced way.

As an Ascension Lightworker, you have the opportunity to understand this and to heal any imbalances with yourself, so that you can express the power and wisdom of both the masculine and the feminine in a balanced way. In doing this, you are contributing that new and harmonious energy to the awakening on the planet.

Clearing Karma for the Collective

Aside from being here to heal yourself in these ways, as an Ascension Lightworker, you are likely also here to help clear karma from the collective consciousness of humanity, as well. This could be the collective karma of a certain group within humanity, such as a particular culture, race, or gender – or perhaps a group of Souls who were involved in a traumatic event that happened at some point in history.

Or maybe you've taken on karma to resolve for your family lineage. This is common for many Ascension Lightworkers who have dealt with dysfunctional patterns in this life, such as sexual abuse, substance abuse, or family violence. If you have dealt with this kind of pattern and you know it has run in your ancestral line, you may well have agreed to take this on for all your family lineage to resolve.

You might also be assisting to clear a traumatic experience a group of people is currently experiencing somewhere in the world. You can know if it's this kind of collective karma you're dealing with, if you rather suddenly feel a heavy load of emotion arise within you, such as despair or hatred or fear, and realize you can't quite relate to it. It doesn't make sense, considering what is currently happening in your life. If this happens, it's helpful to take the time to go within and ask if the emotions have to do with your personal healing or if it's something happening on the collective level you've agreed to help clear.

Be open to an answer that may come in many different forms. It might be a decisive "Yes" or "No"; it could come as an image or a flash of knowing. Trust the response you receive. And if you believe it's something collective, take the time to call in divine Light, celestial and galactic Beings to help you clear the energy – and to transmute the trauma of the collective group of Souls into Light. If this is indeed collective energy you're clearing, you will likely feel a release fairly rapidly of the heavy energy from your body.

Becoming Aware of Your Spiritual Mission

In addition to these tasks as an Ascension Lightworker, you likely also have a particular spiritual mission to accomplish during this lifetime, as well – a service you are uniquely qualified to offer to help awaken and empower humanity during these difficult times of transition.

You may not yet know exactly what this mission is; you simply know you have one. It might be an outer expression of service, such as healing, teaching, networking with people, or building affordable housing. Or you may be called to assist the Earth back to its pristine beauty, such as planting trees or helping to clean the oceans. Perhaps you are what's known as a "frequency holder", someone here to hold a high frequency of Light for the collective as a whole. Trust your intuition as to what your calling may be. Do whatever comes present to you in the moment and watch your mission gradually unfold in greater ways.

If you are already engaged in offering a service to others you recognize as your spiritual mission, allow that to evolve and grow. You might be finding that it's changing in some way to adjust to the increasing intensity of events on the planet. Again, trust and flow with the direction it's taking. For more information about discovering or increasing your effectiveness in your mission, see the chapter in Section 3 of this book discussing spiritual mission.

Securing the Ascension Timeline

So, this is a lot you have likely signed up for! It may feel overwhelming at first to realize it. But it probably makes sense to you, if you have had a number of challenges to overcome in your life. It can help if you keep in mind that, in accomplishing all of these tasks, you are not only raising your own vibration, you are also adding powerful energy to the collective human consciousness as it struggles to awaken.

And, in addition, you are helping to secure in place the planet's timeline leading toward ascension into the Fifth Dimension. This is a process that had been touch-and-go up to 2012, when, according to a number of sources, it finally locked in. Until then, a dire Armageddon timeline had been in place.

Now your work is to help keep the ascension timeline stable and steady, because the dark forces are still attempting to create cracks and diversions in it to delay the shift into the Fifth Dimension. This work is accomplished in the ways discussed above, but also simply through ways that are probably natural to you: staying positive, loving, kind, and empowered, no matter what is happening. Indeed, it is accomplished through your very presence of light wherever you are and your focus on the New Earth you wish to help create.

If you are not convinced this timeline has been locked in at this point, it's certainly understandable. With all that is still occurring in the world, it can look as if things could still shift in either direction. However, even if you're unconvinced humanity is already on the right track, simply keep focusing on the ascension timeline and this will assist in strengthening and securing it into place.

Making Your Ascension Lightworker Tasks Easier

To assist you in accomplishing these Ascension Lightworker tasks, here are some ideas and suggestions of what you can do:

- **Take more time to meditate:** As you have likely experienced, meditation can serve to profoundly deepen your awareness and lift your consciousness. It can help you to become more clearly aware that you are an eternal Being of Light living a temporary life on planet Earth; and this can create a great deal more peace and harmony in your life.

- **Pay attention to your dreams:** It can also be helpful to focus on remembering your dreams, as they may be speaking clearly to you about your life, your awakening, and even about events in the world at large. Your dreams may be one way you are receiving inner guidance about your ascension process.

- **Step into empowerment:** Realize it's up to you, along with all the people of Earth, to create the New Earth. It's important to cease relying on higher authorities to do this. The Alliance and the benevolent Galactics are helping to liberate us on the external level; but it is up to us, in the end, to realize the power we have as a collective group to create the changes we want to see. And, very importantly, to realize that our main power lies in our *consciousness.*

- **Focus on the New Earth**: Focusing in your daily life on the New Earth you envision is particularly helpful, especially if you do it with powerful emotions, like joy and love. In fact, if you can live your life as if this new age is *already* happening, this will add additional power to creating it.

- **See the gift these troubled times offer you**: View these times as an opportunity for deepening your awareness about yourself by exploring such questions as: "What is life?", "What is reality?", "Who am I, really?", and "What am I here to do?".

- **Participate in Global Mass Meditations**: Participating in global mass meditations is a very powerful way to bring healing and power to humanity – and also to feel part of the greater community of Ascension Lightworkers across the planet.

- **Create community:** Do everything you can to create a community of like-minded people around you for emotional, mental and spiritual support. If there are none you know of locally, find these people online.

- **Get politically active:** If you are someone who is called to be politically involved in helping to create change, become active in ways that reflect the dictates of your heart. Trust your intuition as to which outer actions can assist in the transformation taking place.

Chapter 4

Challenges of Ascension Lightworkers

As is clear, your healing and spiritual journey as an Ascension Lightworker is likely a great deal more challenging than that of others not holding the same spiritual purpose. Apart from what has already been discussed, part of the challenge may be due to the length of time you've lived in the Third Dimension (for some people, it's been countless lifetimes through thousands of years). If so, you likely experience times of profound weariness, deep within your soul.

You probably also grapple with a sense of impatience or distress at how long your ascension process is taking. You may find you're experiencing even more than what feels like your share of rapid change and uncertainty in your personal life. At times, you might be dealing with profound loss and change, externally as well as internally. You might feel as if your life is falling apart, or that you are morphing into someone you've not known before.

In a certain sense, what you are experiencing is a very rapid process of spiritual awakening. If you have been on a spiritual path for a while, you can probably remember that your process of awakening in the past was generally a slow and gradual experience. And it took place in a world that was still fairly reliable and predictable, even if you didn't have much faith in that world. Now there's apparently no more time for strolling along your awakening path, slowly discovering new and exciting realms to explore and savor. It's a very different world these days; there can be a sensation that you are being pushed along.

And, if your awakening is fairly new, it may be an incredibly rapid shift for you in your life – exciting on the one hand, but also disturbing in certain ways. You may feel as if you have few reference points as to what's happened to you. You might feel like you're constantly being pushed out of your comfort zone, feeling compelled to let go of formerly-reliable supports and to trust life to a degree you've never had to before.

Ascension Clean-Out

At certain points, you may go through a phase I've called *Ascension Clean-out,* a period of time in which it feels like one challenge after another is arising, without a break. If this is happening for you, you are likely shedding karma very quickly, including collective karma.

In doing this, there are times you are likely to feel very alone, especially since you are also living in a world where everything familiar is shifting precariously around you. You realize you're on a path leading into unknown territory and feel you have few road signs to guide you.

It's important to remember, should you ever feel at times as if something's wrong with you – or that you're somehow lagging behind, because so many "negative" things seem to be happening – that rough times are to be expected when traveling through the higher levels of the Fourth Dimension at the "front of the pack", so to speak.

To prepare you for what you'll be called on to do, all your karma and unresolved traumas from both this life and past lives is now arising from your unconscious to finally be resolved and released as quickly as possible. You can't take your 3D baggage with you into the Fifth Dimension, so it's got to come up now for you to meet, resolve and then release.

Integrating the Dark Material

In addition to dealing with all your healing work of past traumas and woundings, as an Ascension Lightworker, it is also important to fully take in and work through any trauma you experience in learning the information outlined in Chapter One about the dark agenda planned for humanity by the Cabal. It's not necessary to get involved in all the details of it; it's just important to not avoid, deny, or hide from the information.

If you've always assumed that spiritual awakening only had to do with light and love and learning how to connect with a loving Creator, this can be very difficult to do. In taking in this information, either through reading the first chapter of this book or by other means, you are definitely on the "fast track" in your ascension process. It initially demands a lot of courage. But it's important to process it as quickly as possible at this time, due to how quickly events are moving in the world.

This is because, if you do avoid dealing with this information at this point, you will likely be thrown into even greater fear, despair, and anger later on, when the information is finally being released to everyone on the planet. The sooner you choose to deal with this dark material, the sooner you'll be equipped to assist others down the line when they finally have to experience it. The more aware you are of the dark story humanity has been caught in, and the more you are able to integrate it emotionally within yourself, the more effective you will be in helping to transmute this darkness within humanity into Light.

To do this, it is important to remember that, as an Ascension Lightworker, you are a powerful, highly-evolved Soul. You are more than up to the job of not only waking up to who you are as a Soul, but also of taking in all the darkness now being revealed and do your part to help release it into the Light.

Declaring Your Sovereignty as a Soul

In order to accomplish this with as much ease as possible, it is also important during these dark times while the Cabal is still clinging to their power over humanity, to take steps to proclaim your sovereignty as a Soul. This will help protect you from the dark forces at play and also strengthen your ability to stay positive and assist others.

This statement can be in the form of a declaration, either voiced out loud or in the form of a written document you create. In it you would make a statement in some way that you do not accept or give permission to the plan those in the Cabal have in mind to control you.

It's important to understand why such a declaration is effective. Those in the Satanist Illuminati forces who act on the wishes and demands of their "God" – who is a very powerful satanic Being residing in the lower Fourth Dimension – cannot do his bidding to control others unless consent and permission is given by those being controlled. This is one of the laws of the universe.

Of course, we might think we've never given our consent to be controlled. But their asking for permission has been done in a very stealthy manner that has been missed by most of us, and yet has somehow been deemed to be adequate to get it. One of the ways has been to present their plans through dark science fiction and horror films that depict very clearly what they have in mind and what they are already doing. Unfortunately, most people have erroneously assumed these films to be fiction and have had no idea of the truth and reality they have been presenting. And the Satanists therefore have taken people's lack of response to these presentations of their plans as permission to continue doing what they are doing.

The Satanists have also shown their plans through using a number of famous musicians and rock stars who make videos laced with all the dark symbolism of the satanic cult. Certain politicians have also disclosed this symbolism in various ways that go unnoticed by the masses. There are many videos now showing how all this is done.

And very importantly, the Cabal also construes as permission our passive acceptance of the poisoning they've done of our food, water and air, as well as the toxic pharmaceuticals we continue to take and the vaccinations we accept.

At any rate, even if it is not fully clear to you how all of this works, you can still make your declaration of your own sovereignty to protect yourself. You may have to make it repeatedly during times in which you might be feeling the need to. In it, state that you do not consent to their control over you. You might say something like this:

"I do not give you permission to control me. I am a sovereign Being and have power over my own mind, my own body, and my own reality. I do not give you permission for the high-jacking and harm you wish to cause me as a sovereign living human being and as a sovereign Soul."

However, to be effective, you must make this declaration without any anger, fear or desire for retribution and revenge. This may be difficult at first, if all this information about the Deep State and the Satanists is new to you. But do your best to work through your emotions first; do the inner work necessary for this through healing techniques, therapy, and meditation. See if you can first come into a balanced consciousness of love, empowerment, and forgiveness. Only with this consciousness will your declaration of sovereignty be effective.

Feeling Compassion and Gratitude for the Dark

And, once you've done this, you may be able to actually begin feeling gratitude for the whole dark structure that was created on Earth for the part it has played in your ascension process. All that it has created can actually be seen as a catalyst for your leap of consciousness into a higher, wiser, more-evolved state of being.

Perhaps you can even feel free enough to send love and compassion to all those who have participated in the entire energy field of darkness. But, in doing this, it's not that you are making what they have done okay. You are saying "I love you and have compassion for you. But it's not okay what you have participated in, and I do not allow you to control me anymore."

It's similar to the type of "tough love" you might give to a teenager who is out of control, or a friend who has become a drug addict and is abusing your kindness. You love them – but you are setting firm boundaries with them.

If you can accomplish this, you will also perhaps be able to shift into a higher perspective and see how all the pain and suffering now occurring within you and within all of humanity is actually in divine, perfect order. It is all being harmoniously orchestrated by higher powers within us to help us make the leap of consciousness necessary to ascend to the Fifth Dimension.

One way to shift into this perspective is to direct your awareness out into the universe, as if you're viewing the Earth from space. See how the planet and all of humanity are currently in the process of a great transition, moving through a dark period of time in preparation for a profound collective awakening. Feel the excitement of this. Remember how crisis creates great opportunity for enormous change, and that the current situation on Earth is creating this opportunity for humanity.

As challenging as it can be in doing all of this, it is very important to maintain as high a vibration as possible. Do your best to keep feeling strong, positive and optimistic. Act with integrity, kindness and compassion. Your individual vibration affects the collective consciousness more than you might realize.

Sharing the Dark Material

In fact, if you believe you have become aware enough of the "dark plan" of the Cabal and have continued to integrate your emotional responses to it enough to share with others, it may be time to start this. If you think you do not have the confidence or power to effectively share it, be aware that you likely do. Many new spirit guides are coming on board with Ascension Lightworkers these days to assist in this very process. Don't push yourself to share the information with others; simply be open to the opportunities you may have to do this.

At the same time, you do have to use discernment, both with whom you choose to share information, and how you do it. Don't attempt to share it with someone who is very asleep and is prone to fear. But if someone seems open to learning some hard truths, try it gradually, and watch to see how much resistance or panic may arise for them.

It's important to maintain a sense of protective energy around yourself in your sharing and avoid getting entangled in someone else's karma. This information can stir deep traumas for people. Just gently plant seeds where you can and wait to see if the person is ready for more. As someone once said, "Don't water the seeds you've just planted with a firehose."

In addition, be sure to share information from a place of loving detachment, without any expectations as to how they will react. If you start feeling a need for their approval or confirmation arising in you, step back. If you feel yourself getting angry about their denial of what you're telling them, let it go.

Ascension Symptoms

Aside from all these challenging experiences you may be moving through as an Ascension Lightworker, you may also be encountering a number of experiences known as *ascension symptoms* that most people, even those who are not Ascension Lightworkers, are experiencing these days.

Body Changes: One of the most common symptoms has to do with body changes, such as unusual aches and pains – some that seem to appear and disappear, others that jump around to different parts of your body. Headaches that come and go can also occur. Old injuries you thought were healed long ago may begin showing up again. Or you might feel waves of heat or energy passing through your body at odd times. Flu-like symptoms may also come and go in a strange way.

Changes in Sleep Patterns: Something else you may note are changes in your sleep patterns. You might find you seem to need a whole lot more sleep than usual. You may at times wake up feeling drugged and have a sense that you've "been somewhere" and "done a lot" in the sleep state, although you can't remember what.

You may also go through periods of time in which you're having intense dreams every night. You might encounter monsters and battles in these dreams or other fearful scenarios. Don't be concerned with these – they may be signs that old memories are releasing. Or it is possible you might be actually fighting battles with dark energies, as part of your service in the sleep state. If you find yourself feeling exhausted as you wake up, even after a full night's sleep, this is probably the reason.

You may also find that at times during the day, your whole body suddenly pulls on you, demanding a nap. You're afraid to close your eyes, because you know you'll immediately fall asleep if you do. It's important when this happens to give in to these nap attacks if you can.

It may have to do with your body needing the sleep so that important bodily shifts can effectively take place. Or it could also mean that your service in the Inner Realms is suddenly needed. You may or may not remember what you were doing, but intuitively you're sensing you were involved in an important operation or event that required the assistance of Ascension Lightworkers.

There are other times when you may find you get along on a lot *less* sleep than normal. You might actually wake up in the middle of the night for a while, not knowing why you can't sleep. Again, don't be concerned, and don't fret about missing out on your sleep. Use this time to meditate (sometimes the best time to do this anyway) or quietly read. Trust you will somehow feel rested and able to move into your day with ease – and you surprisingly will be able to.

Exhaustion: Yet another common ascension symptom is utter exhaustion. This may happen on and off for a while. It actually shouldn't be a surprise to feel exhausted at times during the ascension process, since so much is happening in both your body and mind.

Sometimes it can be especially exhausting if you're around people who are functioning in low-dimensional types of energies, such as anger or depression. It can be hard to hold your own vibration when you're feeling assaulted by negativity from other people or you're in the presence of a lot of unconsciousness.

Of course, some of the negativity that's exhausting you might be your own. But don't get down on yourself if it is. The emotions you're experiencing are coming up to be released – it's all part of the ascension process. Just realize that you need to be kind to yourself if you feel deep fatigue after experiencing a lot of releasing, either from other people or from within yourself.

Sometimes exhaustion sets in simply because your body is having to adjust to higher frequencies that are flowing in. Remember, you're in the process of being completely rewired: your body is morphing into a much less dense crystalline-body. It's busy absorbing new energies and transforming itself; it's shedding old energies, rebooting itself, disassembling and reconstructing itself. Deep changes on the DNA level are taking place. Your whole system is adapting to a brand new "operating system". It's no wonder if you feel exhausted!

Try to give your body all the rest and sleep it needs. Be kind to it. It will eventually adjust to the new levels of consciousness you're ascending to and you'll feel more energy again.

Heightened Sensitivity: Something else you may be noticing is heightened sensitivity of all your physical senses and your nervous system. Perhaps you realize that bright lights bother you more than before, or strong smells are more unpleasant. Loud noises may affect you in ways they haven't before. And, importantly, you might be noticing a heightened sensitivity to energies: if they're negative, you simply can't abide them like you could in the past.

Physical Disorientation: A sense of disorientation from time to time also seems to be part of the ascension process. Sometimes you may feel ungrounded and dizzy, or even spatially-challenged. You might find yourself bumping into the side of a doorway as you walk through it or actually walking into a wall. Perhaps you go to put a cup on a counter and find that you've missed the edge by a couple of inches. Or perhaps you're driving in your car and have a sudden lapse of memory for a few seconds about where you are or where you're headed.

All this is totally normal when experiencing a wave of ascension: the fact is you're *not* all here. You're living in two or three different dimensions at once. You're in transition into a whole new realm of reality, and your body can sometimes lag behind in another reality.

Psychological Disorientation: Perhaps you're also noticing a sensation of not feeling grounded in what you've known to be your usual, familiar "self". Or maybe you have a sense that the world around you somehow isn't as "real" as it used to be.

It can also be a feeling of being in limbo: you're floating between an older identity you've had for a long time and an unfamiliar one that seems to be moving in. So much of what used to be comfortable doesn't fit or feel right anymore. All your old reference points are disappearing. Or you might describe it as a sense of walking between two worlds, neither of which you're fully in. You know that you're not "all here" – and yet you don't know where the rest of you is.

This sense of living in two realities at once may create yet further strange psychological experiences: like the sensation that you're generally living in a high frequency of love and non-separation – and yet you're still engaged in old third-dimensional activities and relationships based in separation and limitation. It's as if the two realities collide inside you and you can't tell what is real anymore.

At times, you may have the feeling of living in a bubble, feeling separate from the outside world and knowing no way to get out of it. Or you may have a surreal sensation of directing your life by remote control.

On top of all that, you may also be experiencing periods of brainfog in which your mind is fuzzy and your cognitive abilities seem impaired. At times you can't recall names of familiar people, books or movies—or even simple, familiar words like "tree" or "water". You might think you're experiencing dementia as your memory seems to be disappearing.

Of course, this could be a sign of aging or other cognitive issues; if you're concerned, you might want to check it out with a health practitioner. But it also may well be part of the ascension process. The waves of light flooding the planet are causing the release of memories that have negative charges attached to them; and certain words and memories can temporarily get swept away by these waves because they're attached to the dysfunctional patterns being released.

All of these experiences can be very disconcerting if you don't keep in mind that disorientation is to be expected as you traverse the unfamiliar terrain between the Third and Fifth Dimensions.

Ascension Awakenings and Openings

So, all these types of rather uncomfortable symptoms – as well as many more – may be happening for you. But it's important to realize that, despite this long discussion of challenging tasks and experiences you are engaged in as an Ascension Lightworker, the ascension process is by no means all dark and difficult. Many wonderful things are also likely occurring in your life on your awakening journey. There can be many delightful surprises and exciting twists that occur along the way, as well – and it can be important to remind yourself of them.

For example, you might be experiencing spontaneous awakenings filled with light that render you speechless for a while, as you bask in bliss. Or powerful heart-openings that bring you to your knees, as love floods your entire being for everyone and everything in creation.

You may also be having thrilling validations of your inner guidance; you find it is getting louder and clearer and that you're getting a better sense of who your spirit guides are. Perhaps new intuitive abilities are coming online, like knowing who is calling you, even before you look at your phone. Or maybe you're having clear memories of past lives, including those you lived before coming to Earth.

You may also be having very positive dreams or out-of-body experiences which indicate new beginnings or exciting new tasks you will soon be undertaking. Or they're showing you that you're assisting and teaching Souls about spiritual truths in the sleep state, or that you're expressing new talents you never knew you had.

In addition, you may be suddenly experiencing little "miracles" that happen out of the blue – or you're finding that manifestation is suddenly getting easier than it ever was before. Maybe you're noticing that it's easier to heal emotional woundings than in the past and also to resolve relationship issues. Perhaps you're realizing that you barely even realize you have a question, before it's somehow being answered.

You might also be delighted to find you're often seeing triple numbers everywhere you look and sense that they're giving you affirmative signs about what you're thinking about or doing. Catching "11:11" on the clock can be an especially powerful experience, as this is a number that brings in high frequency waves of ascension.

Synchronicities can also occur frequently when you're riding an ascension wave. Some of them may seem meaningful to you, indicating there is something for you to pay attention to. For instance, you might hear about a healing product from someone but you're not sure about it for yourself. Then, the next day, while standing in line at the store, you see someone in front of you has purchased it and they're telling the cashier how great it is.

And then, there are other synchronicities that simply seem to be meaningless, and yet they're still delightful. For example, you might be reading a book that includes a character with the name of "Jamie" in it, and then you're watching a video that evening featuring someone with that same name. Or maybe you've been considering buying new slippers, as your old ones are getting rather shabby; and then the next day, a friend mentions she's just bought a new pair of slippers.

Ascension is a Dance

Between the ascension challenges and the ascension joys, you can realize you're on a strange, yet fascinating, ride. In fact, it can be helpful to look at ascension as a type of dance, one involving two basic moves you are performing simultaneously. On the one hand, you're healing and letting go of old limiting energies and patterns, while also releasing collective karma and assisting others on their path – and, at the same time, you're opening up to the expansive higher-dimensional waves of energy that are now flooding the planet and experiencing new levels of joy, love and empowerment.

At times, it can be tricky and confusing; you might be having both positive and negative experiences at the same time. Adding to that, you now have clear access to all three dimensions of consciousness – third, fourth and fifth – and to some degree, even beyond the fifth. So you may find yourself bouncing around, in and out of all of them. This can be very disorienting.

As time passes, you can expect that the higher dimensional energies currently streaming onto the planet are going to be pushing you even more insistently into higher consciousness. It's probably going to get more intense before it finally eases up. Thus, it's all the more important to learn *now* how to navigate this new territory you're in, so as to find your way through it in as easeful a manner as possible.

Indeed, it would be wise to make a sincere effort to clear out all emotional wounding and mental distortions you are still harboring. You'll find that this clearing will happen whether you take charge of it or not; it will simply be less challenging if you are consciously engaged in it.

This Book

This book is designed to offer you tools to make this clearing/healing process easier. In the next section, "Recognizing the Dimension You're In", I present a picture of what the path from 3D to 5D can look like. I describe how we tend to operate when we're functioning in third, fourth, and fifth dimensional consciousness.

It's important to understand that it is possible to shift into 5D consciousness and live from that perspective, even before the Earth makes its definitive shift into that dimension. We can live, at least some or even most of the time, from this higher, awakened state of being, even as the world around us becomes ever more unstable and life becomes increasingly uncertain.

So, this is the first key I present in describing the dimensions: developing an awareness of which dimension you may be functioning in at any given time. You can then begin, if you choose, to take charge of directing yourself into higher levels of consciousness.

Then, in the following section, "Shifting from 3D States of Being", I offer explanations of a number of specific lower-dimensional 3D mindsets to help you understand what brings them about. I also offer tools for shifting out of them into higher states of consciousness. In a way, these tools are no different from those anyone on a spiritual journey can use for healing and awakening. In fact, this book could initially be seen as just another new age self-help book. But it actually is not.

The information is quite specific in its focus on not simply assisting you to feel better or become more "spiritual". Instead, it addresses low-frequency states of being for which a greatly-accelerated awakening may be needed, specifically in the context of the ascension process. It describes how to view these challenging states from a broader perspective of your evolutionary progress during these times of unprecedented change.

What I include in these chapters is not, of course, an exhaustive list of challenging states of being you'll find yourself in during your ascension process. Nor is the list of keys you can use in turning them around complete. I've just chosen the states that people seem to experience most often, and the keys I personally have found to be most valuable in addressing these states.

You may already be aware of many of the keys I describe. But it's easy to forget them when your mind goes blank in the midst of a particularly challenging experience. So it's helpful to be reminded of them.

The last section of the book, "Remembering Yourself as a Soul", presents ways in which you can hopefully take a break from a constant focus on the 3D emotions and belief patterns holding you back, and concentrate instead on developing more positive and uplifting perspectives in life. These are presented not as an alternative to focusing on what may need healing, but as complementary to it. It's important to not attempt the "spiritual bypass" by ignoring low-dimensional emotions and beliefs still functioning within you. Both approaches to healing – focusing on the negative *and* on the positive – are needed.

This book can be used simply as a reference book for when you're feeling stuck in a particular difficult emotion or belief, so I have alphabetically organized the material in the third section to make it easy to find what you're looking for by consulting the table of contents. Also, because certain keys are useful for more than one challenging mindset, you may find some of them described in more than one chapter.

But the book can also be read straight-through to give you a clear sense of the general type of consciousness helpful to maintain on your ascension journey. It will assist you in understanding clearly what becoming merged with your Higher Self – and eventually with your Soul – entails.

As you've likely discovered, shifting into 5D consciousness is not easy – especially during these times in which most of the population is still stuck in 3D consciousness. There are probably times when, no matter what you do, it feels as if there is no way you can possibly shift into higher consciousness – at least as you may wish to in the moment.

At these times, it's helpful to remember that you are not alone in your ascension process. You have caring spirit guides who are constantly there to support you, whether you are aware of them or not. And there are Angels, Ascended Masters, and Galactics, all eager and willing to help, that you can always call on, as well.

And yet sometimes, it may feel as if all you can do is to continue breathing and ride the wave you're surfing, doing your best to trust the process and somehow hold it together till it finally lands you somewhere.

At times, this landing may be far outside your familiar comfort zone. When this happens, the information and tools offered in this book will hopefully be useful in helping you to stabilize and continue on in the most relaxed, confident and easeful way possible.

Keep remembering that these are times when enormous transformation is taking place within you. Be compassionate and patient with yourself. At some point, you will be able to look back and be grateful for all the effort you've put into facing the challenges you've encountered. You will have awakened into knowing yourself not only as a Soul – but a Soul who has contributed courageously to the evolution of humanity.

In the next chapter, we will begin exploring what the path from 3D to 5D can look like.

Recognizing the Dimension You're In

Chapter 5

Shifting from 3D to 5D

As you're now aware, your task as an Ascension Lightworker during these intense times of ascension is multi-layered and requires a great deal of focus, intention, and deep inner work. Even for those who are not here to assist in the ascension of all of humanity and the Earth, ascension is not an easy ride. But for you, it may be proving to be a tumultuous one, dealing with unresolved issues, profound despair, and even terror at times – all while you are also assisting those around you to stay steady and calm.

It's important to be aware that if you've taken on the task of being an Ascension Lightworker, it means you are equipped to handle it. As an old and highly-evolved Soul, you likely have greater wisdom, stronger endurance, and many more inner resources than you realize. And you likely also have a great many celestial and galactic guides you can rely on to assist you.

And yet, you will likely find that you need to continue focusing on deep inner healing and awakening before your actual ascension to the Fifth Dimension can take place. The rest of this book will therefore be devoted to assist you in this process.

Inner Map of Ascension Journey

To start out, this first section will give you a map of sorts of what the inner journey of consciousness from 3D to 5D might look like.

As explained earlier, although the Earth and all humanity shifted into the Fourth Dimension in December 2012, most people are unaware of this and are still functioning in third-dimensional consciousness. Even if you know about the shift that's occurred and are consciously working to maintain a high vibration, you likely still tend to have habits that take you back into 3D consciousness.

You may at times still operate from a limited and painful 3D view on life without realizing it. Like most people, you just slide back into this view because it is so familiar. It can also be hard sometimes to even discern where your immediate state of being is, because you tend to shift back and forth, sometimes rapidly, between third, fourth and fifth dimensional consciousness. It can be confusing.

To make it easier to discern what's happening, I'm going to describe in this section some general characteristics of consciousness when living in the Third, Fourth, and Fifth Dimensions. Becoming aware of these different states of being is a first key for shifting into 5D. In understanding them, you can begin to make the shift from 3D to 5D in a conscious and intentional way. You realize that your level of consciousness changes your experience of reality.

So much of the ascension process is about awareness: becoming more and more conscious in your everyday life as to what your mind is doing and what old habits you're still unconsciously following.

Merging with Higher Aspects of Yourself

One way to frame the progression of consciousness through the dimensions is to see it as a process of identifying with and merging with higher aspects of yourself. If you have been on a path of spiritual awakening for a while, you are probably already having experiences of merging with what has been called your *Higher Self*. In many ways, the process of ascension includes the increase of such experiences and of actually functioning from this higher consciousness.

You've likely experienced this when you find yourself somehow speaking words of profound wisdom that surprise even you. You wonder, "Where did *that* come from?" Or at times when you experience a sudden sense of spiritual clarity, or a profound feeling of well-being for no reason at all. You just know all is well, all is in divine order. Maybe you've had tremendous heart-opening experiences that happen out of the blue, in which love and compassion pour out of you toward all living beings.

These are some of the signs you are beginning to merge with your Higher Self. But what actually is the Higher Self? This term has many different definitions, depending on people's experiences and understanding.

In this book, I am using the term to describe a more evolved aspect of yourself, an extension of your Soul, designed to guide you toward eventually experiencing oneness with your Soul in 5D consciousness. In reality, you already *are* your Higher Self and your Soul; there is no separation. But from the vantage point of 3D/4D consciousness where most people still reside, the experience is generally one of *having* a Higher Self and Soul, and so that is how I will generally be phrasing it.

In merging more and more with your Higher Self, you get a taste of what it is to be merged with your Soul. Increasingly, you experience love, empowerment, joy, peace and compassion in your life. You become aware that suffering and lack are actually illusions, and you begin to understand the true nature of Source/Spirit.

This journey of merging with your Higher Self, as a bridge into the experience of becoming one with your Soul, is likely not a new experience for you, although it may seem so. If you are relating to any of this material, you are probably a Soul who has known well in the far past how to live in full knowledge of who you essentially are. As stated earlier, this experience occurring now is actually one of *remembering* this knowing, of *re*-merging with the primal Essence of who you are.

The process of ascension in the higher Fourth Dimension at this time tends to include gradually-increasing experiences with your Higher Self: initially just tuning into it unintentionally, then connecting to it intentionally, and eventually merging with it for periods of time. These are all "previews" of experiencing fifth-dimensional consciousness.

Another essential aspect of the ascension process has to do with shifting your attention from your ego-mind to your Heart – and allowing Love to guide you in all ways. Making this transition requires both attention and intention. If you're like most people, you have been trained to live from your ego-mind, not realizing how limited and filled with distorted 3D beliefs it is.

What I'll be describing here in this section is generally based on my own experiences and those of many people I've known and worked with in my healing practice over the years. But do keep in mind that we all have our own unique experiences and reference points. So use what I'll be describing here as a type of map that can help bring some clarity for you and assist you to create or refine your own personal ascension map and reference points.

Chapter 6

3D Consciousness

Let's begin with 3D consciousness and explore what that state of mind is generally like.

3D Sense of Identification

First of all, this is when your sense of identification is with your ego-personality self, the whole little package of your personal human self. You're believing that you're the body, your thoughts and emotions, the roles you play, your relationships, and your situations in life.

Somehow you have forgotten that you have a Higher Self, that you're anything more than an individual human being functioning in this physical world. And, along with this, you feel a natural sense of separation from the Divine, other people, and your forgotten Higher Self. As a result, you feel somewhat vulnerable and alone.

You may usually know better than to think this little you is all you are; when you're more aware or when you're meditating, you know it's not true. But, in your daily life, you may tend to go unconscious at times and fall into the familiar 3D identity you've known for so long – especially when you're triggered by something that creates a reaction of fear, hurt or anger.

At those times, you tend to forget what you know and experience during other more aware times. When you get caught in this small and limited view of yourself, you can be sure you're functioning from 3D consciousness.

3D Relationship to the Divine

If you have a belief in God in one form or another and you're experiencing 3D consciousness, you're likely to conceive of God as a separate entity, a being outside of yourself who needs to be petitioned in order for you to receive the help you need.

If you happen to get really scared about something, you may even be drawn back into the idea of how God was described in a religion you grew up with, in which you may have seen God as a kind of glorified father figure with human attributes. When you're in this state of consciousness, God's love for you can feel conditional.

You may sense that "He" can get angry and punish you if you do something wrong. Or, if you're good and you pray and try really hard, you can maybe be forgiven for what you've done wrong. In other words, you have a feeling that you have to do certain things to deserve God's love, because of an assumption you're inherently not okay the way you are.

These beliefs can be very subtle because they're generally unconscious. They're often there, even if you think you believe otherwise. This lack of a sense of worthiness is something that exists in just about everyone, consciously or unconsciously. It's pretty much hard-wired into 3D human consciousness, along with the shame, guilt, and self-hatred that stem from it. You therefore have a need for external validation in order to feel okay about yourself, to feel valuable and needed.

3D Self-Help Practices

This brings us to the self-help and healing practices you may use to help yourself out of this difficult state of being. Many of these practices can definitely be helpful for shifting into higher consciousness. Yet, you may still be approaching your healing from a limited 3D consciousness in which there's generally an assumption that you're somehow broken, and that you have to fix yourself in order to be okay and deserve happiness. There's something wrong with you as you are.

You feel this because, in 3D consciousness, you're identified with the ego-personality self, and this aspect of yourself is indeed imperfect, and probably always will be. Fortunately, this is not your real or full self, and you probably know this when you're feeling clearer. But when you're identified as a flawed human being, you can become fixated on constantly having to somehow become more perfect.

In the next chapter, I'll describe a more fourth-dimensional type of approach to healing practices. What I'm describing here is the kind of mindset you would likely be in if you're trying heal yourself with a 3D consciousness. At the core, there's the belief that something is wrong with you and you have to be fixed.

3D Emotions and Beliefs

There are a number of other beliefs and emotions that stem from this identification with your smaller self when in 3D consciousness. Probably the most prevalent emotion is fear. There are a lot of different fears, but the most universal are fear of death, abandonment, aloneness, and being either physically or emotionally hurt.

When you're caught in fear of any kind, a sensation of being disempowered and helpless is created, a feeling of being alone in the universe, and a belief that you have only yourself to rely on to really feel safe and to get your needs met. Even if you have loved ones, people who are protective of you, you know you can't depend on them all the time; they are dealing with their own stuff. So a part of you can still feel alone and fearful.

Fear also creates a feeling and belief in lack, that there's not enough of what you need and want, so you have to grab what you can to make it in this world. This belief, in turn, can engender such feelings as survival anxiety, self-pity and helplessness, as well as a movement into blame, competition and complaining — all of which can then turn into hatred, envy, greed, resentment, judgment and control.

You get the idea. All of these states of being are obviously 3D. But it can be helpful to name and delineate them. What's important to realize is they all stem from one thing: identification with your ego-personality self.

Remember, if you find yourself experiencing any of these feelings, none of it is wrong or bad. After living in 3D for so long, such feelings are to be expected. Just be careful not to go into shame or self-judgment if you find yourself feeling these emotions. Just notice in a neutral and accepting manner what you're experiencing. That way, shifting out of these emotions and beliefs is much easier.

3D Relationships

Because you feel an inherent sense of separation from other people when you're functioning from third-dimensional consciousness, you tend to automatically develop patterns of fear, separation and unworthiness in your relationships. You likely mistake a feeling of need, desire or lust to be love.

Since it is difficult for you to experience unconditional love from people, you often feel disappointment, grief, anger and hurt with those you know. You may also frequently experience relationship dynamics that could be called co-dependent, narcissistic, or abusive.

In general, in 3D consciousness, you have the belief that the purpose of relationships with family, spouses, partners and good friends is to give you an essential sense that you are lovable, valuable and important. You believe that your loved ones are there to fill these emotional needs, and you're there to fill theirs.

This belief can sound so right; it's familiar. It's what you've learned and accepted to be true. And, perhaps, to some extent, your emotional needs until now have been met in this way. But you don't realize that the belief that others are responsible for filling your needs has also created power struggles steeped in feelings of hurt, betrayal and guilt. Having given the responsibility to someone else for your happiness, you therefore have no power to create it for yourself and will blame others for its absence in your life.

3D Belief about Happiness

In actuality, when in 3D consciousness, you don't understand very much about happiness or how to maintain that feeling for any length of time. When you think back on your experience in life, your memories confirm that negative thoughts and emotions have been pretty predominant.

When you do manage to feel happy at some point, you ascribe that happiness to something caused by outside circumstances, events and relationships that you have had little or no control over. You are at the effect of these external circumstances.

There's no understanding that you have access to a happiness that resides inside of you – that you can actually choose to be happy, no matter what's happening. There's always a sense of waiting for happiness to happen in the future, a belief that something has to change first before you can be happy. So you're never quite satisfied with what is happening in the moment. There's always a niggling sense of dissatisfaction, even when circumstances are really okay.

Your lack of feeling in charge of your own happiness is further enhanced by the fact that when you are in 3D you aren't aware that you have the power to create your own reality. You forget any information you may at other times know about manifesting what you want and need in life. You feel at the effect of the universe's whims.

Automatic Reactivity and Identifying with Your Pain

In general, when you're in 3D consciousness, you're caught in a space where very little self-awareness or self-reflection is happening. You're not aware that you have any real power over what you're experiencing. This becomes especially apparent when you're experiencing automatic reactions of anger, hurt, pain, irritation or despair—and it feels as if you have no control over stopping these reactions.

In addition, there's often a resistance to meeting the negative reactions you experience in a conscious way with love and compassion for yourself. You're aware of your pain, but you get identified with it. When caught in this state, you have no idea that your pain is not you – that it's something you *have*, something you can relate to, something you can calm down and feel compassion for. You feel you *are* your pain, and you can feel lost in it. You can easily recognize that you're caught in this state when you attempt to escape from painful emotions through drugs, alcohol, sex or workaholism.

Living in the Past and Future

Another sign of being in 3D consciousness is when you have no real awareness of the present moment. You're often caught in the past or a possible future. When living in the past, you tend to get focused on regret and self-judgment; and, when living in the future, you're caught in worry and anxiety.

In doing this, you're essentially creating a future based on your past; you keep it repeating itself over and over again. You forget all you've ever learned about living in the present moment or about being mindful. You're not aware of how you're missing out on all that is currently happening in every moment and how staying present is a portal into higher consciousness. And, most importantly, you're missing the opportunity to create something new in your future.

Your Mind is Your GPS

What makes things even harder is that when you are in 3D, your "go-to" GPS is your rational mind, which offers a very limited source of wisdom. And yet, this is where you make decisions. You've somehow forgotten about the power of your intuition or the wisdom you've often found when in contact with your Heart.

As a result, you find yourself bouncing back and forth between the pros and cons of different options, based on your past experiences and what sounds good, as this is all the mind knows to do. Then, perhaps dissatisfied with this process, you find yourself researching outer sources to help you make your decision – friends and family, who are generally eager to give you their opinions, or experts who claim to have knowledge about what you're indecisive about.

These opinions can, of course, be helpful at times, but they can still leave you feeling indecisive and hesitant, since you're not feeling the sense of having checked in on your own wisdom as to what might be right for you.

Duality and Judgment

Another sign that you're functioning in 3D consciousness is being caught in a mindset of duality and judgment, operating with thoughts and beliefs of what's good and bad, right and wrong. You take polarized stances on issues, feeling you're right, and that people who don't agree with you are wrong.

You may even have judgment and contempt for those who have different views and beliefs. It's really important to become aware of when you find yourself caught in polarized beliefs and judgment, as, for example, in the political arena. Be careful about getting caught in an "us vs. them" consciousness. This is a very common and familiar 3D state of mind.

3D Habit Patterns

So that, in a nutshell, is a description of 3D consciousness. Again, if you find yourself immersed in any of the patterns described here, there's no need to judge yourself for it. It's to be expected. Just be aware of where you are in your ascension process, where you might feel stuck, and have compassion for yourself. Accept whatever is happening as what-is for right now.

If you can stop resisting what is happening in the moment, you will find it's easier to see what you can do to lift yourself out of it into a higher vibration. Resistance to something keeps you stuck in it.

If you can remember that what you're in the process of doing – attempting to shift out of habits you've maybe formed over thousands of years living in 3D – it can help you to be compassionate with yourself. It's bound to take some time and practice to finally shift from these kinds of habits.

Chapter 7

4D Consciousness

Now let's take a look at 4D Consciousness and see how it's different from your state of being when functioning in 3D.

First, it's important to understand that dimensions have levels within them. We don't just shift from one dimension suddenly into another. There are levels within a dimension we journey through.

However, for our purposes here, we can describe the Fourth Dimension at this point as having two basic levels: Higher and Lower. In this chapter I will be describing the experiences of living in the Higher Fourth Dimension. You'll likely recognize what I describe here. If you've been on a spiritual path for some years, you've probably been generally functioning much of the time from this level in your daily life.

4D Sense of Identification

So, what is your sense of identification when in 4D? It's still basically with your ego-personality self – but there is an awareness that you have a higher consciousness, a Higher Self, and you are often identified with this more-evolved aspect of yourself. There's a knowing, at least intellectually, that you are not separate from the Divine; you're one with it.

You also become aware that you are not your "stuff"; you are not your mental and emotional issues. You are so much more: you are a Being who is *experiencing* these issues. Just having this simple awareness, that you are not your issues but rather the one who is experiencing them, can be a great relief. You begin to experience a freedom from the heavy, negative problems you were once identified with, finding it easier to release negative energy and more quickly move forward.

Awareness of Creating Your Own Reality

Also, in Higher 4D consciousness, you become aware that consciousness creates reality. You begin understanding that through your thoughts and your actions in the present you are creating your life, your reality. You're not a passive participant in what happens to you. You know the importance of positive thoughts, emotions, actions and expectations; you realize that in order to create the reality you want to live in, you need to become conscious of your thoughts and emotions and learn to manage them.

You can also realize that you do not have to automatically react with negative emotions to challenging circumstances; you have a choice in responding to situations that trigger you. You have the opportunity to observe a situation you're in, and then choose your response before you act. Because of this, you experience a greater feeling of empowerment, a sense of taking charge of what happens to you.

Another difference that happens in Higher 4D consciousness is you begin to experience yourself more and more as the witness or observer, in which you're watching yourself from a neutral, clear, and balanced place. You see more clearly the stories you tell yourself about your life and who you are. And you know you can change them – or just drop them – if you wish.

4D Time and Manifestation

When you're in 4D consciousness, time begins morphing into an unknown entity. On the one hand, time seems to be going much more quickly than ever before. And yet, at other times, it can feel as if it's slowing down and you are accomplishing an amazing number of things in a short period of time.

You may begin realizing that time is not a fixed reality and that linear time is simply one way to experience time. You may also feel yourself being drawn more and more into present time – and even into the present moment. You don't dwell so much in the past or future.

There are times when you totally forget about time altogether. Rather than a regimented, concrete concept, time becomes fluid, illusory and eternal. You discover that you can actually stretch or condense time, especially if you have strong intention to do this.

You may experience a similar elasticity in your experience of space as you reference your internal experience of it rather than any external measurement. Eventually, you may begin realizing that time and space are actually hooked together; they're one thing – and that they are both moving through you, not the other way around.

You also may begin discovering the Quantum Field, where all time and all space are available to you. There are limitless possibilities and infinite realities you can manifest in this field, through thought, intention and powerful emotions. As you learn this, successful manifestation comes more easily.

Greater Love for Self and Others

In general, you have a greater self-awareness when in 4D consciousness. And you're open to meeting difficult emotions with compassion and unconditional love for yourself, rather than trying to resist them, deny them, or distract yourself from them. You realize it's essential to no longer allow your life to be run by the lower, negative emotional reactions and judgments you have about yourself; you need to learn to love *all* of who you are.

As a result, your love for others also becomes more unconditional, as well. You have experiences of unity consciousness, knowing that everyone is connected. And, with this, you find you want to be of service to others whenever you can.

4D Relationships

However, even with all these experiences, you may still be facing certain conflicts and upsets in your relationships. You're beginning to realize how many unawakened patterns you have developed in relating to people. You become aware of certain dependencies you developed with people close to you. You see how you may be reinforcing dysfunctional dynamics with them, causing suffering and conflict for both of you.

You start questioning the belief that it is the role and duty of your loved ones to give you an essential sense that you are lovable, valuable and important. You see that this is your job, not theirs. You realize how this old assumption includes a belief that you are not inherently whole and not able to experience your own lovableness and inherent worth without someone else's help. Most importantly, you're discovering this isn't true anymore.

You may begin to realize that much of your grief in relationships stems from the feeling that your loved ones don't give you what you believe they "should" give you on the emotional level. You become aware of the times you've felt that people have failed to "meet your needs" and those times when you've been accused of not meeting theirs. You see how you have blamed others for your emotions, your actions, and your beliefs about yourself – and how this has disempowered you.

As a result, you stop blaming other people so much and start taking responsibility for your own emotions and reactions. You see when you are projecting your own issues onto them and can apologize for this.

You also begin to realize how conditional your love may be for your loved ones and discover that perhaps you've never felt unconditional love being given to you, either. You begin contemplating how it may be possible to develop unconditional love in a relationship.

This can get complicated if you are someone with low self-worth, as you may tend to allow others to take advantage of your kindness and treat you without true caring or respect. You may discover that you've been confusing what you've thought to be unconditional love for people with allowing them to take advantage of you due to your lack of self-worth. You discover the need to heal wounding around this pattern.

Indeed, when in 4D, you begin seeing that all the challenges you have in relationships point to the need to truly develop unconditional love for yourself. You realize that it is the love for yourself that you must rely on, first and foremost, for your sense of feeling valuable, loved and respected.

You understand that, if you're going to find true freedom from hurt, blame and resentment in your relationships, it's not the job of others to give you this sense of emotional wholeness. It's up to you. Whatever love and validation others may offer you can simply serve to enhance this sense of wholeness you already have within yourself.

With these realizations, you are taking charge of your own healing around relationships and making unconditional self-love a primary goal.

Healing in 4D

In your process of healing when in 4D consciousness, you no longer have a belief that you're broken or that you need to be fixed. You understand that who you are is a Soul – an eternal Being. You're much larger, more powerful, much more complex than a body/mind being with issues. And you recognize that you, in your most authentic Essence, are already perfect, just as you are.

You're simply in the process of letting go of old inaccurate 3D beliefs that something is wrong with you. You're releasing all the traumas and emotions you've experienced in multiple lifetimes in 3D that you've thought were a part of you, but you now see clearly are just energetic debris that has attached to you. And you're learning to let it go.

With this understanding, you can begin to see yourself clearly as the beautiful Being you are. Even if you can't feel it or know it all the time, you do now have a reference point. This is all very different from how you might approach your healing process within 3D consciousness – as someone who needs to change or be fixed in order to be okay or worthy. You know you are already okay and worthy. You just need to let go of old 3D ideas of how you've thought you were not.

Experiences of Awakened Consciousness

When you're operating in 4D consciousness, you also find you're having an increasing number of experiences of awakened consciousness – such as periods of profound well-being, deep love, peace, expansive freedom, or a profound stillness you've never experienced before. These sometimes seem to happen for no reason at all.

You notice you're experiencing more appreciation for the world around you. As you go through your day, you find that your senses seem to be somewhat heightened and that the world is more lovely than you've noticed before.

In addition, when in the Higher Fourth Dimension, you notice you are having experiences on multiple levels of awareness and are awakening into a knowing of yourself as a multi-dimensional being. You may even have experiences of yourself simply as vast consciousness – a sensation of having no personal boundaries.

There are generally increased synchronicities that occur in 4D consciousness. You see how things can magically work themselves out at times. You begin to feel divinely guided. You feel as if the Universe is giving you signs, gently directing you in where to go, what to do. You realize that everything is possible. There's a greater trust that you're being taken care of by unseen forces. And although your GPS is still basically your rational mind, you have increasing reliance on your intuition and your Heart.

You can also notice that intuitive and psychic abilities are being activated – such as telepathy, remembering past lives, becoming aware of your galactic heritage, channeling, or receiving downloads from some higher source. You are feeling a greater presence and guidance from angelic or other celestial beings, giving you a feeling of greater safety and support.

Challenges to Staying in 4D

All these aspects of consciousness are probably familiar to you, and you may have noticed how they are increasing lately. Although it's possible to still get caught in 3D habit patterns of thought and emotional reaction, higher 4D consciousness is probably becoming more and more your default consciousness.

But, due to the amount of change that's likely occurring in your life and the speed at which it's happening, it can also be challenging to stay in this higher consciousness. It's natural for emotions like fear and uncertainty to arise; but, it can all go a lot more smoothly if you can learn how to gracefully accept what is happening and not resist it when you're encountering change, loss and confusion.

Again, it is all about awareness of which level of consciousness you're functioning from – and making a choice as to which level you wish to live in.

Fantastic Dinner Party

There's a question that author Jim Self poses that I find helpful in understanding the dimensions and how we function when we're in them. He asks you to imagine the most wonderful gathering you can think of with your best friends and loved ones – an occasion that would bring great joy to you.

This could be a whole group of people you know, or maybe just two or three; but they're people you trust and love and are totally comfortable with. They also, in this scenario, all get along really well with each other.

And perhaps you're having a great dinner party with them. Imagine this for a moment. Feel what it's like to be with these people you love – feel the joy, the sense of comfort, the intimate trust, the love. And let's say you've been having so much fun, you've lost track of time. And you're just looking around and seeing that everyone is really happy. There's been intimate sharing and deep connection among you, and a whole lot of laughter – as well as great food you're all sharing.

You're feeling the love that's present in the room, the sense of well-being. It feels so complete; your whole being is humming with pleasure. And you're thinking, "It just doesn't get any better than this!" Deep gratitude and joy are washing through you.

If you can feel all this, understand that this experience is a reference point for you: What you're feeling with this imagined scenario indicates that you're experiencing the highest level of energy in the Higher Fourth Dimension. And this is really wonderful.

But then you may be wondering: if this great feeling is still 4D, what could 5D possibly feel like? Well, it's not that this wonderful dinner party couldn't happen in 5D consciousness; it certainly could. But there would probably be some differences. In the next chapter, let's look at my description of 5D consciousness to see what they might be.

Chapter 8

5D Consciousness

Again, as when I described fourth-dimensional consciousness in the last chapter, some of what I describe here may also sound familiar to you. You may well slip into 5D consciousness, at least for moments, in your daily life. And it can be validating and encouraging to be aware of this.

5D Sense of Identification

In 5D consciousness, your sense of identification is quite different from when you're in 3D and 4D. Your identification is as a multidimensional Being – or as the Soul, the eternal aspect of who you are. You're fully aware that you *are* the Soul that is expressing itself in a human body. This is not just an intellectual understanding; it's an ongoing experience of it, the full knowing and living of it.

There's an understanding that you, as the Soul, have extended part of yourself into lower, denser dimensions to have an experience in human form on earth – but that the human form is just one part of you. Because you experience yourself as a multidimensional being, you're aware of living in a number of different dimensions; and also, simultaneously, as part of the collective consciousness of all that exists.

There's a profound knowing of your oneness with all people, with all of existence. There's no sense of separation or duality; you're one with all of creation. You may experience yourself at times as a point of awareness in the Ocean of pure Consciousness. And, with this, there's an expansive sense of freedom, a knowing of the vastness of yourself, a huge spaciousness.

5D Mood and Emotions

In 5D consciousness, you know yourself to be free of all suffering, all lack, and all limitation. They no longer exist for you in your 5D reality. Your mood is generally clear, peaceful, happy, harmonious. There's often a sense of quiet bliss. This state of being is not dependent on any outer circumstances, events or relationships. It's just there as a natural, basic default mood.

At times, you might experience a period of intense bliss, joy, love, or gratitude; but generally, it's a mood that's quiet, peaceful, balanced, neutral, and optimistic. The monkey mind is gone, leaving you with a feeling of clear spaciousness in your mind. And, with this, there's a sense of exhilarating inner freedom.

Very importantly, what you can notice in 5D is a total and complete lack of negative emotions. There's an absence of fear, anger, depression, hurt, shame, judgment, self-doubt, and loneliness. These were all left behind in the lower dimensions.

There may still be "lessons" to learn, but there is no sense of guilt or that you've done something "wrong". When it becomes apparent you've said or done something that's off track or hurtful to someone, it's more of an experience of "Whoops – this didn't work!" And, in a neutral and compassionate way, you take action to redirect your words or actions back to a position of "right action". Integrity and trasparency guide you, and yet self-doubt and self-judgment are absent.

There's an easy acceptance of what-is – no longing, no desires for anything to be different from how it is. The constant niggling dissatisfaction that has always been present in your 3D/4D consciousness, usually on a subconscious level, is gone. Whatever is happening in your life is just fine. And there's a curiosity about whatever may be next – even an anticipation, knowing it will be interesting and engaging.

Trust in the Benevolence of the Universe

In fifth-dimensional consciousness, there is a knowing of the nature of the Universe and life that is very different from what you believe you know in the Third and Fourth Dimensions. In 3D/4D, the world never feels totally safe. There's always some sort of fear about survival on the subconscious level. And there is also a sense of separation and aloneness.

When you're in fifth dimensional consciousness, all that is absent. There's a simple trust in life, a knowing that the Universe is inherently benevolent, and that, of course, you're going to be taken care of. There's no anxiety, no fear. You feel precious and valuable for the unique contribution of consciousness you offer to the world.

Openness to the "Impossible" Happening

In 3D/4D consciousness, you can often feel caught in the limitations of what your rational mind thinks it knows, based on your experiences from the past. The limitations you believe in when in 3D/4D consciousness can seem formidable, and there is little or no belief that you can get around them.

In 5D, you understand that what might sound impossible to your lower-dimensional awareness is actually very possible. You understand that there are actually no limitations to what you can create. And you know as well that you inherently possess the power to bring about creations you are inwardly directed to manifest.

5D Interactions with the World

At times in 5D, it's not just you that feels different; the actual world around you can feel changed too. You're not actually in a different place – you can still see all the same objects and people around you – but they are all somehow vibrating with life you've never been aware of when you've seen them through 3D/4D eyes. It's almost as if all cells in everything are lit up and dancing.

And strangely enough, there can also be a sense that everything you see is happy, even objects: trees, doors, tables, your printer. Needless to say, you, yourself, are charged with happiness. You may find yourself smiling widely at everyone you meet, feeling warm and friendly, wanting to engage with them. A profound love may simultaneously envelope you and pour from you.

In general, there seems to be no separation between anyone or anything and yourself. You're light and clear, without any feeling of density. And yet you're very full – of love, of light, of joy. There is no sense of the small egoic-self present. In a way, there is nothing of you left – just pure consciousness expressing through a physical body.

But at the same time, there can be a feeling of being very large and expanded. There is no time, no space – just a vibrating joy that sings throughout your entire being.

Unconditional Love and the Sacred Heart

At the core of 5D consciousness, there is an expansion and openness in the Heart, an outpouring of love from your whole being. There's a feeling of warmth and emotional receptivity and a flowing of love toward all you encounter and for all of life, including yourself. Within you there's a total absence of judgment or separation, replaced with a field of love you can feel both within and around you. At times, you can be visited by what could be called "love attacks" — a surge of love that pours through you with a power that can bring tears.

A graciousness moves through you, making way for a deep desire to be of service. And you know this to be your natural state of being, that having an open Heart is innately natural to you.

In fifth-dimensional consciousness, you're also aware of how Love is a powerful force; it's at the core of all existence. Your GPS has therefore shifted fully from your rational mind to your Heart. Unconditional Love naturally guides your every action. You know your mind is much too limited for making decisions about your life; your Heart's wisdom is much more reliable. When you enter into this space, you have clear access to Universal Mind where all truth resides.

Being constantly centered in your Heart, you also experience a natural, unconditional love for everyone – and for yourself. There's no more judgment. There's no working at getting rid of judgment; it's just absent. The love you feel for people has no attachment with it. It's a clear, more detached type of love, with no strings attached, no expectations or demands.

5D Relationships

In 5D consciousness, you feel no need for approval, love or connection from others. You enjoy all that people give to you, but you have no *need* for it and therefore no expectations or demands on them to meet your needs. These are all met by your own self-love and your knowing of your inherent value.

A relationship without the agreement to take responsibility for each other's needs may sound, from a third or fourth dimensional point of view, as if it would be a dry, unemotional and disconnected type of relationship. But in 5D you realize that, without these emotional types of demands, you can have warm, loving, and highly-fulfilling relationships that run smoothly, without a lot of drama.

You find that although another person can offer you a great deal of love, respect and support, you are not dependent on these qualities to feel lovable, valuable and important. The love you receive from others is a bonus, an overflow that is much appreciated and valued; but it is not needed within your being, because you are able to provide the love you need from within yourself.

And, very importantly, your love for others springs solely from your true caring and compassion for them – not from a need that they provide you with something in return. It's an unconditional love, free of demands or expectations that a person act in a certain way or be something different from who they are.

There's actually no emotional need for *any*thing in a relationship – and yet, paradoxically, it's all there for you to enjoy: love, connection, respect.

New Abilities

When in 5D consciousness, you can also find that your senses are even more enhanced than when in 4D. Everything looks more alive at times, as if lighted from within. Colors can look brighter. You may even see new colors that don't exist in the lower dimensions. At times, you might hear what has been called the "music of the spheres" or the "eternal OM".

Because you can communicate telepathically, there's also no real need to speak. Nor is there any need to hide anything you're thinking or feeling; you're fully comfortable being completely transparent.

You realize that other psychic abilities are waking up in you, as well. As you shift into the higher levels of 5D, you will actually be able to do things such as levitation, moving objects with your mind, or passing your hand through solid objects.

Manifestation in higher levels of 5D is instantaneous. In 4D, you became aware of the Quantum Field and began learning how to create and manifest within it. In 5D, you realize you can create something just by thinking of it – it's immediate. You think of an apple; it appears in your hand. All things come to you through simple thought.

Also, in the higher levels of 5D, you may discover you can actually time travel with your body to other worlds and dimensions.

5D Time

In 5D, all time as you've known it actually disappears. You fully realize that linear time is just one form of time. You now have access to any moment in any location – to all timelines, past, present and future. There's a sense that, rather than you moving through your life, life is actually flowing through you.

In 5D you live completely in the present moment – not just in present time – but actually in the moment itself. All low-vibrational thoughts of past and future are irrelevant, simply absent. You have a trust in the constant, effortless flow of life in each moment. You find it's a very comfortable zone in which to function.

The same number of events happen in your daily life, but there's a sensation of timelessness. You flow from one event to the next. There's no frustration about how things are unfolding, even if something happens that you would have previously thought was terrible. There's just a knowing that all will work out and you'll be fine. You're neutral, accepting, empowered and peaceful.

Once in a while, when you're immersed in the present moment, you'll suddenly remember an appointment or something else you've scheduled, but have not held in your mind until this moment – the exact time you need to remember it. You see that, without fail, you are always somehow reminded precisely when you need to remember something scheduled to occur at a given time.

You are never really early or late when you function in this present moment zone. By the clock you might seem off, to some extent. But as for being right on time for the circumstance you're in, it's always right on time for both yourself and for the other people involved in a meeting or appointment with you.

5D Focus

When in 5D consciousness, your focus is often on creating and co-creating. You also find you love learning and expanding your awareness. And you feel a sense of wonder and excitement, even with the smallest things you discover or experience.

You also enjoy the adventure of exploring and discovering new worlds, both in physical form and beyond form. You may sense that eventually, in the higher levels of 5D, you can probably learn to visit other galactic civilizations, your star sisters and brothers. Although you are following what interests and excites you, your focus in all your activities also naturally centers on serving others.

In essence, you're totally enjoying life that's filled with joy, peace, freedom, and a sense of fulfillment. This, of course, is very different from your experience in 3D and 4D consciousness. Gone is any irritating dissatisfaction with your life, no more waiting for something better to happen.

In general, when living in 5D, there's a buoyant optimism about life, a feeling of being totally alive and aware. You are confident that whatever is ahead for you is going to be just as wonderful, intriguing and delightful as life generally is for you.

Creating Your Own Map

So this is a general map I've come up with, depicting these three levels of consciousness. You may find you have additions or corrections you'd like to make to your own map as you're experiencing ascension. But, hopefully, these words have stimulated thought and realizations that will be helpful to you.

As I've noted earlier, we now have access to all three dimensions at this point – and to some degree, even beyond 5D. So, with awareness, you can begin to choose the level of consciousness you'd like to live in.

In the following section of this book, you'll find I've broken the material down into specific challenges you may experience on your ascension journey that tend to pull you into lower states of consciousness – along with keys to assist you in shifting out of them and into higher consciousness.

Shifting from 3D States of Being

Chapter 9

Understanding 3D Mental-Emotional States

This section of the book includes chapters on specific low-dimensional mental-emotional states. They are in alphabetical order for easy access. I initially give a short description and explanation about the particular state of consciousness and then I offer ways in which you can work with it to shift into a higher vibration.

Ascension Symptoms

In a way, as I described in Chapter 3, each of these mind-states could be seen as an Ascension symptom. You can expect to experience them, simply because you are in the process of rapidly transforming in consciousness. Much is shifting around within your mind and body, as they struggle to keep up with the changes in consciousness you are experiencing.

Certain long-dormant aspects of your brain are now awakening, new strands of your DNA are activating, the electromagnetic field around you is shifting, and old beliefs and emotions are arising to be released. At times, you may feel as if not "all of you" is present, and you don't know where the missing parts are. This may manifest with an experience of dense mindfog, as if not all parts of your brain are available to you.

It can be frightening if you don't understand that this is a common symptom for when you're going through an ascension "upgrade" in your brain. It's as if your Soul needs to rewire parts of your brain for a while in order to ready it for a higher vibration.

With all this happening, it is no wonder you can find yourself in uncomfortable emotional states and confusion at times. However, since they seem to happen most frequently when the high-dimensional waves of light now flowing onto the planet are most powerful, they will likely be temporary and eventually dissipate.

Picking up Energies from the Collective

Occasionally, as also described in Chapter 3, you may also be responding with fear, anger or other low-vibrational emotions to something you are picking up from the greater collective consciousness of the planet, or from particular groups of people experiencing specific challenges. This is often the case if you are especially empathic and you can find nothing going on in your own life that could be causing you to feel such emotions. There is a great deal of turmoil in the world at this point, and you are likely very tuned into it on the energetic level.

These emotions can be met and then released relatively more easily than if they were your own, so it's helpful to determine if the emotions have originated from within you or not. When you suspect that certain confusing, unexplainable emotions that have suddenly arisen in you are not your own, ask your inner guidance if this is the case. If you receive an affirmative answer either in words or on a body/energetic level, call in divine Light, ascended masters and angels to help release the emotions back to Source. It may take a few minutes, however, you will eventually feel a release of the energies.

3D Baggage Up for Releasing

However, if a low-vibrational state lasts for any length of time, it's important to delve more deeply into its cause and find a way to meet the emotions successfully, so as to resolve them. During these times of accelerated ascension, when dark and disturbing information about the world and humanity's plight is being released, deep emotions and memories are surfacing from your unconscious mind. These can be from this lifetime, but they may also be from past lives when you were involved in deeply painful situations.

Often when you've experienced trauma in your life and felt overwhelming emotions you could not handle at the time, these emotions, along with negative core beliefs attached to them, have retreated to a resting place in your unconscious. They reside there with the memories from past lives you are also not yet ready to meet and integrate.

This is helpful in that, with these overwhelming emotions and beliefs tucked away in your unconscious, you can usually find a way to continue functioning in your life. You're not entirely free of them, as they can get activated in similar future experiences. But, for the most part, you can pretty much forget about them in your day-to-day life.

However, during these times of ascension this is no longer true. When your vibration is rising, all this unexplored emotion and trauma must surface from the unconscious to be understood, processed and then released. It cannot go with you into the Fifth Dimension.

Raising Your Vibration

In a way, it doesn't matter whether the cause of your upset or confusion is an ascension symptom, tuning into the collective, or your own 3D stuff surfacing from your unconscious. You can always benefit from a deeper explanation of all of these mindsets and learn keys to shift from them.

The basic key to keep in mind when feeling stuck in any of these 3D places is *doing something that will raise your vibration*. Almost anything you can find to do that will be helpful. Even if you can shift into just a somewhat higher vibration, your mind will be clearer, you will feel less anxiety, and your body will be calmer. When you've achieved that, you can then more easily tune into your inner guidance to understand what to do next.

In a clearer state of mind, you can also tune into what can be seen as benefits of what you are experiencing, even if it's painful. You can ask such questions as "Why is this happening?" "What can I learn from this?" or "Is something else at play here?". There is always something you can learn from any challenging situation. And just recognizing this benefit – without going into self-judgment or shame – can automatically raise your vibration.

At the same time, it's important to also keep in mind as you read the material in this section that, if you are experiencing any of the emotions discussed, you should never judge yourself for it. Negative emotions are part of what the realm of creation known as the Third Dimension is all about, and it's what you came here to experience. Now, as part of your continuing learning process, you're figuring out how to shift out of them.

And, as an Ascension Lightworker, you are also developing greater compassion for all human beings, so fully experiencing the emotions yourself can prove extremely helpful. Therefore, be compassionate and patient with yourself in the whole process of learning how to shift out of low-dimensional emotions.

Chapter 10

Angry

Anger really has a bad rap in most cultures in the world, and perhaps especially within spiritual circles. It's an emotion often considered "inappropriate", "immature" or "unspiritual". It's a feeling to be kept hidden, denied or somehow healed.

If you experience anger often, perhaps you've found yourself judging it and demeaning yourself for feeling it. If so, like many people, you may be confusing the *emotion* of anger with the common *expression* of anger, which generally entails blaming and directing hostile energy at someone. That type of expression, of course, projects low-frequency energy and is usually very uncomfortable to receive on the other end. And it's generally not helpful, anyway, in accomplishing what is desired.

What Lies Beneath Anger

It's important to understand the nature of anger – why and how it develops. First, anger is not considered by many psychologists to be a "primary" emotion. This means it tends to arise in a person to cover up other emotions that are even less desirable to feel, such as hurt or fear. Often both of these emotions lie beneath anger. The feeling of anger serves as a defense against them.

This is not necessarily a bad thing, in that the vibration of anger is actually a higher one than that of either hurt or fear. It has a sense of greater power with it. However, if you only focus on your anger and the issues that come up around your expression of it, you may never get to the bottom of why it has actually arisen within you to begin with.

It's important to investigate the feelings of hurt and fear that lie beneath the anger. Ask yourself what it is that has been hurtful or caused you fear. In general, what you are going to find is a situation or relationship in which you feel disrespected, uncared about, or disempowered. You feel your needs are not being met, and you feel helpless about getting them met. These are the situations you need to resolve.

Anger is Your Ally

To resolve them, you need to realize that your emotion of anger is actually your ally. It arises with a great deal of energy in order to give you the power to DO something about the situation in which you're feeling hurt or fearful. Anger wants Action. But it wants *constructive* action that will change the situation so you are feeling more empowered, respected and cared about. Throwing hostile energy at someone will not accomplish this. Indeed, it generally does just the opposite.

To be able to express anger in a constructive way, you need to use its energy to give you inner strength to resolve the situation and not merely dissipate it by blowing it out in some way. You need to set a firm intention, based in self-respect, to not again allow anyone to treat you in a way that is not respectful and kind.

With this resolve, you can then begin finding more effective ways to interact with someone who is not treating you well. As you speak what is true for you, you may find you can actually speak quietly, containing the anger within you – and achieve success. Because you are lined up inside yourself with a new sense of determination and self-respect, a sense of quiet authority emanates from you.

If a person isn't being kind or respectful to you, and they are unwilling to shift into this new mode with you, you can just walk away. Not with hostility – just with a quiet sense of knowing you don't have to take what they're dishing out. You make decisions based on what's important to you, not allowing someone else's self-centered needs to sway you in another direction.

When you realize you have allowed people to treat you with disrespect and lack of consideration, you discover you have the power to *not* allow that dynamic anymore. You see that you're the one who has allowed it; so you're also the one who can decide to stop allowing it. Taking responsibility for your own situation gives you power.

In essence, what you're doing is treating yourself with greater respect and kindness. You have made a commitment to yourself to not allow any more disrespectful, unkind dialogue or action against you. In projecting this empowered and self-loving energy into the world, you begin finding that other people also start treating you that way.

Initially, this may not be the case, however. When you first begin standing up for yourself, attempting to demand respect and consideration, if you're with people you've been interacting with for a while, they are likely to resist this new energy from you. They're probably going to want you to go back to the way you were before, allowing them to continue taking advantage of your generous or disempowered nature.

This is not necessarily out of any malice on their part; it's just that people, dealing with their own issues, tend to automatically take advantage of people who allow them to do so. It is therefore up to you to stop this dynamic.

At first, you may find that you're losing friends – or people you thought were your friends. Some people may eventually disappear from your life, unwilling to make the shift in their interactions with you. But those who do truly care about you will eventually shift back to interacting with you, adapting to your new mode of taking care of yourself.

In addition, you will begin attracting new people into your life who naturally treat you with respect and kindness. It will become clear to you that *people tend to treat you the way you treat yourself.*

Stepping Outside the Blame Game

Another approach to resolving anger issues is to look at how you may be participating in the "Blame Game". When you get caught in third-dimensional habit patterns, it's very easy to fall into blame for what is not going well in your life. Either you land on something or someone who is responsible for the difficulty you find yourself in, or you decide you're the one to blame. You soon discover that neither of these approaches assists you out of anger patterns.

Yet, in 3D consciousness, this is a common way to approach negative situations. There is always someone or something to blame, and there is always the victim. With this perspective, it's deemed important to punish the party responsible for the problem. It's all part of the game plan in 3D, a way people keep themselves separate and divided.

And yet, it's important to understand that when you're participating in the Blame Game as the blamer, this also keeps you in a powerless victim role. It serves to keep you from taking responsibility for any part of the negative situation. And therefore, as described above, if you're not responsible for creating the situation, you're not in a position in which you can change it.

Blaming someone else for your suffering can initially feel good, because, at least, you're not blaming yourself. But, eventually, you'll find that the blaming stance doesn't really free you from your pain. Instead, it locks you into a position of anger, self-righteousness, hatred, and self-pity – not where you want to be, if you're on a serious ascension path.

Taking Responsibility for your Life

It's important to be able to see this dynamic of blame clearly, and to avoid it whenever you can. To raise your vibration, you need to take responsibility for what is occurring in your life; you need to take charge of your thoughts, emotions and actions. In doing this, a sense of empowerment will arise within you, and anger will dissipate.

However, do remember that, in taking responsibility, you are not confusing this with blaming yourself. Responsibility and blame are two different things entirely. One frees and empowers you; the other creates victimhood.

At the same time, it also doesn't mean that someone or certain government entities – or whoever – haven't done things that have helped to create difficulty in your life. They often have. But focusing on blaming them and starting down that road will just keep you disempowered. Instead, if you take responsibility for your own life and what happens in it, you will find that fewer and fewer people do things that affect your life negatively.

Remember: you create your own reality. Your continual thoughts and emotions keep sending out messages to the universe that attract back to you experiences and events of a similar energy that will continue to happen in your life.

Chapter 11

Anxious, Insecure

Feeling anxious is perhaps one of the most challenging 3D states of being – especially if it's chronic. It's as if you can never quite catch your breath or fully relax and just allow life to be as it is. During these times of ascension, and especially since the beginning of 2020, periods of anxiety understandably seem to be occurring more frequently for many people.

Collective Anxiety

And yet, occasionally, during the ascension process, anxiety can seem to arise out of nowhere. It has no context for you. Your life seems to be relatively okay for the time-being; there's nothing going on that should be causing you anxiety. It can be really confusing.

If this happens, know that these spells of anxiety may not even personally relate to you; as mentioned earlier, they involve something you are picking up from the collective consciousness or from people with whom you're connected. This can often be the case if you are especially empathic.

So when you're feeling anxious, particularly if it doesn't make sense, the first thing to do is tune in and ask if what you are picking up is collective anxiety. If it is, you'll find that just this questioning will begin to relieve the anxiety. And you can then do whatever you can to bring love and compassion into your awareness and release the anxiety into the Light. If it *is* collective anxiety you're experiencing, it will dissipate.

Trauma Arising from the Unconscious

However, your anxiety could also mean that an old trauma from this life, or from past lifetimes, is now being released from your unconscious in order to be consciously dealt with, so your ascension can continue.

As humans, we have a particular type of "escape valve" around trauma. Whenever we experience something too difficult to deal with at the time it's happening, in order to continue functioning, the traumatic emotions and core beliefs we're experiencing eventually descend into the unconscious.

This is convenient – and at times life-saving. But it's common to think that, once the trauma sinks down and essentially disappears from your conscious mind, you're past the experience and you can forget about it. Unfortunately, this is not true.

First, you can notice that those same emotions and beliefs you avoided feeling do keep popping up in consistent ways whenever they are triggered by new and similar events. You keep stumbling over them, even though you might have forgotten what caused them to begin with. But secondly, during these times of shifting into ever-higher levels of consciousness, all these negative emotions and beliefs need to be cleared out, because you can't take them with you to the Fifth Dimension.

Therefore, dealing with any of this material from past traumas has become all the more important during these times. The anxiety is a clue that there is something presenting itself to you in order to be cleared.

Shifting from Anxiety to Calm

Fortunately, higher-dimensional energies of light now streaming onto the planet are making this clearing process easier and easier. And, if the anxiety isn't overwhelming, there are a number of simple things you can do to shift yourself into a calmer state of being – so that you meet the traumatic emotions and successfully heal and release them. One of the first suggestions is to take slow, relaxed, diaphragmatic breaths, which will cause your body to trigger a natural tranquilizing effect. Consciously relaxing your body will help shut off the stress response in it.

Darren Starwynn, in his book, *Finding your Calm Center*, offers a number of other insightful techniques and approaches for calming yourself. For instance, an interesting one he describes is the *Body Energy Hook-up*: Touch the tip of your tongue to the roof of your mouth, right behind your two front teeth. This is a particular acupuncture point. When your tongue is in this position, it is difficult to feel anxiety or stress. This simple act can provide a gentle but immediate feeling of inner connection and calming.

Another practice that can really assist in creating a sense of calm is one you may be familiar with: The Emotional Freedom Technique (EFT) or "Tapping". This is a form of acupressure, based on the same energy meridians used in traditional acupuncture, but without the invasiveness of needles.

In this practice, simple tapping with the fingertips is used to input kinetic energy onto specific meridians on your head and chest while you think about your specific problem and voice positive affirmations. This short-circuits the emotional block from your body's bioenergy system, thus restoring calm to both your mind and your body. EFT can be used for a great number of issues, but calming anxiety is an especially important one to use it for.

Survival Anxiety

All these kinds of techniques to calm anxiety are helpful to learn. And, for most people, they may be all that's needed. But there is a certain kind of anxiety that the usual tools can't assist with very well, and that is "survival anxiety". This can come about when there is so much loss and change in your life that you begin to feel unstable and insecure, and you're anxiously grasping for anything familiar or any safe ground to stand on.

Maybe you're at a point in your ascension process in which you're constantly being moved out of your comfort zone. Or you're being compelled to let go of important supports you've always relied on, one after another, without a break. Perhaps you're even losing your home, your work, your health, or a dear friend. Or your financial situation looks dire. You barely catch your breath and you're being pushed to the next level of letting go of what was feeling safe. With all this, "survival anxiety" keeps snaking around in your belly.

True Security Originates from Within

When these things happen, it can be helpful to know there is at least one upside. And that is you have the opportunity to discover something very important: that your only true security comes from within you – from your trust in Source/Spirit. It does not originate from anything outside of you. Outer security, in the end, is only an illusion. And often, for you to finally discover this, all outer supports you mistakenly thought were keeping you safe may disappear, at least for a while.

When you're in this kind of situation, you can see you often have the choice between two different approaches to life: the third-dimensional choice of "survival anxiety", and the fifth-dimensional choice of trust.

The third-dimensional mode of survival in this context doesn't just apply to getting your material needs met. It refers to a generally unconscious approach to life in which you may be trying to stay in control of everything happening in your life. There's the feeling that if you're not in control, you maybe won't survive. You'd better have enough money (which may mean a reliable job, a lot of clients, money in the bank, or someone who will support you). And you'd better have good relationships so you can get emotional support when you need it.

The important thing to realize is that when you're in the mode of survival, you are looking outside yourself for all you need. And you're using your limited third-dimensional mind to determine how you're going to get it in order to survive here on the planet. This can keep you in a low-level, continuous state of anxiety, especially as you come to realize that in the end you may have very little control over your outer conditions.

As you move toward fifth-dimensional consciousness, you will find that you need to let go of this limited perspective and mode of operating in life. You'll see that your belief that your needs are going to be met by things and situations you've set up outside of you isn't working very well anymore.

When survival fear arises, instead of panicking, see if you can drop inside yourself and align with a trust that you will find the means of survival in other ways, perhaps in ways that will bring you an even greater sense of security, joy and freedom. Find the trust that Source/Spirit is taking care of you. And remember that Source/Spirit, being infinite, has countless – and, sometimes, very surprising – ways in which to do this.

In these experiences when deep insecurity and loss of outer supports occur, know that this call to fully trust Source/Spirit is probably what's happening. See if you can have faith that it knows exactly what it's doing in bringing about changes in your life, including losses that initially seem painful. Know that the things you are losing are likely essential for you to lose, so as to prepare you for entering the much higher vibration of the Fifth Dimension.

Living in the Present Moment

If your survival anxiety includes the fear of not making it financially, this can be a particularly difficult anxiety to handle – especially if it is ongoing, month after month. An important key in learning to stay balanced in this situation is to realize that in stressing over something that is not yet happening, you are living in the future. This is a very limited, 3D approach to life. See if you can try, instead, to focus on living in the present moment. It is in the present that you have the power to create your life.

You may, for example, be concerned that you have no idea where your rent money for next month is going to come from. Become aware that you are not yet living in next month – you're here, right now. And probably relatively okay. If you can hold your focus on what the present moment holds, rather than what you're imagining your future will present, you can begin to calm yourself.

Staying in the Center of your Head

Keeping present in the moment, however, isn't always easy. In his Mastering Alchemy course, teacher Jim Self presents a useful tool to achieve this. It involves bringing your awareness into the center of your head, behind your eyes, into what has been called the *pineal center*. And then, from there, looking out of your eyes into the outside world.

You may think you're always looking out at the world from within the center of your head; but if you check, you'll probably find you're not. Your mental and emotional bodies extend out much further than your physical body; and, if you're like most people, you probably spend a lot of time with your point of attention somewhat out in front of you, especially when you're interacting with the world.

When you bring your attention into the center of your head, you can feel something shift. It suddenly brings you to "right now" in this very moment, in which you have a clear sense of YOU. You also discover that this is your power center. You feel aligned and grounded.

When you shift into this space while contemplating your financial issues, you can think more clearly about your situation and realize, "Right now, I'm fine – I have a roof over my head, food to eat. I'm safe."

Then you can take some deep breaths and make the choice to enter into trust. You can look initially at the options your mind comes up with. If none of these ideas offers a solution, you can remind yourself that the universe has countless ways you know nothing about that can help you to pay your rent.

In staying in trust in the here and now, new possibilities can begin to flow into the clear and open space you've created. Your openness to the limitless possibilities that exist can begin to create a different scenario for you in the future.

Planning for the Future

Attempting to plan for the future in any kind of way at this point in time is getting increasingly difficult – even if it has nothing to do with money and livelihood. So much is changing so quickly, both in the world and in people's personal lives, that not much of what used to work for planning ahead seems to work very well anymore.

It seems best, no matter what, to stay as much as you can in the present moment – as this is where you'll be living constantly when you're in the Fifth Dimension. This doesn't mean you should never think at all about the past or the future. There's nothing wrong with seeing if there's anything to be learned from the past, or in attempting to plan for the future.

It's when you get lost in the past or future that a problem arises. This is because you can form identities around them, regretting what has happened, or desiring what could be. This takes you out of the flow of reality that's happening right now.

Another term for living in the present moment is *mindfulness*. This teaching involves being a witness to your moment to moment experiences. And the most important experiences to be mindful of are the sensations within your body – as your body is always living in present time. Being mindful of the actual experience of being here and now is very different from focusing on your thoughts, judgments, and emotions about your life. Those are your "stories" and are not very helpful in easing anxiety.

If you are fully aligned with the present moment, you can find that you have access to all timelines, past, present and future. You have the ability to let go of the past, and you can visualize the future you wish for – all while living in the present moment. And you can also have the opportunity to discover what could be called the *eternal moment* – a deeper experience of the present moment – a sense of knowing that you are a Being living in eternity.

Anxiety Attacks

As anyone who has suffered from chronic anxiety knows, dealing with this condition can be exhausting. But when you actually have severe *attacks* of anxiety or panic, it can be terrifying.

Experts offer many different tools for dealing with these attacks. The first is to take charge of your thoughts. For example, rather than thinking, "This is awful, what if I completely lose it?", use more affirmative language, such as, "Okay, this doesn't feel good. But it's just my body's emergency response and it will end as I stop scaring myself."

Or instead of thinking, "What's causing this horrible feeling? What if I'm dying or having a complete breakdown?", think instead: "This feeling is strong, but it's not dangerous. All bodies react this way when we think we are in danger or are overly stressed. It's not something to be concerned about. It will end soon, and I'll be fine again."

Taking charge of your thinking puts you in control of your body's emergency system. As you get proficient at taking control, you can completely shut down anxiety attacks and prevent them from starting.

Other tools include distracting yourself, such as counting, calling a friend, organizing materials on your desk, playing a game, etc. Or with powerful sensory experiences that jolt you into present moment awareness, such as cold water, ice, strong flavors in food, and touch. And, very importantly, recognizing that all panic attacks do end – no one experiences unending anxiety attacks, even though it can sometimes feel that way.

Of course, if you feel a need for help with your anxiety attacks, there are professionals who are well-trained to assist you. Two of the most successful anxiety attack treatments are cognitive-behavioral therapy and exposure therapy. Both focus on changing behavior rather than examining your underlying psychological structure stemming from conflicts and past events.

And then, of course, although perhaps not the preferable way to go, there is medication that can also assist you, at least temporarily. Even if you don't like relying on drugs, sometimes you have to do whatever you can to bring in a sense of calm. If your entire being is racked with anxiety, it's well-nigh impossible to focus on raising your vibration.

Attack It with Gratitude

Healer Mark DeNicola has an interesting and somewhat unique approach to anxiety attacks. He calls his approach "Attack It with

Gratitude". It involves, as the name implies, countering an attack with thoughts centered around things you are grateful for.

What makes this tool so powerful is that, even though anxiety attacks can overwhelm you, your thoughts are the fuel that keeps them going. It's your thoughts that tell you that you are not okay. It's your thoughts that make you believe you will never be able to function normally again.

Therefore, the focus is to reclaim power over your thoughts, since they are at the core of what you are currently experiencing. By focusing on things you are grateful for, you're guiding those thoughts in another direction – one that starves, rather than feeds, the anxiety.

You may think you have nothing to be grateful for. It may seem so, when you're in the throes of dealing with anxiety. But, if you consider it for a moment, there's always something to be thankful for. And, think about it – things could always be even worse. It's always relative. But what's important is that feeling gratitude for even the smallest things can work to stop your anxiety attack.

It's also important to note that the primary goal of the exercise is not to list off as many things as you can, but instead, to refocus your mind away from the anxiety. In focusing on things you're grateful for, you're stealing the power away from that part of your mind that is trying to convince you that you should be panicking.

Chapter 12

Conflict with Another Person

As your vibration rises and you become freer of negative emotions and thoughts, it can be very painful to find yourself in conflict with another person. This is particularly true if the person is someone you love and respect.

As with all other areas of your life, if there are low-vibrational patterns you still tend to follow in your relationships, these patterns are going to arise and show themselves clearly. This is so you can learn how to recognize and understand them, forgive yourself, and then release them. Like all other aspects of your life that do not resonate with fifth-dimensional consciousness, you need to leave these patterns of relational conflict behind.

So – how can you approach conflict from a higher frequency of consciousness, so it's not just another method or technique you learn but then forget about when you get triggered? How can you approach the conflict in a way that actually frees both of you involved?

Basic Guidelines for Communication

You can start with some basic concepts and guidelines that are suggested by a number of methods that are available from what I'd call "higher 4D" consciousness.

The first guideline generally involves speaking with "I-statements". This means you only speak about yourself, what *you* are feeling and thinking. You don't tell the other person what *they're* thinking or feeling – or why.

For instance, rather than saying something like "You hurt me when you said that" or "You wanted me to feel bad about what I'd done" – you'd say something, instead, like "I felt hurt when I heard what you said" or "It felt to me like you wanted me to feel bad."

These responses may sound rather similar to the first two, but they're not. First, you're not telling the other person they're responsible for how you feel – and you're not telling them about their motivation for doing what they did. In other words, you're speaking about yourself, and you're not blaming the other person for how you feel. In doing this, you're stepping out of the victim position and assuming responsibility for your own responses.

What you can find in speaking this way is that it's very empowering. You have control over your own sense of well-being, you have a choice over how you're going to respond to them. And secondly, when you're not blaming them for how you feel, you're making it easier for them to hear what you're saying. So, this is the first guideline: in speaking, you use "I-statements" and only speak about yourself.

Then, the second guideline usually given is that there's no interrupting the other person when they're speaking – no contradicting them, no interrupting them to say something about yourself. You actually listen to them, sincerely wanting to hear them speak about their feelings and thoughts and motivations. You wait till they're finished before you start responding. When you can both do this, taking turns to listen, knowing that you'll get your turn to speak, you can both relax and truly listen to each other.

Although not always easy, these guidelines are simple to follow. And often they eventually create a desire in each person to apologize for whatever it is they have done to contribute to the conflict and misunderstanding.

Reflection Technique

So just following these two guidelines can greatly assist you in resolving conflict. But there is a third component you can add to this process that can really heighten your awareness and understanding of each other's emotions and thoughts. And this is to begin by focusing on one of you at a time. Let's say you'd go "first".

1. **You Speak:** You have the opportunity to speak at length about yourself, your point of view about the conflict, what your feelings and thoughts are – all, again, using "I" statements, and without blaming the other person for anything – taking responsibility for

yourself. And the other person would listen quietly to you.

If there's a whole lot you want to say, then at first, you just say a part of what you wish to communicate. This is because, when you've said your piece, the other person will then need to reflect back to you what they've heard you say, and you don't want to overwhelm them with too much information at once for them to remember.

2. **They Reflect:** So when you've finished speaking your first piece, the other person then reflects what you've said back to you, perhaps with words like, "So what I've heard you say is that...". You listen to their reflection of your words. If they get something wrong or they miss something, then you gently correct them and make sure they've gotten it in their reflecting it back to you. And when they do, you let them know.

3. **Anything More?** And then, once that is clear, they ask you, "Is there anything more?" And you have a chance to continue on, if you need to, and go through the same process till you feel satisfied they've listened and understood all of what you've had to say.

4. **They Express Empathy:** Then finally, it's time for them to express in some way how they can understand and empathize with your feelings.

5. **Switch Roles:** At this point, of course, it's time to switch roles. They speak and you reflect what you've heard.

6. **Continue Taking Turns:** If there is yet more to share for either of you, you continue on, taking turns like this until you both feel complete.

This works well, because if you both stick to these guidelines, you each know you're going to have your own time to speak and the other is going to have to really listen to you. You can feel patient when it's your turn to listen and reflect. And again, in taking responsibility for your own feelings and actions, you may automatically want to apologize and express your empathy and compassion for the suffering they have been experiencing. You're not taking responsibility or blame for their suffering – you're simply expressing your understanding and your love for them.

So these are some simple and effective ground rules to start with in resolving conflicts with another person. So long as you're both following these guidelines, you'll find that solutions will come to both of you in how you can work through the difficulty you're having with each other – just because you're really understanding each other better.

Watch for Projection

If you and the people you experience conflict with are both really motivated and mature enough, it may be possible to resolve all conflicts in your relationships by using these kinds of techniques.

However, you've probably discovered that, with certain people, no matter how carefully you try to communicate with them, you still tend to get triggered over and over again with them. Even using communication skills to the best of your ability, you never feel you can fully relax around the person. Things they say and do just continue to set you off into defensiveness, judgment, anger or hurt.

Sometimes this may indicate that the person reminds you a great deal of someone else, probably in your past, with whom you had similar difficulties (like Mom or Dad or a sibling – or a former spouse). Once this is seen, it's easier to look more closely at this current person in your life and see clearly that they are not this other person. You may even realize they aren't really like them at all. You've somehow projected motivations and characteristics onto them that aren't actually there. They're similar maybe – but your projections have heightened and distorted these characteristics.

Karmic Relationships

But often it also means you know this person from past lives in which you created karma together, and that you have brought this conflict into this lifetime to hopefully resolve. Most close relationships you have – with the people in your birth family, your spouse, your children, good friends – are very likely Souls you've known in former lifetimes, often multiple times. And you're brought together in this life as an opportunity for all of you to resolve any karma with each other you've brought in with you. Or simply to have experiences that you as a Soul decided you wanted to have in this lifetime.

With some of these people in your life, of course, there is no negative karma – there's simply an easy, natural love you have and maybe a soul contract to be there for each other in difficult times. You just know and love them, without any question. But with those you have challenging relationships with, it is likely you have been in this position before with them in somewhat similar situations.

Your roles may be roughly the same as they were in past lives – or they may be reversed. But you have likely written into your soul contract that you would be together with this person to hopefully resolve former conflicts.

When you step back and view these relationships from this vantage point, it can finally make some sense out of your conflicts, especially with people close to you. It can be helpful to find practitioners who can perhaps "read" these past lifetimes for you to give you a clue as to how the automatic conflicts with them first developed. Or you can perhaps learn how to remember these lifetimes yourself, through hypnosis – or through inwardly asking in meditation for this information.

Responsibility Creates Empowerment

However, it isn't even necessary to ascertain how the conflicts originally came about with these people. The main questions to ask yourself are, "What is it I'm here to learn and resolve in this relationship?" "Why does this pattern happen over and over again between us?" "What is it I'm doing that continues to cause my pain, and how can I shift my beliefs and behaviors to no longer do this?"

If you're in a pattern of blaming a person for your pain, this may be difficult at first. As I say, this is because, in blaming them, you are placing yourself in the role of the victim – a role which offers you no power to change your situation. You're constantly waiting for them to stop doing to you what they're doing, so you can feel better. And this rarely works.

It always, always takes two to tango in a relationship. No matter how cruel or inexplicable a person's behavior and attitude toward you may be, it is your response to what they say and do that is the key to stop your suffering.

This does not mean that you then should blame yourself for the conflict. There is no need at all to blame either one of you. Blaming is a third-dimensional reaction to pain that really gets you nowhere. See if you can step completely out of this low-dimensional Blame Game altogether. Just see the situation as a conflict that's occurring between two people, both of whom probably want to resolve it.

Again, as I say, for you to resolve it for yourself, you need to take responsibility for your own actions and reactions, your own thoughts and emotions, and your own sense of well-being. You may not be able to change what they do or say, but you *can* change how you respond to them. And this, in turn, will change the whole dynamic between the two of you and eventually set you free.

Misunderstanding about Forgiveness

Generally speaking, finding freedom in a relationship requires forgiveness of whatever you perceive the person has "done" to you. This is where many people get stuck. They think they have to let the hurtful actions toward them be okay and just accept them. They think this is what forgiveness is. Hurtful actions are *not* okay, and you don't have to accept them. And you certainly don't have to continue being at the receiver's end of them.

But if you are feeling disrespected and hurt by someone's behavior, it's up to you to take yourself out of that situation. You've probably found that reactions like blowing up at them, getting small and hurt, or stuffing your feelings do not bring results that feel good to you.

What you need to do is take care of yourself in an effective and mature way. Sometimes it may mean actually leaving the room when an unstoppable interaction occurs. Other times, it may be helpful to state that you're not willing to be part of this pattern with them anymore, and maybe the two of you should talk later when you've both calmed down. This is taking charge of yourself; it's taking care of yourself in a mature way.

And then it's important to take the time to delve deeply inside yourself to hear what it is you're needing to learn from the situation. You have to be honest with yourself and be prepared to hear something you may not want to hear, how you are at least partially responsible for the conflict happening with them. And then be ready to change your behavior toward the person and not fall back into old, automatic reactions to them.

Empathy Brings Forgiveness

In doing this, you can then see more clearly that what's actually true is that you are two Souls in pain who are attempting to resolve karma with each other. Neither one of you is right or wrong, good or bad. Most likely, the other person is also suffering, although it may not be clear to you due to your focus on your own pain. Do your best to see the situation from their point of view, as well as your own.

They're a human being, just like you. Can you feel empathy for them, realizing that, in their own way, they are attempting to find balance and joy and freedom in their life, just as you are? Can you see their struggle? Can you feel compassion for them?

With true empathy, forgiveness for what they have done becomes much easier. You're still not making their actions okay – but you're forgiving them for their inability to unconditionally love you and to understand spiritual truths. You realize that, as different as your positions may look, they are like you in their confusion, pain and ignorance. They're caught in the karma too.

You may be surprised when you have this experience of true empathy at how your relationship with them can shift to one of greater ease and openness. You have changed so much that, even if they haven't reached the truths and understanding you have, they cannot help but shift their emotional reactions to you, and so the dynamic between you will be different.

Higher Self Conversations

One way to assist you in experiencing empathy for the person you're in conflict with is a process you can do by yourself, which can be especially helpful if the other person is not willing or able to agree to guidelines when communicating. This process entails communicating with the person in the Quantum Field with both of your Higher Selves present.

As you may know, the Quantum Field is a field of consciousness you live in, whether you're aware of it or not. In this field, infinite possibilities on every level of creation are available to you. There are no limitations and there is no space or time. You can draw anything in creation to you – including another person in their etheric form. This is because you are energetically connected to absolutely everybody and everything in existence.

Knowing this, you can call to you someone you wish to speak to from a higher and clearer perspective. Say, for example, you've had an argument with your boyfriend and you can't seem to get past it. One or both of you tend to get activated each time you attempt to talk; and when you do, miscommunication constantly seems to happen. Here's what you can do:

1. **Get into Meditative State:** Take the time to bring your attention to your Heart and shift into a meditative state in which you feel as calm and centered as possible. See if you can move past the monkey-mind chatter in your head and lift into a state in which the thoughts that come into your mind are unhurried and undemanding – a quiet mode of contemplating or pondering. Sometimes this is easier to do at night, maybe before you go to bed when things are relatively quiet.

2. **Be aware of Quantum Field:** Then, become aware of the space of the Quantum Field all around you. It will feel empty and vast – but it is actually filled with any and all possibilities you might wish to create. State your intention for a quiet and productive conversation with your boyfriend.

3. **Call in Higher Self:** Then call in your Higher Self to be present with you. See if you can feel the loving support that comes with this presence. Even if you can't see or feel anything, trust that your Higher Self is there to be with you when you have your conversation with your boyfriend.

4. **Tune into your Love:** Next, tune into the love you feel for him. Then call him to you, along with his Higher Self. You will probably feel the presence of both of them come into your field. Even if you're not sure, have faith that they're present and proceed anyway. Tell your boyfriend you'd like to have a friendly and heartful conversation to clear up the difficulties the two of you have had with each other.

5. **Speak and Listen from your Heart:** At this point, as you feel the support of your Higher Self with you, begin speaking to your boyfriend from your heart. And then stop to listen to what he may have to say. You'll see that, with both Higher Selves present, the talk can occur on a very high level in which unconditional love exists and in which

full understanding can take place. You may feel yourself filled with a sense of compassion and harmony, along with a new understanding of what the conflict has been about. And perhaps a new way of communicating with your boyfriend, when you're physically together.

You may be astonished at how such a conversation can shift a relationship into one of love and understanding. The other person probably won't have a clue what you've done, but it won't matter. What happens may seem miraculous. But, if you really understand what the Quantum Field is about, and how you're connected to everyone and everything in creation, it really isn't so surprising.

"Channeling" the Other Person

A variation on this exercise is one that could be called *"Channeling" the Other Person*. The term isn't really accurate, in that you are not bringing the actual spirit of the other person through you to speak. However, you are expressing from a deeper level within you that knows the heart and goodness of the person. This aspect of you is intuitively aware of the person's struggles, limitations and suffering. And this is what is valuable to you in learning to both understand and forgive them.

To "channel" another person in this way, sit at your computer or with pen and paper and shift into a meditation mode. Then see if you can tune into the person you're feeling in conflict with and "channel" what they may be saying about their feelings and their life. See if you can allow yourself to experience the person from within their consciousness – in a way, merge with them – and become aware of their personal pain and suffering.

Write whatever comes to you, as if the person is speaking to a third party, just sharing what's true for them, what's difficult for them, what they're feeling. And see if, by becoming more fully aware of the struggles they experience in everyday life, any negative feelings or thoughts you still have toward them can naturally dissolve through your empathy and compassion.

Switching Roles Technique

Yet another variation on this theme is to find a third party to join the two of you in conflict to facilitate a process between you. In this exercise, the two of you switch roles – you become each other – and have a conversation about what's true for you. As the other person, from their point of view, you speak, using "I" and "me", about their feelings, their experiences, their perspective about any areas of conflict which may exist between you – as if you *are* them.

Let's say you and your sister are going to do this process together. The two of you decide that you're going to start out with your sister playing you.

1. **Tune into Each Other**: First give yourselves a few moments to tune into each other.

2. **She speaks as if She's You:** Then your sister would begin speaking as if she is you, expressing in first-person your feelings and experiences, as she understands them.

3. **Gently Correct Misunderstandings:** You might be surprised initially at how much she actually does understand you. But with anything she is not accurate about, wait till she's spoken for a bit, and then gently correct her, expressing what she's said more accurately and have her repeat that.

4. **You Speak as if You're your Sister:** Then it's your turn to speak about her feelings and point of view as you understand them, as if you are your sister.

You can go back and forth this way, playing each other, till you both feel clear that the other one really "gets" you, understands your point of view, and has empathy for you. The person facilitating the process can also gently ask questions of each of you as you play each other to more fully bring out hidden feelings.

Sending the Holy Spirit

There is yet another powerful key that can help resolve a conflict with another person, and this is to send them the Light of the Holy Spirit. This term may sound like a Christian concept; but actually, it's just something the Church adopted many centuries ago as its own. The Holy Spirit is actually one of the aspects of Source, itself, that, among other things, is here for us to use for resolving conflict, suffering and ignorance. It is an extremely powerful tool for shifting consciousness into a higher vibration.

You can call it in simply for yourself to experience a greater awareness of Spirit – or to clear your mind, body and aura of negativity. You can draw it in through your crown chakra and ask for it to fill, surround, and protect you for the highest good of all concerned. If you focus in doing this, you will likely feel a sensation of Light entering your body and flowing all around you. You'll feel clearer, more centered in your Heart, and more greatly protected from outside energies. It's actually a great tool to use on a daily basis to keep your vibration high.

Once you do this for yourself, you can then send this Light through your third eye and/or Heart to places, groups of people or situations, either currently happening or in the future, in order to create greater love, harmony and peace wherever you're sending it. And, very importantly, you can also send it to an individual you are feeling conflicted about.

So what you'd do is this:

1. **Call in Light for yourself:** Call in the Holy Spirit for yourself for the highest good of all concerned, and feel it filling, surrounding and protecting you. You can do this with your eyes open or closed.

2. **Send it to the Other Person:** Then draw it down into your third eye and/or Heart, and send it out toward the person. See it surrounding, filling and protecting them.

3. **Watch it Flow Back:** Then, as you do this, watch how the Light flows right back to you, forming a connection of Light between the two of you. Feel it dissolving all anger and hurt and creating a sense of harmony and understanding.

You can do this process when you're alone in the Quantum Field: just envision them as you are sending the Holy Spirit to them. Or you can do it when you're physically with them, especially when you are interacting with them. It will work either way.

Again, the other person will likely have no idea what you've done to create a softening of the conflict and the shift into Heart energy. But you'll find it will be much easier for you to resolve your differences if you have not only sent them the Holy Spirit, but also continue to keep it present for both of you as you interact. It will hold you in a higher consciousness, filled with love and understanding – which, in the end, is what resolves all conflict.

"I Love You - God Bless You"

A final simple but powerful key for creating greater harmony and understanding with another person is to repeat to yourself a phrase all the while they're speaking to you: "God bless you – I love you." This not only helps to keep you focused on being non-reactive while listening to them; it also injects a positive energy into the field between you that they can also experience. You can begin to feel an emotional shift between you that feels more harmonious and loving.

Chapter 13

Decision Difficulty

During these increasingly-uncertain times, it can get quite stressful to make important decisions, especially those regarding your future. Fearful of making the wrong decision, you may find your mind bouncing back and forth between pros and cons of all the possible choices. Perhaps you then turn to other people to hear their opinions about your decision. This can be helpful at times, but other people's opinions can often add to your confusion.

Some people might advise, "You just need to follow your heart." This always sounds good – so warm and fuzzy. There's an emotional feel-good quality about that answer. But as you've probably discovered, if you've ever tried to "follow your heart", this may not always be the best guidance, after all. Your heart will tell you how you feel emotionally about the situation, and what you hope may happen. But it may not know what is best to do.

Emotions can certainly tell you something important about yourself, and sometimes the best decision is one that satisfies your emotional desires. But often, these desires arise from such emotions as fear or greed or anger, and end up not directing you in the best direction.

Then there is always the guidance you probably hear about "following your intuition". This can be helpful if you can easily discern the voice of your intuition from the voice of your mind and your emotional desires. But what if you can't make this discernment? You may need a little more than vague instructions of where to go to get your answers. The idea of "going inside" just doesn't give enough direction.

Using the Wrong Tool

If you find yourself in this situation, be aware that in trying to decide on the best decision, especially a potentially life-changing one, you've probably been using the wrong tool: your rational mind. For small matters in life – like what to eat for breakfast or when to set a dentist appointment – the mind can be an excellent tool. It stores tons of information from past experiences and things you've read or heard about, so you can decide about things like it later on in life.

But at this point on your ascension journey, when it comes to more important decisions in life, your mind can be clueless as to what the best decision might be. It's not equipped to make it – and actually never has been. All it knows to do is list pros and cons and give data about what it thinks it knows about situations based on its past experiences. For really important decisions which may change the course of your life, the mind can be woefully inadequate.

The Body's Intelligence

On the other hand, the body can be a marvelous tool for giving you information on certain matters. It can, as you probably know, provide answers about what's going on inside of itself and what it needs. If you have engaged in muscle-testing, you can probably testify to this. But perhaps surprisingly, it can also give you information you need about other matters in your life, especially when used in conjunction with your imaginative faculty.

Let's say you're trying to decide whether it would be better for you to go to San Francisco to see a friend this weekend or to stay at home to catch up on your work. Your mind would probably give you the pros and cons of both decisions, and you'd find yourself bouncing back and forth. And your heart would undoubtedly decide on going to San Francisco, because it sounds like it would be more fun. But you'd still wonder if this was really the best decision, because you also know your work is important to do. So you're stuck.

However, if you put the question to your body, you might get a clearer answer. Here's how:

1. **Don't Use Active Imagination:** First of all, imagine yourself this coming weekend in San Francisco, seeing your friend. What's important in this imagining is this: DON'T use your active imagination, where you might

remember the fun things you've done in the past and then imagine these things happening again. And don't think of things you want to do when you're there and imagine them. That's using your imagination to guide you in a particular way.

2. **Do Use Passive Imagination:** What you need to do is use your *passive* imagination. This is where you just kind of float in your imagination up into next weekend and simply see yourself there in San Francisco with your friend. Period. Don't put any thoughts or desires into this – just see yourself there and be open to see what spontaneously begins coming to you. It can be surprising. What you see might not be the scenario you've been day-dreaming about. Your friend might turn out to be in a sour mood, the weather might be chilly, you might see yourself coming down with a cold.

3. **Pay Attention to the Feeling in your Gut:** Whatever it is that comes to you, pay attention to it. Then focus on what is happening in your gut. Is it contracted and tight – or easy and relaxed? The gut responds to what it knows.

4. **Do the Same with the Other Option:** Then, the next step is to do the same thing with the second decision: staying home and catching up with your work. To your mind or heart, this decision might not seem very good or pleasant; but if you move ahead in time with your passive imagination and see yourself staying at home, working, you again might be surprised. You might discover that staying home feels exactly right for you for this coming weekend. You're feeling energized and clear. You're realizing that your energy has been low, the work has been nagging at you, and it feels really good to get it done. By the end of the weekend, you're feeling great. Again, feel into your gut when you're tuning into this possibility. What is it telling you?

Of course, the opposite experience could also happen: you may realize that going to San Francisco is the better decision. Either way, you experience a *felt experience* in your gut that feels like a solid knowing – not just a mental kind of knowing in your mind. And it feels like you can trust it.

Seeking Right Action in Your Sacred Heart

So, for those kinds of decisions that feel a little difficult – but probably aren't life-changing – using the body, along with passive imagination, is a good tool for helping you make decisions. But what about the really big decisions in life, the ones you know could alter your course in life, or maybe permanently change an important relationship? Your body can probably tell you some things about parts of the situation, but it's probably not the best tool – or the only tool – to use for making a big decision.

Where you need to focus now, during this time of ascension, is on your *Sacred Heart* – or sometimes referred to as your *Higher Heart* or your *Spiritual Heart*. It is here that your answers reside. When I refer to your Sacred Heart, I'm not speaking of your emotional heart. As I say, there is definitely intelligence and love in the emotional heart; but you'll probably also find all the conflicted emotions you're feeling about the decision you're trying to make.

Your Sacred Heart is actually something quite different. It's located somewhat above your emotional heart and your fourth chakra. It's not emotional in the same way as your emotional heart. There is love – but it's a more detached, unconditional kind of love. This love has no opposite and never morphs into resentment, need, or hatred. It is more of a profound, energetic sensation that resonates in your whole being and takes you into a deeper dimension of being.

The Sacred Heart is a doorway into your Higher Self, your Soul, your higher wisdom, God – whatever you might call it. It is where you as a human being connect to that higher Source of wisdom and Truth within you.

You undoubtedly know this place in yourself. It's what just seems to break open and expand with love and joy at certain times in life when you feel greatly moved – or when you suddenly experience a spiritual opening or understanding. There's often the sensation of being able to see vast vistas of Truth for a few moments and know who you really are, beyond this human existence. There's sometimes a profound sense of freedom felt in these moments and the knowing of a Oneness with all that is.

There seems to be no way to purposely produce these experiences for yourself (although you may try!). But the reason I refer to the Sacred

Heart is to point to the place within you to go to, when you have an important decision to make. It's this center of your being that is a portal into your higher knowing.

Sacred Heart Meditation

Here is one way to approach contacting your Sacred Heart to help you make a decision:

1. **Think about your Decision:** Start out by closing your eyes, taking a couple of deep breaths and centering yourself. Begin thinking about the decision, the questions you have, or anything you're confused or concerned about. Be aware of what both your mind and your body begin experiencing as you think these thoughts, without any judgment or resistance.

2. **Set an Intention:** Ask for guidance from all celestial sources that might be available to you. Set an intention that you're going to receive the answer to your question. Picture yourself finally having the answer and feeling all parts of yourself comfortable and aligned with that decision, whatever it is. Then release your question for now—stop thinking about it.

3. **Focus on your Sacred Heart:** Then move your awareness to right above your heart chakra and focus on your Sacred Heart there: this lets this Heart know you're seeking its intelligence and its comfort. Place your hand on your chest and breathe deeply. Feel into this sacred center; feel yourself falling into it, deeper and deeper.

   If you can't actually feel yourself moving more deeply into it, don't worry – just keep focusing on that area and pay attention to any sensation you begin feeling. You may begin feeling a softness, a calm relaxation – and a sweet, deep sense of safety. There's a Divine Presence that can pervade your whole being. You can sink into it and feel a type of quiet bliss. You can become aware that you are unconditionally loved, just as you are. There's nothing to change, nothing you need to do to be deemed worthy of love. Again even if you don't initially feel all this, don't worry. You may simply feel too stressed about your question or concern. Just become as still as you can.

4. **Ask "What is Right Action?":** Now focus again on the decision you've been pondering, or the situation you're confused or concerned about, and ask: *"What is right action in this situation?"*. Note that this is the important term: *right action*. You're not asking how to get what you want or what will make you happy – and you're not asking what you *should* do. You're asking what right action would be in this particular situation, what action would create the most benevolent outcome for you and for all others concerned.

5. **Wait for the Answer:** And then wait quietly and patiently. Do your best, despite any fears or desires you may have, to sincerely want to know what the right action would be. Keep breathing, and see what happens. Everyone gets answers a bit differently. You may actually hear words – if so, you'll likely hear a clear, concise answer. Especially pay attention to the very first thing you hear. But you may instead get a body sensation that gives you the answer, or see an image. Perhaps a clear knowing will just appear.

6. **Distinguish Where Answer is Coming From:** You may initially have trouble distinguishing whether an answer is coming from your Sacred Heart or from your mind – or from desires you have – or messages from your Inner Critic. The way to know it's your Sacred Heart is the feeling or sensation that comes with the message. If it's your Sacred Heart, it will be a feeling of unconditional love, of softness, compassion. It's not emotional, like the emotional heart; there's no fear, anger, anxiety or desire. It's not judgmental, like messages from your inner critic; it doesn't induce guilt or shame in you. And it's not just old recycled thoughts from your mind; there's a freshness to the energy of the Sacred Heart. There's a sense of receiving higher-dimensional wisdom that creates a feeling of trust in you.

7. **Be Patient:** You may not get an answer immediately. Not a problem. Because you've asked the question with intention and sincerity, the answer will come one way or another – often through synchronicities that appear in your life. These are outer signs or indications of your answer.

8. **Trust the Answer You Receive**: Once you get the answer, you then need to trust it. At first, your mind or emotions may not like what you're getting. You'll feel a sense of resistance within you. Remember, you don't have to make any decision at this point about taking action on the answer you're getting. You're just asking the question. Knowing this will calm any fears you may have about the answer.

Responding to Truth

But do sit still with the answer you've received and let it be for a while, without reacting to it one way or another. What will happen may surprise you: you will see how your mind and emotions begin to respond to the Truth you've become aware of. They begin aligning themselves with it.

It can be an amazing experience – watching how your emotions and your mind suddenly recognize the majesty of the Truth as it enters your being and you begin to interact with it. It can be especially surprising if the answer is contrary to what you would have thought it would be. But you naturally begin trusting it, because there's a pleasant sensation vibrating in your being as you reflect on it. There's a clear and resonant "bong" of a bell that is sounding within, an increasing feeling of an openness, an expansiveness you experience.

You will also likely begin experiencing a profound sense of relief throughout your being, as your mind finally surrenders and you can no longer deny what is true for you. Your emotions begin moving from fear and grief to a sense of calm and reassurance.

You may realize that this decision is going to cause some upset in other people, and perhaps a lot of work in changing your whole life to fit with it, but this is not important now – you can't imagine yourself not following what is right for you.

Magic Happens

At this point, the real magic can start happening. Once making the decision to follow right action, everything in your life starts lining up with it. Doors open, outer blocks and resistances disappear. Supportive people show up to help you make the necessary changes in your life. The universe cooperates, and everything flows. All this is strong validation that you are moving in the direction of right action.

In the end, you come to realize you want all your decisions to come from your Sacred Heart, you want everything you do to be right action. It becomes a way of life, a way of going through your day, constantly touching into that depth of your being to see if you're on track, in alignment with right action. You no longer have to sit down, go within and do the whole process of tuning in and getting your answers. It becomes a quick and natural process, stemming from your desire and intention to be in tune with your Sacred Heart.

In living life this way, you truly become a divine instrument not only in your own life – but in the life of all those around you. Life becomes simple and straightforward. Struggling with decisions, both big and small, is something of the past. You are allowing your Sacred Heart to lead.

Chapter 14

Depressed

There are dozens of reasons these days for why people are experiencing depression. Many cannot function without the aid of medication. Others, attempting to avoid drugs, drag through their days in a bleak haze. If depression lasts for any length of time, it can be absolutely devastating.

Depression may have always been part of your life. But now, during these days of rapid ascension, you may be finding that dark moods seem to occur more often. There may be good reason for this, especially if your whole life seems to be falling apart and you no longer know who you are or what you need to be doing. But depression can also happen for seemingly no reason at all – as if ascension, itself, can cause it to arise.

Physical Health and Depression

However, before you start looking for "ascension reasons" for feeling depressed, it's important first to look for physical health issues that may be either causing or contributing to your depression. Mental health professionals now acknowledge that physical health can greatly impact mood, especially the part of the immune system that is in the gut, as there is a direct connection between the gut and the brain.

As you're likely aware, there are certain foods and chemicals, which can particularly affect your mood. Therefore, it's helpful to pay attention to your diet and watch to see if there is a connection between what you're eating and how depression may result from certain foods, such as sugar or gluten, in particular.

Depression is also acknowledged to be symptomatic of increasingly-common disorders such as Lyme disease, Hypothyroid, Fibromyalgia, and

Electromagnetic Sensitivity Disorder. So, it's helpful to check all these things out with health professionals before you begin thinking about medication or other measures.

Your Body's Trying to Keep up with You

However, depression can also develop simply because your body consistently feels bad, no matter what you eat, how much you exercise, or how many health supplements you take. Body pain and discomfort may occur simply because you are expanding rapidly in consciousness, and your body (especially if it is also aging) is struggling to keep up; aches and pains occur in the process. Also, if past unresolved emotional issues are arising to be resolved, physical issues attached to the emotional ones are likely going to manifest.

In the ascension process, your body is attempting to lighten its density from being carbon-based to crystalline-based. It's therefore very important to learn to love your body unconditionally, and to have compassion for all it is experiencing during this period. Your body serves you constantly in the best way it knows how – especially considering the unresolved mental and emotional issues it holds in its DNA. Try to catch yourself feeling irritable or impatient when your body is in pain, and, instead, shift into compassion.

In essence, you and your body are a team. You, as a Soul – and your body, as a consciousness known as the *Body Elemental* – have created the human being form you are currently inhabiting. It may be obvious, but it can be easy to forget it at times: If you treat your body with respect and love, it will respond in as positive a way as possible.

Anger Beneath the Depression

Another possible cause of depression, as mental health experts also explain, can be due to anger turned inward. While this may sound like an overly simplistic approach for describing depression, there is no doubt that repressed anger can play a significant role in it.

If you're suffering from depression, you likely have a powerful Inner Critic that perpetuates feelings of unworthiness and shame. When you listen to this Inner Critic, you not only feel more depressed, you probably also find it much more difficult to stand up to your depression. You find it harder to take positive actions that could help you feel better about yourself (like engaging in activities you enjoy), and being more social.

It can be helpful to verbalize your critical inner voice as though someone else were telling you these judgmental thoughts, and to express the feeling behind the thoughts. By hearing the thoughts spoken in this way, you can begin to feel some separation from the harsh, critical attitudes against you. This separation or distance offers the opportunity for you to answer back to these attacks. It can also help you develop more self-compassion and a kinder, more realistic point of view toward yourself.

To learn more about the Inner Critic and what it really is, read the chapter called "Shame, Guilt and Self-Judgment".

Ascension Void

So, all these ideas and suggestions can be helpful, especially for people who are not yet fully engaged with their ascension process. But, as someone reading this book, you probably are very much engaged.

And it's important to understand that depression can easily arise when you're working your way through what I call the *Ascension Void*, a period in the ascension process when your whole life begins feeling flat and meaningless, and you're losing all interest in things you used to be passionate about. It feels like nothing interesting is happening for you, and there's nothing much to look forward to in the future either.

This rather painful period of time seems to occur at least once for people going through the ascension process. And it can be a bit scary, because you don't know your purpose anymore; the goals you've had to guide you in the past now feel meaningless. And you find that your life feels rather small.

When you're in this phase, you're generally also not very much interested in being with people, and you find yourself staying at home a lot. You start losing a sense of who you are: You seem to be in the process of releasing much of your 3D identity and you don't know yet who you're becoming. Overall, you feel raw, vulnerable, and very uncertain about life.

And yet, this phase of the ascension process is a very important one – and probably essential. It's a time in which you are being called to enter into deep healing and to surrender to whatever may be coming up for you. You're needing to let go of all ego identities, attachments, and beliefs you've had, often including what you've thought were spiritual "truths". Your whole identity is up for question.

In essence, it involves a letting go of all of who you've always thought you were, all you have accomplished, all the roles you've played – perhaps even including what you might have thought of as your spiritual mission.

It's a time to see how much truth resides in all these former identities and goals. You discover that whatever turns out to be 3D baggage will be falling away, as you will not be able to take it with you into the Fifth Dimension.

Indeed, all the low-vibrational energy aspects of yourself you've taken on during your time in the Third Dimension must be left behind – including all roles, relationships, and images of yourself that are based in 3D ego consciousness. And all unresolved issues you have developed in 3D must also come to the surface to be acknowledged, resolved, and released. This is the core of what is occurring while you're in the Ascension Void.

This experience is obviously not a very comfortable one. A lot of inner change is occurring, leading you ever more deeply into unknown territory. All your old reference points are disappearing. And you may experience loss in many different arenas of your life.

All this can easily lead to depression, if you're not aware of what is actually going on. It may bring up basic identity survival fears in you. It can feel like a stripping away of who you've known yourself to be. But remember, it's only a stripping away of who you *think* you are. It's the dismantling of the ego structure you've taken to be your "self."

The good news is you'll find that, throughout this whole deconstruction period, the essential YOU – your Higher Self – will remain intact. In fact, this true reality of who you are will finally be able to shine through all the more clearly. You can experience a thrilling sensation of freedom, when you realize that what is actually being released is *all of who you are NOT*. When all this is cleared out, leaving an empty space within you, it makes room for your Higher Self to move in and begin expressing through you more clearly.

Ascension is a Rebirth

Ascension into the Fifth Dimension is truly a form of rebirth. And, in order to be reborn, you have to essentially die first to what you have been in the past. If you can move into trust of your ascension process, you'll find that the wave you're riding into the Fifth Dimension is bringing you to a place of greater security, peace and joy than you can even imagine.

So it's important to flow with any changes that are happening and not try to hang onto what's leaving – even though it may look scary to step into the unknown without familiar reference points. When you're out the other end of this Void, you discover how much freer, more stable, and more authentic you are. You may pick up some of the same roles you were previously playing and some of the same interests, but you're engaging in them with fewer ego agendas.

The Ascension Void may happen more than once; but all successive ones tend to be shorter than the first one. And, if you've been through it once already, you're ready for another one when it appears. However, when you are in the middle of one, it can sometimes feel awful; your life can seem pointless.

The main thing to remember is that you will make it through. It will not last forever. Let it play out and do its job. Surrender to it, trust it, and be willing to dive deeply into your healing process. Let go of trying to bring your old life back. It won't work in the end, and it will only slow your ascension down.

Remember that what is occurring for you is all in good order, as the Ascension Void is a necessary step. There is nothing, in the end, to be depressed about, because nothing is wrong. It is a required step in the journey you're making from the Third Dimension into the Fifth.

See yourself as the butterfly still in the cocoon. Cocoons are always a mushy mess when the metamorphosis is in progress. You need to be patient and continue loving yourself, while the magic of ascension is in the process of freeing you from your old, distorted 3D identity and birthing a whole new You.

Unresolved Traumas from the Past

And yet, depression can also happen at times other than when you're in the Ascension Void – sometimes out of the blue with no apparent cause. As you look more closely, you may discover that the depression was caused when something unresolved from your past entered your conscious awareness because some similar event currently happening is triggering the earlier memory and unresolved emotions. These emotions are waiting to be acknowledged, accepted, resolved and released.

Surrendering to the Depression

If the experience of depression is something relatively minor, there are many tools in this book and elsewhere that can be helpful. But, if you've really fallen into deep depression or despair, it can often feel too difficult to do any of those things. You just feel too overwhelmed.

If this is the case, then it is time to fully surrender to the depression. In using the term *surrender*, I am not referring to giving up or resigning yourself to the depression. Surrender in this context involves a conscious and purposeful choice to allow what-is – whatever it is you're experiencing – to simply be and not resist or try to change it.

To do this, you need to first make the decision to move out of your mind, where negative thoughts keep cycling around and creating negative emotions; and then to focus, instead, on your body where the emotions of your depression are actually centered. When in emotional pain, you'll find that your tendency is to try to move away from the pain and to go into your mind in hopes of somehow escaping it. But all the mind can do is keep recycling your thoughts about your depression, trying to get you away from it, distract you, or in some other way get you out of it. As you've likely discovered, this doesn't work.

Instead, if you can move your focus down into your body to where the depression (and any other difficult emotions) reside, without any judgment or resistance to them, you can begin to shift it. You need to just allow your emotional state to be what it is – and do your best to feel compassion for the part of yourself experiencing the depression.

Being-With Process

Here is a way to do this:

1. **Think about your Depression:** Start by thinking about it. Allow all your familiar thoughts about it to come present – how it feels and what might be causing it. Watch your mind carefully. Note all the familiar ideas and strategies you've tried in attempting to get away from feeling the depression – how to get rid of it, change it, distract yourself from it, fix it.

2. **Become Aware of the Emotions that Appear:** Then become aware of the emotions that are coming present. Realize that when you're thinking about your depression, matching emotions follow. And be aware that, as you think about it, your mind really does not know what to do about it.

3. **Focus on your Body:** So, now switch your focus to your body. Where in your body do you feel the depression and

other negative emotions that go with it? Usually, you'll find it's somewhere in your gut or your chest. Bring your full awareness to this place and focus your attention there. This may be difficult at first; you might find yourself wanting to escape back into your mind. But remember, your mind does not have the answers. You need to stay with the depression, itself, to know what to do with it. Keep your attention on that part of your body where it resides and take a deep breath or two into that place. You may wish to also put your hand on that part of your body.

4. **Be Totally Present to the Depression:** Then see if you can just be with this part of you that is experiencing the depression. You can see it as your "inner child", your "emotional self" or your "pain body". But know it is a part of you that is not the adult, conscious self you generally use to engage in life with. It's a part of you that only knows emotions and bodily sensations.

5. **Breathe into the Emotions**: Again, be aware of the tendency to want to escape back into your mind, away from the emotionally-centered experience of the pain. Instead, just stay there with it – and breathe into the emotions. You don't have to have answers or know how to fix things in any way. You just need to *be with* this little one, without any resistance or judgment. Just allow it to be, as it is – the depression it's experiencing is part of your reality at this time. Just accept this for now. Understand that emotions always want to be felt and fully experienced without resistance or judgment. This doesn't have to be for a long time: just long enough for you to feel this emotional self relax and let go to some degree, as it starts feeling acknowledged and allowed.

6. **Listen to Your Little Self:** Then see if there is something it may wish to say to you. Be willing to listen closely, without feeling defensive, guilty or judgmental. If you can find loving, compassionate words of wisdom to respond to it, great. But if you can't, you can just keep repeating "I love you" with every breath, and continue to listen. Just doing this will bring a deeper sense of relaxation and a lessening of the suffering – and probably some insight about

yourself and the depression you're experiencing. Something else you can also do at this point is to allow this suffering aspect of you to express its feelings and thoughts through writing, either by hand or typing.

7. **Allow Tears if they Come:** In this process of communicating with your inner child, tears may come — let them. Tears release energy stored in this part of your body and allow new healing energies to pour in. But do be aware that overdoing the crying does not help your release. When you are in the process of crying, you can feel when the energy has released. The tears stop and there's a sense of relief. It is good to stop here and not go back into crying. If you do relapse, you'll find you're just recycling the pain through your body and falling into self-pity. This does not assist in the release of the emotions.

8. **Tune into your Sacred Heart:** So, once you've felt a sensation of let-go, it is then time to tune into your Sacred Heart – your Higher Heart that exists just above your heart chakra. This is your sacred sanctuary – the seat of your Soul. It's where you can feel the presence of Spirit; it's calm, peaceful, and filled with love. Once you're fully aware of this part of yourself, enter into it – and bring with you the one who is experiencing the depression. See how it responds once it enters this sanctuary of Love, how it relaxes and maybe even smiles.

9. **Call in your Higher Self:** At this point, you can call in your Higher Self. This Self has infinite love and compassion for both you and your inner child self. It brings a sense of safety with it, a protectiveness. Both you and your child self can feel embraced by this unconditional love.

10. **Release Emotions into the Light**: You may also hear a message from your Higher Self about what to do with the sense of depression you are suffering. And, at some point, you may feel a shift and know it's time to release any negative emotions and thoughts that may be contributing to your depression – as well as the depression, itself. See them enter and disappear into the divine Light that is present.

This "being-with" process can be done more easily with a partner or friend holding space for you, keeping you on track. But it can also be done alone, if you call in help from your Higher Self and other divine Beings who are with you. It's all a matter of shifting out of your head and into your body to be fully with the emotions, with compassion, rather than resistance and judgment.

Inner Critic – Primary Implant

Yet another way to approach your depression is to be aware of the existence within you of the aspect mentioned earlier that's been called the Inner Critic or superego. This is the part of you that is constantly judging you and making you wrong, the voice that keeps telling you you're never quite good enough.

It's the aspect that can cause a great deal of depression and despair. When you listen to it and believe what it's telling you, as most people habitually do, you can't help but feel bad about yourself. And if the messages get really loud and constant, you can fall deeply into a darkness that feels impossible to get out of.

Often, the advice from mental health experts is to get to know this judgmental part of you, learn to accept it and love it – because it's a part of you. To some extent, this advice can be helpful. The Inner Critic is something that is present with you and it's important to pay attention to it, see what it does, and how you respond to its messages.

And yet, if you really attune to this part of your psyche, you may realize that it doesn't actually feel like a natural part of who you are. In actuality, it's not. The Inner Critic is not a part of the original human blueprint. As strange as it might sound at first, according to information given by a well-respected whistleblower named "Cobra" within the "disclosure community", the superego is something foreign – a type of advanced AI technology that is attached to the frontal lobes of your brain on the etheric level, designed to keep you feeling separate from Source.

As with other things discussed earlier, this may sound like science fiction or conspiracy theory, and you need not believe it. But be open to the possibility that it might be true, as it can be helpful to explain so much. According to this source, this implant was something we all had to agree to before incarnating into 3D Earth. The requirement was set in place eons ago after the Fall of Consciousness occurred, when dark non-terrestrials, known as the *Archons*, arrived on earth and entered the inner realms of the lower Fourth Dimension here. From that position, they managed to take a significant amount of control over the developing human race. The implant attached to the brain, known as the "Primary Implant", has been part of every human being since those early times.

Among other things, this implant has the effect of giving you a feeling of a split between your inner Soul presence and your ego-personality self. The programming in the implant is designed to cause you to experience self-judgment, self-doubt, self-hatred, guilt, shame and fear. Partially this is achieved through recording all negative messages you've received from important adults as a child and then playing them over and over again in your mind throughout your life. But there's also a programming within it that keeps sending you negative energy, so that you feel disempowered, unloved and weak. It's so designed because the Archons feed and thrive on these emotions.

As I say, if this information is new to you, it probably sounds too strange and fantastical to be true. This is understandable. But if you contemplate the possibility of truth in this information, you may realize that it makes sense somehow. And as frightening as this may be to ponder, some part of you may respond with a huge "Yes!", as if you've known this before and you're just remembering it.

Either way, whatever seems to true to you, realize that at this point, this superego/implant is not something you can just get rid of. But you *can* definitely diminish its power over you, by not believing the messages it gives to you and not allowing it to control you. Instead, you can be aware of its presence, and catch it when it speaks – and not fall into guilt, shame, self-hatred or depression. You can stand up to it in an empowered way and not let it control you.

At some point, this implant, along with other similar AI devices like it, will be gone from Earth. In 5D, they can't exist. They will not go with us. But it is important now to be especially aware of the Primary Implant and not let it control you. Primarily, remember that emotions such as self-hatred, shame and guilt are not a natural part of you.

Yes, healing these feelings is important. But if you can keep aware that the implant is not telling the truth about you, and is actually something foreign within you, healing can be much easier. Self-love will be simpler to develop. You can more easily remember that who you are is a powerful, glorious, Spiritual Being – an ancient Soul who is on Earth to assist the human race to awaken and evolve.

And to be here to do this, you have had to enter into the darkness of the Third Dimension and lose the memory of who you really are. It has all been part of the game here. You knew in coming to Earth that you'd be subject to all the darkness here, lifetime after lifetime. And be subject to a karmic wheel that had been tampered with after the Fall of Consciousness to keep you endlessly incarnating.

Being aware of all this can make it much easier to let go of shame, guilt, self-doubt and self-hatred – and depression. You realize that this is all just stuff you've picked up while traveling through the corrupted Third Dimension, thanks to the implant and other means of control. It has not been a part of who YOU actually are.

Dissolving the Primary Implant

Something else you can do if you are interested in further diminishing the impact of the negative voice within your head is to focus on dissolving the Primary Implant. Cobra, the Pleiadian contactee who describes this implant, states that the use of the Violet Ray is helpful in achieving this.

Using this ray simply involves calling it in and seeing it penetrating the frontal lobes of your brain where the implant is located. Also call in St. Germaine, the keeper of the ray to assist you. You may or may not actually see the violet color; do not worry if you don't. Just have the intention to hold it there to essentially melt the implant.

You may become visually aware of what the implant looks like: it might appear as a dark object attached to your brain – or perhaps like something that penetrates in different ways into your brain. Or there may be an energetic feeling that begins to occur. Just keep with your intention to dissolve it with the Violet Ray.

Using the Violet Ray in this way might be something you feel drawn to focus on for a while, perhaps during a five-minute period of time during your daily meditation practice each day. As time goes on, you may wish to check within yourself to see if the same tendency toward self-judgment, guilt and shame are still there. You will likely realize that this has diminished, and that you are freer, feeling more empowered and loving toward yourself.

Discarnate Entities

A final thing to be aware of if you're dealing with depression is that sometimes you are experiencing it due to discarnate entities who have attached to your aura. This is something else that can sound scary if you're new to this idea. But understand that many people walk around with entities, unaware they're there. At times, they can also take over the emotional and verbal expression of a person.

These entities could be "earthbound Souls", human Souls who have left their bodies behind in death but who have gotten lost on their way into the afterlife. They have not found their way into the Light and tend to wander around among the living, looking to enter the aura of someone with an energy that's familiar and comfortable for them. For example, if they were people who felt depressed a lot when they were alive, they will find someone who tends toward depression, because this is what is familiar to them.

However, these discarnate entities may also be non-human beings who have no soul and know only hatred and disdain for humanity. They were originally created in the inner realms of the lower Fourth Dimension by the Archons, and they tend to create a heaviness and despair in people to whom they attach. These kinds of beings have been referred to in countless cultures throughout history as "demons" of some sort and are very real.

Both types of entities are now being activated since humanity entered the Fourth Dimension and the process of ascension began. Because so much of humanity is now waking up and raising its vibratory rate, especially now since the Great Awakening has begun, these beings are feeling threatened about their extinction and are becoming somewhat more aggressive in attempting to invade the fields of human beings.

In fact, the more light you carry, the more you may attract these entities, as they do not want humanity to evolve in consciousness and they seek out awakening Souls in order to dim their light. This is not something to feel fearful about; you simply need to be aware of this possibility and learn how to keep yourself safe, which I will outline below. Be careful also to not feel you're doing something wrong if you're attracting them. The lost Souls, in particular, may be seeking you out because they need help, they want to be free.

However, you will want to be especially careful because some of the entities approaching awakening Souls are very clever and can deceive people who are able to hear them, introducing themselves as Jesus or Buddha or some other high energy form. When believed, they will then begin to flatter the person, telling them such things as they are fully-enlightened, they're an embodiment of the Christ Consciousness, or they're the reincarnation of someone famous.

For this reason, it's important to be aware of any tendency you might have to want to be special or spiritually superior to others – and any need you feel to have others hold you in awe. If so, you might be susceptible to these kinds of "faker-spirits" who feed off of a person's need for aggrandizement.

If you begin to hear messages from an invisible source that feel overly-positive, you need to clearly feel into the energy they hold. Does it truly feel clear and loving – or is there something "off" about it? You can't be too suspicious. If it's actually a high-energy Being wanting to contact or guide you, it will patiently allow you to doubt its identity and continue to be with you lovingly until you discover its true nature.

Clearing Entities from Your Aura

If you suspect you may have negative entities of some sort with you, it would be wise to attempt to clear them out. It can take some skill; but with practice, you can probably do it. In general, it demands a level of self-authority and a knowing that spiritual Love is a powerful force for healing even the darkest of energies.

The following are guidelines for clearing entities from your aura, along with any other negative vibrations caused by thoughts forms, implants, or psychic bonds that may come with them:

1. **Call in Divine Light:** Call in and visualize divine Light entering your body and your aura.

2. **Call in Guides:** Call upon angels, specific ascended masters, or galactic guides you resonate with to be present and assist you to clear your energy.

3. **Healed and Forgiven:** Speak compassionately to the entities, telling them they are healed and forgiven. Ask that they be surrounded with the Christ light and the Christ love.

4. **Into the Light:** Ask your guides to take them to their perfect place in the Light. Visualize all dark energies being gently carried out of your aura into the Light.

5. **Implants & Thought Forms:** Request that all negative thought forms and implants left behind be dissolved and lifted in the light of truth.

6. **Psychic Bonds & Cords:** Ask that all psychic bonds and cords be severed, and to surround and protect your auric field from all but that which is of the highest vibration.

You may need to repeat this process until you feel clear. It can feel amazing to suddenly feel clear of something dark that felt like a part of you – but obviously wasn't.

If you don't feel successful with this clearing process, you may wish to seek assistance in this process from a practitioner who is skilled in doing it. You can find them online by typing in research words like "entity releasing" or "depossession".

However, be aware that getting these energies cleared once doesn't mean you can continue on in your old thinking and emotional patterns that may have attracted the entities to begin with. You will just attract more. And, very importantly, understand that if you drink a lot of alcohol or use drugs, you are creating holes in your aura that invite them in.

It's important to develop a practice of clearing your aura on a daily basis and of holding divine Light around you as much as possible to keep you safe. This is especially necessary if you work in a public setting where there are many people. And, particularly so, if you work in a hospital, where recently-transitioned Souls sometimes wander around, feeling lost.

In addition, be especially careful if you tend to frequent low-frequency places like bars or homes of drug addicts where lost Souls and dark beings tend to hang out. If you've had entities with you before, it will be all the easier to attract more.

* * * * * *

As you can see, depression is a tremendously complex emotion and has many possible origins. One way or another, if it tends to hang in there and keep you in a low vibration, it's important to do something about it. If all you can do is take a pill at first to stop the chronic suffering, then it may be wise to do that. If you can at least feel a lift in your mood, you can then decide to use some of the techniques and explanations offered here and elsewhere to further empower you to overcome the suffering.

Chapter 15

Disoriented, Scattered, Mind-Fogged

If you're feeling disoriented, scattered, mind-fogged, and generally exhausted these days, know you are one of many who increasingly bring this complaint into doctors' offices. It's not uncommon to feel ungrounded, confused, and dizzy – or to be walking into things, forgetting where you're going, or unable to come up with the most common words.

Physical Causes

There are numerous possible reasons for these symptoms. Many of them could be physical, as they are listed as symptoms of a myriad of diseases and disorders such as hypothyroidism, fibromyalgia, Lyme and Candida. These are also symptoms of electromagnetic sensitivity certain people experience due to the electronic devices and cell towers that have proliferated everywhere in the last twenty years – especially now that 5G towers are being erected in many communities.

So it can be helpful if you're feeling this way for any length of time to be checked out for these disorders.

High-Frequency Waves of Light

However, during these times of ascension, it is common to experience these symptoms for a reason most health professionals are unaware of: the high-frequency waves of Light that are now streaming onto the planet.

Although these waves can bring a great deal of joy, inspiration and love, they can also cause many uncomfortable ascension symptoms as they move into your field and body – including a sensation of feeling disoriented, scattered and mind-fogged.

When these light waves hit, you can begin feeling confused, ungrounded, and unable to concentrate. It may appear as if everything around you is surreal or not solid, and that your body is very dense and heavy. Or as if only part of you is present, and you don't know where the rest of you has gone. All of this can be very disquieting if you don't know that it's your ascension process that's causing it.

Activation of New Crystalline DNA

One thing that might be occurring in these experiences is the activation of your DNA, causing the outdated 3D carbon-based DNA that has maintained your identity with physical realities to shift into a more crystalline form.

This is a huge transformation. Because you have spent the majority of your life identified with patterns rooted in your carbon-based DNA, this shifting naturally creates an experience not only of disorientation, but also exhaustion, and greater sensitivity to sound, smell, light or energies.

Other sensations, such as a feeling of great expansion or a buzzing from a natural high, may also occur as your crystalline DNA gets activated. This can feel great, of course; but it may take you a while to learn how to function as a physical human being with the new heightened level of awareness you are experiencing. Because these experiences are rooted in simple BEingness, you can be confused, thinking you don't know how to accomplish physical tasks when feeling so expanded, relaxed and altered.

The key is to move slowly and allow being and doing to merge as one embodied expression of consciousness in action. It's also crucial to stay hydrated and grounded in the present moment and to rest as much as possible.

As your DNA continues to shift, more of the outdated 3D patterns of ancestral and familial conditioning will continue to drop away and return to Source. Instead of focusing on trying to clear out this conditioning, it is more essential to get to know how to function in your life in expanded states of consciousness. This will allow what no longer serves you to dissolve on its own accord.

Grounding Yourself

Meanwhile, on a practical level, it's helpful to not only keep hydrated and move slowly while staying in the present moment, but also to ground yourself as much as you can. Spend time out in nature, barefoot, if possible. Lie down in grass, feel your connection to Gaia. Talk to the trees. You can discover that all of Nature is already in the expanded field of consciousness you're shifting into. Your mind can begin to clear; you can feel more alert and present.

If you can't get outdoors, then you can send an energetic grounding cord from your perineum or tailbone down into the center of the earth. This can steady and ground you surprisingly quickly.

Naturally, if you are experiencing these disorienting sensations, they could well be a mixture of emotional/physical stresses and ascension symptoms. In a way, it may not matter: whatever the cause, you still need to slow down and rest as much as you can to allow your body to go through the changes it needs to during these challenging times.

Chapter 16

Failure

One of the most painful sensations you can create for yourself is when you've decided for some reason that you are a *failure*. Not that you've failed at something specific – which is something everyone does all the time – but actually labeling yourself as a "failure".

The emotion this labeling creates is obviously third-dimensional; but so is the act of labeling itself. It is understandable, however: labeling someone is one of the many limiting and distorted patterns people adopt in the Third Dimension. It's a pattern that springs out of the idea of duality, another 3D habit: You're either a success or a failure. There's always good/bad, black/white, right/wrong.

It can be helpful to understand this dynamic so you can try to avoid it. But, if you're already stuck in the feeling of failure, it doesn't do much. The pain is too great. So it's important to understand more clearly how this belief and feeling of failure originate.

Identifying with What You Do

Most often a sense of failure begins through identifying with what you *do* – rather than who you actually *are*. This type of identification has been prevalent in the West, especially in the US, but now is also very common in the East. Success in what you achieve at work, in school, and at home is seen as essential for anyone to feel good and valuable as a human being. What you do and accomplish is who you are.

Believing this can make you very vulnerable. If what you choose to do at any point turns out to not be "successful" in the eyes of others or yourself, then your intrinsic sense of value as a person falls. If you watch closely, you may find that much of what's occurring on your ascension path is steering you away from identification with what you do and is pointing instead to a focus on who you are as a Being.

People who are spiritually-oriented tend to want to avoid the trap of identifying with the "doer" by focusing on being "spiritual". And this can work, if you truly can place your value on who you are as an embodied Spiritual Being. In doing this, you know your sense of value lies within the light and love you hold as a Consciousness. Your very presence is what is valuable. You see not only past the roles and activities you engage in, but also past all your personality characteristics. You find the higher, more authentic YOU, and identify with that -- and you find there's no way you can fail; you are already YOU.

Fourth, Fifth and Sixth Rays of Creation

In the Mastering Alchemy course offered by Jim Self, there is a technique that can be helpful in shifting out of a failure mode and learning to manifest a more positive reality for yourself. Especially valuable when you wish to change an entire set of emotions, beliefs and experiences you're having around an issue, this technique involves using what are known as the Fourth, Fifth and Sixth Rays of Creation. These are rays that can assist you in creating what you desire. They include countless codes and frequencies of light, sound and color.

You don't need to understand the intricacies of how they work – you simply need to be aware of how to use them. The way to start is by reflecting on a difficult issue you're working with inside yourself, and becoming aware of all the negative emotions, beliefs and conditions the issue has created within you.

As an example, let's say you are having a difficult time with a family member who has achieved much success in the world. You are feeling resentment and hurt by something they've said about you, causing you to feel like a failure. You also feel intimated by them and anxious about having to confront them about this. In addition, you realize you're judging them pretty harshly.

Here's what you can do:

1. **Call in 4th, 5th & 6th Rays of Creation:** Move into a meditative state of mind. Then call in the Fourth, Fifth and Sixth Rays of Creation. There's no particular way in which these fields of consciousness will manifest to you; just call them in and know they're there.

2. **Release Emotions & Thoughts in the 4th Ray:** Become aware of all your uncomfortable emotions and thoughts about your issue. One at a time, allow the emotions of resentment, hurt, intimidation and anxiety, along with your judgments, to be released into the Fourth Ray. Here they will be pulled apart into clear and separate components of the problem.

3. **Take them into the 5th Ray:** Now take all you've placed in the Fourth Ray up into the Fifth Ray, which is like a workbench. Here you can get a good look at each component and make sure you'd like to remove them. You may wish to retain some part of the issue that might be valuable to you in some way.

4. **Toss what you don't want into the 6th Ray:** But all the rest of it you can then "toss" up into the Sixth Ray, one at a time, and see each piece disappearing. The Sixth Ray is the repository of absolutely everything in creation, a grand cosmic "library". You can borrow anything from it and also return anything you no longer want. It's another term for the Quantum Field. You may feel a surprising relief in throwing unwanted emotions and patterns into the Sixth Ray. It can be amazing how a simple act within your imagination can so affect how you feel.

5. **Ask the 6th Ray for what You Want:** Now it's time for you to think of what you would like to be *given* in return from the Sixth Ray, what emotions, beliefs, and experiences you would prefer to have regarding this family member.

6. **Bring it all into 5th Ray, then the 4th – and into yourself:** You can ask for anything; but generally, what you focus on you will likely be the opposite kinds of things of what you've given away. You might choose such things as success, compassion, confidence, harmony, trust and strength. Feel and see these qualities flow, one at a time, from the Sixth Ray into your arms, and bring them all into the Fourth Ray to be brought together into a new integrated package of positive emotions and energies. Pull this into yourself.

This exercise may sound too simple; you may doubt it could change a situation you have in mind. But remember the extraordinary power of the imagination. It's where you create your reality. This technique may greatly surprise you.

Chapter 17

Fearful

Fear underlies just about all emotional suffering that occurs in the Third and Fourth Dimensions. It is what reduces a human being to the weakest and least effective state of mind. For that reason, while going through all the challenges you're facing in your process of ascending into the Fifth Dimension, it would be a good idea to do your best to focus on healing all trauma that has created fear within you and leaving it behind.

To be clear, all fear will not be left behind, in that there will still be a warning signal that activates when you are in any actual danger. This will be more of a sensation in the body, however, than an emotion of suffering. It is the devastating emotion of fear that will be absent.

There are many kinds of fear that people suffer from: fear of rejection, failure, intimacy, loneliness, change, being judged, not being good enough. And now, with the process of ascension, a big one is fear of the unknown. There are a number of methods therapists use to assist people in overcoming their fears; one of the most successful is behavior modification. If you experience a great deal of fear about life, it may be wise to try therapy.

Shifting from Fear to Calm

However, if you just occasionally experience fear arising within you, it can be helpful to know that the higher-dimensional energies of light now streaming onto the planet are providing assistance for shifting out of fear. And, if the fear isn't overwhelming, there are some simple things you can do to shift yourself into a calmer state of being – so that you meet the traumatic emotions and successfully heal and release them.

Deep Breaths: One of the first suggestions is to take slow, relaxed, diaphragmatic breaths, which will cause your body to trigger a natural tranquilizing effect. Consciously relaxing your body will help shut off the stress response in it.

Tapping: Another practice that can really assist in creating a sense of calm is one you may be familiar with: The Emotional Freedom Technique (EFT) or "Tapping". This is a form of acupressure, based on the same energy meridians used in traditional acupuncture, but without the invasiveness of needles.

In this practice, simple tapping with the fingertips is used to input kinetic energy onto specific meridians on your head and chest while you think about your specific problem and voice positive affirmations. This short-circuits the emotional block from your body's bioenergy system, thus restoring calm to both your mind and your body. EFT can be used for a great number of issues, but calming anxiety is an especially important and easy one to use.

However, if the fears you are experiencing, especially ones that feel irrational, have arisen since you've been awakening to the Fifth Dimension, it might be helpful to be aware of what may be causing these.

It's actually very understandable that fear might come up as your ascension process accelerates: you are shifting very rapidly into higher and higher levels of consciousness, without a reliable map. It's natural to experience fear from time to time, not really knowing what's ahead on your path or even where you might be headed.

Unconscious Fears of Awakening

Negotiating the new and unfamiliar structures and spiritual laws of the higher Fourth Dimension can be daunting. And, strange as it may seem, the fears you experience might actually be about fully awakening to who you are.

Although you naturally want to fully awaken to who you are as your Higher Self and to shift into fifth-dimensional consciousness, you may have unconscious fears about actually doing this. For instance, what would it mean about your current relationships and comfort in being around people you know? How would you relate to them? Would they draw away from you? Would they envy you or judge you? Fear of the shift it might cause in your familiar relationships could subconsciously cause you to resist a change you might consciously desire.

Past Life Fears

Other fears you experience may stem from experiences in past lives.

Punishment: One fear might be that if you fully awaken, something terrible might happen to you. This may be due to unconscious memories of past lifetimes in which you attained a high degree of awakening; and for some reason, you were either tortured, hanged, imprisoned, or otherwise punished for expressing what you had come to experience. Thus, you may have a subconscious fear (although intellectually understood to be unfounded) that this might happen again.

Fear of Repeating Mistakes from the Past: Another past life scenario that may cause a fear of awakening is one in which you might have awakened and then assumed the role of a spiritual teacher, prophet, or leader of some kind. And in that role, you abused your power, bringing harm to others. Subconsciously, you fear being back in that position again and making the same mistakes.

If this is so, you may naturally experience anxiety about moving forward into a position of power for fear of abusing it once again. With this fear, you might manage to sabotage every opportunity you are given to rise into a greater position of power and visibility in your life, subconsciously believing you'd be struck down and somehow punished.

If you suspect either of these fears to be present with you, it can be helpful to find help from a hypnotherapist or other past-life practitioner to assist you in consciously remembering these lifetimes. In bringing the memories and the beliefs and emotions connected to them into your conscious awareness, you can then begin to heal them.

No Need to "Fix" Yourself

Even if you find that fear is keeping you stuck in 3D consciousness, it's helpful to remember that moving back into a mode of attempting to fix yourself is not the answer. There is nothing broken. There is nothing wrong with you. There is simply a fear waiting to be met.

Effective ascension work is different from what you may have learned in the past in the Third Dimension in which you "worked on yourself" through digging up the past and then re-experiencing the suffering and analyzing it in depth – all in hopes of somehow fixing and healing yourself. Although it's important to explore dysfunctional patterns that come up, especially if they are new to you, what can often work better in the Fourth

Dimension is keeping a focus on what is already perfect and whole, and enhancing this awareness through being positive and compassionate with yourself.

An intention to focus on love is also very important. Just as remembering that loving everything that appears in your life is the most effective way to face the existential fear of emptiness that can occur on the path of ascension, this approach is just as effective in addressing a fear of awakening. And, of course, learning to love yourself – even with the fears you experience – is also essential for your awakening.

But, most importantly in overcoming fear is to meet it head-on with trust and courage, feel it completely with acceptance and love – and then gently push past it and do what you fear doing. You know the old saying: "Feel the fear, and then do it anyway." What you might discover is that the fear, being illusory at its core, dissipates and finally disappears. And you are left standing, not only unhurt, but stronger and more fearless than ever.

This process of facing fear may take a while and a number of sessions with yourself before the fear totally dissipates. But it does work. In the end, you'll generally find that the fear is merely a third-dimensional reaction to an illusory threat.

For further approaches to healing fear, see the Chapter on Anxiety.

Chapter 18

Frustrated, Blocked

A feeling of frustration can sometimes happen so suddenly, it can be hard to stop it. If you notice, it usually occurs when you are either trying really hard to achieve something and it isn't working, or you're attempting to resist something that won't go away. Life just isn't going the way you want it to, or how you think it "should" be going.

Stop the Struggle

It can be especially frustrating when you're trying to achieve something in your life, something that feels so right – and yet, every effort you make in that direction seems to get blocked and hindered. If you find yourself in this situation of struggle, and it's clear over and over again that what you're trying to do is not working, it can be smart to just stop the struggling, to cease your striving to push forward, trying to make something happen that isn't wanting to happen.

Instead, you can be open to what else might be trying to happen. You can surrender to what's occurring and watch to see what else may unfold. You may initially feel that what's happening is not right, not what's "supposed" to be happening. But if you have trust and stay tuned to your inner knowing, you'll probably realize in time that it's actually perfect.

In fact, you have the opportunity to see that probably everything coming into your life during these times is what will help you ascend in the fastest, smoothest way possible. You will begin to see this more clearly if you can shift your perception of yourself and your life from your mind to your Sacred Heart. From this intuitive place, you will sense the rightness of all occurrences and experiences in your life, even as they are happening.

Stop the Resistance

A similar type of frustration can come from your resistance to situations, events or relationships that are occurring in your life. There is an important teaching in many different spiritual traditions about ceasing to resist what life is giving you, and to simply accept what-is. The teaching continues to suggest that what you are resisting is the very path to attaining ongoing inner peace, joy and freedom. If you approach life by resisting what-is and attempting to change things from that position of resistance, not only will nothing really change for the better, but inner peace, joy and freedom will continue to elude you.

It's easy to forget this. Resistance can be so automatic, and it can be to anything at all: a situation you find yourself in, something someone says to you, a quality in yourself you don't like, the death of a friend. Big or small, if it's unpleasant or painful in any way, your first reaction is probably to resist it, judge it, or try to quickly change it. And, if you check closely, you can find that reaction probably stems from a sense of fear or hurt.

If you try to change something from the position of resistance, you'll likely find that nothing really changes – or, if it does, that change won't last long. Your mind may simply continue its annoying, resisting chatter, while your negative emotions settle in more deeply and your actions become less effective. You're stuck in your resistance.

Whereas, if you can move quickly into acceptance, you can feel a sense of relief in realizing that the impatience, irritation or pain you're experiencing is due to the fact that you're probably resisting what-is. Once you become aware of this and shift into acceptance, everything within you can relax. Your mind chatter will likely stop, a clarity will move in, and a soft sense of peace and let-go can occur.

You may still not like what is happening, but you can experience a peace and a sense of relaxation with this acceptance. And then – from this place – you are ready to begin focusing on what you'd like to change about the situation.

Acceptance vs Passivity

There is often confusion about this acceptance approach to life. There's the belief that if you don't resist things you don't like and don't try to change them, you're going to stay stuck in the same rut you're in. You may judge acceptance as a position of passive resignation, of being a victim or doormat, as a kind of giving up and giving in.

This is not what the path of acceptance is about. First of all, the practice of accepting what-is is anything but passive. It requires a very active, conscious approach to life, in which you have to constantly stay awake and pay close attention to your thoughts, emotions, and reactions. And, importantly, it demands making a conscious choice to not follow along with the automatic programming of resistance to something unpleasant.

Secondly, the path of acceptance is not passive in that it requires a great deal of courage. In order to fully experience acceptance, you need to be open to feeling all the emotions present within you regarding whatever it is you're wanting to resist. This often isn't easy. But it's important to feel these emotions fully, at least briefly, or you will be stuck with them. And they will continue to bring more of the same into your life.

Thirdly, the path of acceptance does not mean you can't move to change anything. It simply means that to be effective, your attempts to change must come out of a state of acceptance and clear understanding of what you want to change, rather than one of resistance and avoidance.

Effective change derives from an understanding of how something got to be that way to begin with – how you, yourself, created it to be that way. And until you first accept that something is the way it is, you can't hope to understand how you created it. Or how to avoid creating it again in the future.

As you're likely aware, what happens to you in life doesn't just come out of the blue; in one way or another, you have created it, you have called it into your life. You have brought it in, in order to learn from it. If you immediately resist what comes in, you miss the lesson – and it will either continue to plague you, unresolved, or it will come in again and again, until you get it.

Trusting What Comes into your Life

So the first step is to simply allow and accept whatever appears in your life, trusting that it's there for a good reason. You accept that it is your reality for right now. It need not stay with you forever; it's simply here now to help wake you up and move you further along on your path to freedom.

As you do this, you can then open yourself to learn what the lesson is and accept it. You can take responsibility for creating it, which gives you the power to do something about it. And you can then also let go of all negative feelings and judgments you may have toward yourself or others involved in the situation you wish to change. You are then ready to move toward change and effectively manifesting what you do want in your life.

Misconceptions about Manifestation

At first glance, it can look like the teachings about acceptance run counter to the teachings about "creating your own reality" – which involve taking control of your life, getting rid of what you don't want, and manifesting what you do want.

These kinds of teachings also hold a lot of truth. Yes, we are powerful creator beings who can manifest what we want in our lives. We can change ourselves, change our lives, change the world. So how can these two seemingly opposed approaches both be effective?

There is misunderstanding about the teachings of manifestation, just as there is about the teachings of acceptance. It's often assumed that manifestation arises out of resistance to reality as it is. This is not true. Effective manifestation cannot happen if you're focusing on the opposite of what you're attempting to manifest – and this is what you're doing if you're resisting the opposite situation. You're caught in negativity by your resistance.

Effective Manifestation

Clear and effective manifestation happens when you are focused entirely on that which you're attempting to manifest. And this focus can only happen if you begin with acceptance and understanding of what you're trying to change. It's this state of being that brings about the power to change something.

In the end, the change must be an organic kind of shift that emerges – a natural one toward a better, more positive place. There can't be a pushing. Or anger, hurt or fear motivating you.

The Bonus of Gratitude

You truly do have the power to create and change whatever you want in life. You simply need to know how to use this power effectively. And this starts with the age-old teachings of accepting whatever appears in your life with open arms and fully experiencing what-is – first – before trying to change it.

And, if you're really smart, you can bring in gratitude, as well, gratitude for all you're experiencing. For gratitude not only feels good; it's also one of the greatest keys for effective manifestation.

For more keys on effective manifestation, see the chapter on Manifestation Difficulty.

Chapter 19

Grief and Loss

The ascension path most often includes a certain amount of loss and grief. It   seems to be an inevitable part of the process as we let go of our limited, distorted 3D lives and all we've created in them. Some of our creations simply exist in too low a vibration to accompany us into the Fifth Dimension.

Although the term "grief" can be used to describe the emotion that arises due to losing anything in your life, it generally refers to what is experienced with the loss of a loved one. And, since many Souls are currently leaving the planet, you may well be losing loved ones to death and struggling to deal with this kind of major loss.

Losing a Loved One

The first thing to understand in experiencing grief over the loss of a loved one is that there is generally no better or worse way to grieve. It is a highly individual experience. How you grieve depends on many factors, including your particular coping style, your life experiences, and how significant the loss is to you.

However, no matter how you may grieve, the grieving process generally takes time. Healing tends to happen gradually; it can't be forced or hurried. There is no "normal" timetable for grieving. You could start to feel better in weeks or months, or it may take years. However it happens, it's important to be patient with yourself and allow the process of grieving to unfold naturally.

It's also helpful to understand that the pain you experience over your loss of a loved one will not go away faster if you try to ignore it. This can only make it worse in the long run; it will simply recede for the time-being into your subconscious mind – and then start surfacing in somewhat distorted ways when certain events occur that trigger the emotions. For true healing, it is necessary to face your grief and actively deal with it.

Responding to your loss with sadness, fear or loneliness is normal and to be expected. Be careful not to believe you have to be "strong" to somehow protect others in your family or friends. Expressing your emotions openly will not only assist you in your own healing, it can assist others to do the same. But, at the same time, don't think you need to cry in order to express your feelings. Not everyone does. Just express your grief however it comes naturally to you.

You may have heard that grieving should last about a year, or some other prescribed time. This is a myth. It takes as long as it takes. At the same time, do not think that moving on from your loss means you forget about it. You will likely never forget it; but you can eventually go on with your life and keep the memory of someone you've lost as an important part of you.

You may have also heard about the "Five Stages of Grief" – denial, anger, bargaining, depression, acceptance. These are typical states people often pass through in their mourning process; but they are not necessarily sequential, and some people don't experience any of them in their healing process. Again, allow yourself to feel all emotions that arise within you and as deeply as you can, whether they make sense or not.

Trying to Hold onto What You're Losing

However, loved ones may not be the only losses you're experiencing since you've been on the path of ascension. You might find that certain situations and things that have been important to you in your life are also disappearing. And sometimes, profound grief can occur with these losses, as well.

Aside from the grief caused by the losses, a further challenge can often be a struggle to hold onto the thing that's leaving. If, for example, you are losing a comfortable home you've enjoyed for years, or a long-time mode of making a living, or a relationship you've relied on for years, it can cause a lot of fear and distress.

If you're losing something important, it's natural to clutch at it, attempting to hold onto it. But if it's actually leaving, it's wise during these times of ascension to realize it probably needs to go. See if you can consciously let it go and trust that, if this is happening, it's likely necessary for your awakening. It can't go with you where you're going – and there is probably something else in store for you that will lift you into a higher vibration. Find the faith that you will be taken care of without it, probably in ways you might never have thought of before.

It's important to realize that the more you try to hang onto things that are disappearing, the more difficult your life will become. You need to trust the process, and consciously choose to let go of whatever is being taken from you.

Perhaps, in the process, you can explore old beliefs, attitudes or distorted perspectives you've had about life that are not actually based in truth. You may find that what you've thought was totally essential for you to be able to live in comfort and joy really is not essential, after all.

In realizing what is really essential to your Being, you can discover who you are beyond all your ego identities, attachments, and limited beliefs about yourself. Once you decide to just cooperate with the loss that's happening, it can actually be exciting to watch and anticipate whatever may be next coming toward you in life. You can rest, knowing that whatever it is, it's coming in order to lift you yet further into a higher vibration.

Until you've found your way through the losses, it can certainly be unclear what their positive and freeing purpose might be. But if you look closely at any point, you can see that everything – absolutely everything – is happening for your ascension in as expedient a way as possible. You just need to trust this and cooperate in the best way you can, so you are skillfully and trustingly riding the ascension energies as they flow in, rather than resisting them.

Surrendering to your Grief

If the experience of grief is for something relatively minor, there are many tools in this book and elsewhere that can be helpful. But, if you've really fallen into deep and overwhelming grief, it can often feel too difficult to do any these things.

If so, it is time to fully surrender to the grief. In using the term *surrender*, I am not referring to giving up or resigning yourself to the grief. And I'm not saying that wallowing in it and feeling self-pity is helpful. Surrender in this context involves a conscious and purposeful choice to allow what-is – whatever it is you're experiencing – to simply be and not resist it or immediately try to change it.

To do this, you need to make the decision to move out of your mind, where negative thoughts keep cycling around and creating negative emotions; and to focus, instead, on your body where the grief is actually centered. You'll find that your tendency, when in emotional pain, is to try to move away from the pain and to go into your mind in hopes of somehow escaping it. But all the mind can do is keep recycling your thoughts about your grief, trying to get you away from it, distract you, or in some other way try to get you out of it. As you've likely discovered, this doesn't work well.

What you need to do is move your focus down into your body to where you actually feel the grief, without any judgment or resistance to it; you're just allowing your emotional state to be what it is – and doing your best to feel compassion for this part of yourself experiencing the grief.

Being-With Process

Here is a way to do this by "being-with" it. (It is the same process offered in the Chapter on Depression, a similar type of powerful emotion.)

1. **Think about your Grief:** Start by thinking about it. Allow all your familiar thoughts about it to come present – how it feels and what might be causing it. Watch your mind carefully. Note all the familiar ideas and strategies you've tried in attempting to get away from feeling the grief – how to get rid of it, change it, distract yourself from it, fix it.

2. **Become Aware of the Emotions that Appear:** Then become aware of the emotions that are coming present. Realize that when you're thinking about it, matching emotions tend to follow. And be aware that, as you think about your grief, your mind really does not know what to do about it.

3. **Focus on your Body:** Now switch your focus to your body. Where in your body do you feel grief and other negative emotions that go with it? Usually, you'll find it's somewhere in your gut or your chest. Bring your full awareness to this place and focus your attention there. This may be difficult at first; you might find yourself wanting to escape back into your mind. But remember, your mind does not have the answers. You need to stay with the grief, itself, to know what to do with it. Keep your attention on that part of your body where it resides and take a deep breath or two into

that place. You may wish to also put your hand on that part of your body.

4. **Be Totally Present to the Grief:** Then see if you can just be with this part of you that is experiencing the grief. You can see it as your "inner child", your "emotional self", your "pain body", or some other concept. But know it is a part of you that is not the adult, conscious self you generally function from when engaged in life. It's a part of you that only knows emotions and bodily sensations.

5. **Breathe into the Emotions:** Again, be aware of the tendency to want to escape back into your mind, away from the emotionally-centered experience of the pain. Instead, just stay there with it – and breathe into the emotions. If tears come, allow them to flow. You don't have to have answers or know how to fix things in any way. You just need to be with this little one, without any resistance or judgment. Just allow it to be, as it is – the grief is part of your reality at this time. Just accept this for now. It's important to understand that emotions always want to be felt and fully experienced without resistance or judgment. This doesn't have to be for a long time: just long enough for you to feel this emotional self relax. As it starts feeling acknowledged and allowed, it will finally begin to let go.

6. **Listen to your Little Self:** At this point, see if there is something it may wish to say to you. Be willing to listen closely, without feeling defensive, guilty or judgmental. If you can find loving, compassionate words of wisdom to respond to it, great. But if you can't, you can just keep repeating "I love you" with every breath, and continue to listen. Just doing this will bring a deeper sense of relaxation and a lessening of the suffering – and probably some insight about yourself and the grief you're experiencing. Something else you can also do at this point is to allow this suffering aspect within you to express its feelings and thoughts through writing, either by hand or typing.

7. **Allow Tears if they Come:** In this process of communicating with your inner child, tears may come – let them. Tears release energy stored in this part of your body and allow new healing energies to pour in. But do be aware that overdoing the crying does not help your release. When you are in the process of crying, you can feel when the energy has released. The tears stop and there's a sense of relief. It is good to stop here and not go back into crying. If you do relapse, you'll find you're just recycling the pain through your body and falling into self-pity. This does not assist in the release of the emotions.

8. **Tune into your Sacred Heart:** So, once you've felt a sensation of let-go, it is then time to tune into your Sacred Heart – your Higher Heart that exists just above your heart chakra. This is your sacred sanctuary – the seat of your Soul. It's where you can feel the presence of Spirit; it's calm, peaceful, and filled with love. Once you're fully aware of this part of yourself, enter into it – and bring with you the one who is experiencing the grief. See how it responds once it enters this sanctuary of Love, how it relaxes and maybe even smiles.

9. **Call in your Higher Self:** At this point, you can call in your Higher Self. This Self has infinite love and compassion for both you and your inner child self. It brings a sense of safety with it, a protectiveness. Both you and your child self can feel embraced by this unconditional love.

10. **Release Emotions into Light:** You may also hear a message from your Higher Self about what to do with the sense of grief you are suffering. And, at some point, you may feel a shift and know it's time to release any negative emotions and thoughts that may be contributing to your grief – as well as the grief, itself. See them enter and disappear into the divine Light that is present.

This "being-with" process can be done more easily with a partner or friend holding space for you, keeping you on track. But it can also be done alone, if you call in help from your Higher Self and other divine Beings who are with you. The main focus is to shift out of your head and into your body and to be fully with the emotions with compassion, rather than with resistance and judgment.

Using the Violet Flame

If "being with" your grief feels too difficult, there is a simpler technique for finding relief. And it involves using the *Violet Flame.* The Violet Flame is a gift of light kept by the ascended master, Saint Germain. Existing in your Sacred Heart, it is a powerful tool you can use to heal yourself from anything. Whatever you may have manifested in the past through your words, thoughts, or actions that needs to be cleared can be transmuted and released into this flame.

The Violet Flame contains compassion, forgiveness and mercy and will transmute all of your lower-dimensional emotions, including grief. You invoke it through connecting to your I AM Presence, and asking for its help with sincere intention. One way to invoke the Violet Flame is to focus on your Sacred Heart, and say words similar to the following:

Through my I AM Presence, I now invoke the Violet Flame. I ask it to flow through my crown chakra into my heart and into every cell of my physical, mental, emotional bodies. I ask it now to transmute my grief into light.

You may actually see or feel the Violet Flame in your Heart. If so, gently place your grief there to transmute it into light. It's not a problem if you do not see or feel it. Just trust the process as you call upon the Violet Ray and release your thoughts and emotions into it. You will likely feel a sense of release; the heaviness of the grief will lighten.

You may also wish to simply step into the Violet Flame and feel yourself enveloped and bathed in its healing light, as your grief dissolves in the flames. In doing this, it will transmute the grief you are experiencing into light. By releasing negative thoughts and emotions into the Violet Flame, you are releasing them not only for your own personal ascension, but also for the collective ascension.

Chapter 20

Irritable, Dissatisfied, Blah

There may be times you realize you've been in a "bad mood" for a while, feeling kind of flat or blah, or even somewhat irritable and dissatisfied with just about everything that's happening in your life. You're not really down, but you're not feeling good either. Just somewhat sour and negative.

Perhaps it's hard to pinpoint what's happened to cause the mood, and you keep trying, without success, to do things that will distract you from it. But all you can think of are the things going on in your life that are negatively affecting you.

If this kind of mood persists, one thing to look into is the body-mind connection. It's true that the mind definitely affects the body; but it's also true the other way around. For instance, if you're having problems with your digestion or other health issues, this may be affecting the chemical production in your brain that could be impacting your mood.

Focus on Positive Things Happening

But if you're thinking it doesn't have to do with your health, and you can't figure out any other reason for your mood, the first thing you can do is rather obvious: begin focusing on positive experiences you're having in your life, rather than the challenging ones. Although obvious, it may not occur to you when you're in a negative state of mind. You will find that the more you focus on positive thoughts, especially with a sense of gratitude, the more positive experiences you begin creating and the higher the vibration you'll experience.

At times, your mood may be severely impacted by the high-dimensional waves of energy streaming onto the planet, which tend to cause some disruptions in those areas that are caught in 3D energy. But you can notice that even when these waves are really impacting you in these ways, there are times in between them when everything seems to calm down and smooth out for a while.

During these times, you have the opportunity to relax and breathe – and begin integrating what has been occurring for you. You can stand back and look at your life from a broader view and become aware of all the positive things that have been also occurring, right alongside the challenging things.

For instance, aren't you more aware than you were a year ago—maybe even a month ago? And I don't mean just a little more so, the way you might have experienced changes in the past. I don't mean slight change. Isn't there something inside you that is now much stronger and more resilient? Perhaps you have a better understanding of what love is about – true, unconditional, spiritual love.

Think about it: Do you ever have days in which joy just bubbles up in you out of nowhere for no reason at all? Or times, in the middle of great irritation or even despair, when you're suddenly inexplicably drawn into a profound inner peace? Maybe you're at times so filled with love, you're in tears?

And perhaps you're even having experiences in which you sense a karmic contract has just completed itself. Indeed, that, as intense as your experiences are, maybe all karma in your life is coming to a close.

You may realize that, in general, there is simply a greater inner peace you now walk around with. Less mind-chatter. More self-love. More acceptance of life, simply as it is. Greater detachment and ease. And more and more prolonged glimpses of utter freedom and knowing who you are on a much higher and broader level than ever before.

All these experiences are signs of ascension, both the difficult and the wonderful. Occasionally, these two types of experiences – joy-filled ones and painful ones – happen all in the same day, or even simultaneously. It can feel crazy. But, if you keep focused on the positive, you will find your mood will grow steadily lighter and more optimistic.

Waiting for Something Good to Happen

You may also discover when you're feeling in a flat and uninspired mood, that you are caught in waiting for something positive outside of yourself to happen that you believe will make you happy. Maybe you're waiting for more money to come in so you can afford to buy or do something you believe will bring happiness. Or perhaps you're waiting for a new and wonderful relationship to appear, or the opportunity to move or to go on vacation. Or maybe something hopeful on the news to happen.

You have experienced enough change by this time in your ascension process to realize that waiting for something in your life to make you happy rarely works. In believing that outer sources and circumstances will bring you happiness, you are disempowering yourself. You are helpless over your own state of being.

First, the thing you're waiting for may never even happen. Secondly, even if it does happen and it brings you a sense of happiness, it's probable this feeling won't last, because something else negative will likely happen to bring you down again.

In addition, even if you're happy about the thing happening once you get it, there's always going to be something else you want that will arise. This is the nature of desire – it's a hungry mouth. There's always more desire that's going to arise – and if you can't fulfill that new desire, you can fall into unhappiness again.

It's important to realize that going after, and even receiving, all the things you think you want in life is probably not going to create lasting happiness. You will always be dealing with a niggling sense of dissatisfaction.

There is nothing at all wrong with trying to manifest things, relationships, and situations to create a more comfortable and satisfying life. Learning to successfully create the life you wish to have is all part of the ascension process. You just need to realize that depending on these outer sources to create and maintain your happiness is not likely going to work very well. Happiness is an inside job. You can discover that it is actually a choice. You can make the decision to feel happy, no matter what appears to be happening in your life.

And, if you are really depressed, outer sources probably won't cut it at all. The depression will color any new uplifting emotions you may feel, even with the most wonderful events or relationships that come into your life. (If you're dealing with depression, read the chapter on Depression for keys on how to alleviate this challenging state of being.)

Focus on the Miracle

As dull and unexciting as your life may feel in the moment, it can help to remember that, in the bigger picture, ascension is still happening. And whether it takes you a short while or a number of years to complete the transformation into your fifth-dimensional consciousness and merging with your Soul, it won't matter, if you keep in mind how miraculous it is that it's happening at all. Remember, you're finally on your way Home!

So rather than getting lost in the "ascension blues", focus on the miracle. And watch carefully for all the little, but very important, changes that are happening within you. You may be surprised at how very different you currently are, compared to a few years ago – how much more awake, loving, peaceful and joyful.

Look at Life through Your Sacred Heart

And remember, if you feel discouraged, you're probably looking at everything through your rational mind, that limited 3D lens that really can't grasp the higher Reality of what's going on.

Try instead to move into your Sacred Heart and look through its wider lens. You may find it's easier to recognize that your irritable, dissatisfied mood has to do with the story you're telling yourself about what's happening in your life or about yourself. And that you can just as easily tell yourself another more positive story – or maybe no story at all.

You will discover that, behind your stories of discontent, there is a knowing that ascension is indeed happening and all you have to do is keep moving forward, one step at a time. And remember that you are being guided perfectly with meticulous loving care through your own unique process.

Magic of Gratitude

Something else you can do when you're feeling stuck in a low-vibrational 3D mood is to focus specifically on the feeling of gratitude. It can sound corny – but it really does work: gratitude has a high vibration. Focusing on what you are grateful for in your life and allowing a feeling of gratitude to come into your body and heart will automatically raise your vibration.

You might even consider keeping a "gratitude journal". Or make it a practice to review your day at night before going to sleep, naming what happened in the day you can be grateful for. You can even just repeat the word *gratitude* a number of times to yourself and, surprisingly, feel yourself shift to a higher awareness, a greater openness, a deeper sense of peace. Try this, while focusing on your Heart.

There are actually a number of scientific studies on the brain and gratitude that have found that when someone's feeling gratitude, the brain's chemistry starts changing. More endorphins and serotonin are created. One study was especially interesting. It reported that if a person is feeling gratitude – and then also starts feeling a sense of compassion, as well – this produces what they call a "happy brain". When someone's feeling both of these emotions together, the brain emits even more chemicals which create a state of deep well-being and happiness.

So this is a very simple recipe for well-being and a high vibration: Focus on gratitude and compassion and create a happy brain.

Move into the Witness

Sometimes, if you get too involved in a problem you're facing, it's difficult to see things clearly. When this happens, you might try shifting into the point of view of the loving witness or observer. This is where you move your awareness into a space somewhat outside yourself and just watch what's happening inside you from that somewhat detached perspective.

As you watch your thoughts and emotions, you can realize clearly that you are not your thoughts or emotions. You're someone who *has* thoughts and emotions and who has the power to change them. This simple realization can quickly loosen up your identification with your mind and emotions, which, in turn, automatically raises your vibration.

Other Simple Ways

There are some other simple things you can try to nudge yourself out of a flat or irritable mood.

Physical Exercise: Physical exercise is sometimes all it takes. Just get out there and start moving to get your energy flowing. Breathe deeply. Focus on the sensations in your body. This can shift the chemicals in your brain and clear out stagnant energy.

Clear Your Aura: Clearing your auric field is always something else you can try. If you tend to be empathic, you likely pick up stuff from other people without knowing it. Call in divine Light, call in Angels, Ascended Masters, Galactics – and request they help to clear anything out of your field not belonging to you. You may be surprised how quickly your mood can shift with this simple request. It's like a gray cloud has suddenly lifted.

Focus on the Present Moment: Focusing on the present moment and bringing your awareness to the immediate reality within your body and your mind, can also move your awareness into a deeper place within you, past the irritability and into a softer, calmer place. You may realize your thoughts have been either in the past or the possible future – or both – and the thoughts are negative or anxious. Coming into the present moment takes you out of your mind with all its stories and brings you fully present with yourself in the reality of Now.

Chapter 21

Judgmental

Probably no spiritually-oriented person likes to think they're judgmental. It's not considered to be kind or awakened. This is perhaps because there's a reminder in most spiritual teachings that we are all one consciousness.

As someone committed to your spiritual awakening, you likely have had experiences of this oneness that exists among all human beings – and indeed with all of creation. Perhaps you have felt a profound love and compassion for people, no matter who they are or what they do.

And so it has probably distressed you when a feeling of separation has arisen within you at times, especially when it's come with a sense of judgment toward others. Perhaps you've attempted to be less judgmental but have found the habit difficult to overcome. As much as you may not want to judge, your mind might seem to have a mind of its own.

It can be especially difficult to avoid judgment if you've observed so much of what's wrong with the world: violence, wars, injustice, lack of compassion. And from what you've experienced, perhaps you've naturally drawn the conclusion that there exist "bad" people who are greedy, selfish and uncaring who perpetuate all that's wrong with the world, and there are "good" loving people who align with peace, justice, and harmony.

It's even more difficult to avoid judgment if you see that the "bad" people have pretty much been in control of the world forever, keeping humanity suppressed by starting wars, ignoring the poor and downtrodden, and preventing justice. Maybe you've even believed that these people should be exposed and brought down. It may feel natural to jump into the camp of those fighting against the Cabal and the Deep State and to be glad when they've been brought down.

The Attitude of Spiritual Superiority

You probably recognize that your longing for kindness and caring emanates from a deep spiritual part of yourself, a precious aspect of your being. But a problem can arise if you develop an attitude of "againstness" and separation from certain people who are *not* kind and caring, especially if this is coupled with an attitude of spiritual superiority. This attitude feeds struggle and dissension both within you personally and in your world.

To move toward a merging with your Higher Self consciousness, it's important to be aware when you're judging others. As the old saying goes, if you want peace, unity and love in the world – you need to start with yourself. In the Fifth Dimension, there is no separation, no sense of "us against them". Indeed, there is no right and wrong – all polarities are non-existent.

When you're living in alignment with Truth, you can know that every human is a Soul journeying through this challenging experience of incarnation on planet Earth. Everyone is attempting, consciously or unconsciously, to find their way Home. It's true that some people look like they've taken some twists and turns along the way, getting caught in negativity and darkness. But that's the only difference – they're simply not yet very awake to the truth of who they are.

Every one of us is doing the very best we can with what we know and understand. We're all in this together, bumbling along, trying to find our way through the density, separation and fear here in the Third Dimension. Despite all the confusion, disappointment and suffering, it's important to remember there is a divine plan unfolding that is beyond the understanding of the rational mind. So, to hold judgments against anyone or anything often simply points to our ignorance.

This doesn't mean you should never do anything to try to set things on a better path or bring a situation into a better alignment with Truth as you see it. If you see something you can help change, or someone who could use your assistance in understanding a truth, of course, you should take the opportunity to do these things. It's probably part of the divine plan that you do so.

The point is it's important to do the things that feel right without the attitudes of self-righteousness or superiority – and to also be aware that "feeling sorry" for people may be just another way for the ego to feel superior.

All this can sometimes be tricky, as old attitudes and feelings can so easily slip in and motivate you to speak or act in a self-righteous or superior way. But being aware of them and being honest with yourself can help you steer clear of these pitfalls.

Perhaps the most painful judgment that can emerge is one toward people you love. In fact, at times, you may find yourself judging most harshly those who are most beloved to you.

You've probably noticed that judgment of loved ones seems to arise naturally whenever stress appears in your daily life, when things aren't going the way you want them to. It's easy to lash out in judgment at someone you know will understand and forgive you. The mind just automatically seems to do this.

Trying to Stop Yourself from Judging

So, what can you do to stop this automatic reaction? How can you cease the tendency of the mind to judge people, even those you love?

Generally, you have probably attempted to stop yourself from judging someone when you've noticed yourself doing it. You've known it doesn't feel good and that it drags you into a lower consciousness. Perhaps you've tried to convince yourself you need to be more compassionate and understanding. Everyone has their stuff they're working through, everyone is trying their best, etc. But how often has that self-prodding really worked?

Judging or berating yourself for being judgmental is not usually successful in stopping the automatic judging that occurs. You probably simply feel guilty or ashamed for a while, before the judging again reasserts itself.

You're Hurting Yourself

The first thing you can do to actually make a shift from this automatic judging is to fully understand why judging others is harmful. It's not because it's morally wrong. It's not even primarily because it may hurt the people you're judging – although this is, of course, important.

It's because when you're in judgment, you're hurting yourself. It separates you from another person, and this denies the oneness that actually exists between the two of you. You can't experience it. It also lowers your vibration, keeping you at the level where separation, conflict and suffering exist.

But, at the same time, again, be careful to not feel shame or self-blame if you find yourself in judgment of someone. Don't fall into thinking you're a "bad" or "unspiritual" person. The truth is you're simply not seeing the spiritual truth of oneness clearly.

Telling yourself you "should" be compassionate and understanding is rarely effective. This may work for a short while (shame can be a powerful motivator), but it usually doesn't work in the long run. Judgment will continue to show up and you can only push it away just so much before it backfires on you.

Why We Judge

It's important to understand why people judge in the first place. It's actually quite simple: When we're judging someone, it indicates we're not feeling very good about ourselves, we're judging ourselves about something. And we're trying to do something to make ourselves feel better by pushing someone else down.

Here's how it works: When you're judging yourself, this brings on a feeling of low self-worth. This in turn creates a feeling of loneliness and separation, which then generates a feeling of wanting to strike out at someone else to try and ease the pain.

Very simply, judging others is an attempt to alleviate a feeling of inferiority and inadequacy. It's the mind's way of trying to feel superior in order to counteract this negative feeling about oneself. The unconscious belief is: "If I align myself with those people I deem to be superior, more spiritual, more successful, more intelligent than others – then I too can feel superior, spiritual, successful, intelligent. If I can feel morally right and better than rich, greedy, lazy, aggressive, stupid, ugly, uncaring (fill in the blank) people, then I can feel better about myself – I can respect and like myself more."

Judging is also often an attempt to alleviate a feeling of loneliness and separation. The belief is: "If I can align with another person or group opposing another group, I can feel less lonely, separate, left out. I can feel a sense of identity of belonging to a group of people I respect and feel an alignment with."

But, of course, it doesn't really work in the end. When you judge others, it doesn't make you feel any better in an ongoing way, because it doesn't resolve the underlying issue.

If you're wondering if all this is true, think about it for a moment: When you're feeling good about yourself and you're feeling connected to others, do you tend to be judgmental about anyone?

Compassion for Yourself

So, when you find yourself being judgmental, it's clear it won't do you any good to berate yourself or to try to be accepting and compassionate about someone. Instead, *turn toward yourself with compassion.*

Realize that your judgmentalness is just a sign that you're not feeling good about yourself, that you're judging yourself in some way – and what you're trying to do is feel better. You're trying to feel a bond with others you respect and like, so you can feel less lonely and separate.

In doing this, you have the opportunity to gently explore how you're judging yourself and see how you might stop. You may find that what you're judging someone about is the same thing you're judging yourself about. But not always. You may just generally be feeling judged or criticized.

Either way, once you discover what you've been judging yourself about, you can find understanding and compassion for yourself. And then you can explore ways in which you might create a greater sense of self-worth and feel a bond with people you like and respect in a more effective and healthy way than through judgment.

Eventually, when you start turning from being judgmental about people, you may begin to find it actually painful if you hear yourself saying something negative about someone. You may even feel pain when you hear someone else being judgmental about another person.

This is a sign of a growing awareness of the oneness that exists among all of us, the truth that all of humanity is really like one multi-celled organism. Your response to someone else's pain is like the automatic response of your hand when you bump your knee: it immediately reaches out to your knee to comfort and protect it.

Stepping Free of Polarization and Division

Another practice that can be helpful when attempting to avoid judgment is becoming extra vigilant about the thoughts and emotions you seem to dwell upon as you go about life. It's important to really take charge of the thoughts and emotions you are allowing your mind to focus on. In particular, if you are still engaging in a lot of negative thinking and emotional reactions to events happening around you and in the world, you might stop to contemplate this.

It's understandably difficult to accept with equilibrium much of what is occurring – or at least *seems* to be occurring (as it is hard to know for sure, due to all the fake news being reported these days – both by the mainstream media and the alt media). But negative reactions of anger, fear, blaming, or despair to anything you hear or read are neither helpful in keeping your vibration high, nor in assisting the collective consciousness to rise out of fear and anger.

In particular, it's really important that you become aware of any of the ways you may be adding to the elements of polarization and separation that are currently increasing in the world, through your judgments and your reactions to certain political personalities. Staying in your heart with compassion for *every*one, no matter who they are, is essential. And remaining neutral when others around you begin judging or complaining about others is also important.

At the same time, it is helpful to process negative emotions if they continue to arise. If you find yourself obsessing about them, it is time to be with those emotions and not try to push them away, distract yourself from them, or try to change them. Take time to be *with* them compassionately, allowing and accepting them as part of your experience at this time. Know that if they are arising during these times, they are attempting to be released to prepare you for the new energies coming in.

Also remember that you have much help available to you from the inner realms at this time – Beings who are eager to assist you through your healing process into higher awakening and transformation. Ascended Masters, Archangels, and benevolent Galactics are all accessible to you. You simply need to ask for their assistance.

If your difficulty is in being mainly judgmental about yourself, you may find the chapter on Shame, Guilt, Self-Judgment helpful.

Chapter 22

Lost

If you've been feeling lost lately, due to experiencing a lot of change and uncertainty, you can know you are well on your way to the Fifth Dimension. This is a common indication that you're in the process of journeying through the higher Fourth Dimension, preparing you to eventually enter the Fifth.

But it can get scary. You may find that so much is changing in your life and within your being, you don't know who you are anymore. You feel lost, without a compass to guide you through the ever-shifting reality you've entered.

Perhaps it seems to be harder than ever to know which decision to make in any moment, not knowing where it might take you. The old ways of feeling certain about your life seem to be falling away: the old relationships that used to provide comfort, the old situations that gave you a sense of stability, and the old beliefs that used to guide you. There's not much to hold onto anymore to feel safe and certain of who you are and where you're going.

You are a Trail Blazer

And this is because you are a trail blazer on this path into the Fifth Dimension. Most people haven't a clue yet about this journey. It's a whole new experience for humanity – and one also that evidently no other Beings in the universe have ever made before while taking their physical bodies with them. So much of it is still unknown.

But you, as a courageous Ascension Lightworker, before incarnating, volunteered to go ahead as a pioneer to help forge this path. As a result, you may find there are not yet a lot of road signs where you are traveling or obvious pointers as to which way to go at any given moment. You may feel totally alone on the path. Unidentified crossroads may confuse you; apparent dead ends may cause you to doubt yourself. You may have to backtrack and choose a different unknown road to take, often to another unknown destination. It's no wonder you can feel lost for a while until you find your bearings again.

On the other hand, when you're feeling lost, you may find that it is not so much a lack of knowing where you're going; it's more an inability to feel soothed and safe at this point by your familiar known ideas, beliefs, and viewpoints about life. You probably haven't actually strayed off course. You have simply veered in a new direction which you will eventually find is part of a greater plan for your ascension.

When you're in 3D consciousness, there is a tendency to feel as if you've gone astray in your journey whenever you find yourself heading in a direction that differs from the one you believe will take you where you want to go. But it's not as if you won't ever get where you wish to go. It's more that, in order to take the path necessary to reach your desires, you need to first change something about yourself – about your beliefs, your emotions, or your way of operating – so you can successfully take that path. So you may feel as if you're lost, but you're actually right where you need to be, learning to change something.

Another way to look at it is that you are purging the low-vibrational frequencies of your known reality and are stepping forward into an exciting new frontier. This doesn't mean you can't move toward what you desire or that you have to give up hope about what you think you'd like to have in your life. It's just that this fading away of your old ideas and habit patterns is an opportunity to release the way in which you've previously thought outcomes you desire should come.

Trust is the Only Option

And yet, there may be times when you truly cannot see your way forward with any sense of safety. And your only option is to make the leap into total trust, trust of the Universe, Source, your Higher Self. Simply relying on outer sources of information – opinions of friends and family, or experts you find – just doesn't cut it anymore.

Nor do the thoughts your rational mind is generating, based on information you've received from the outside. Your mind only knows how to fruitlessly spin its wheels when trying to understand things that are beyond its capabilities.

What you hear from outer sources or your rational mind may have worked in the past when you were still functioning fully within third-dimensional consciousness. But you're now in unknown higher-dimensional territory, and your guidance at this point has to come from *within* you.

Trusting the messages from this inner source requires a trust you may have never had to develop before. In the past, it was relatively easy to determine how to survive – physically, financially, and emotionally. You could usually figure out how to get the things you needed and the emotional support you craved from people and circumstances around you.

But now, you may have come to realize that old strategies don't work very well anymore. And, if you're really self-aware, you may also see how trying to continue living in your accustomed ways keeps you in a low-level state of anxiety, especially if you inevitably come to realize in the end that you have very little control over many outer conditions.

It can be helpful to come up with an affirmation for when you start feeling overwhelmed by loss and a sense of feeling unsafe. For instance, "I am always given everything I need and desire for a happy, healthy, comfortable life – no matter how my journey unfolds."

This kind of affirmation can instill in you the vibrations of faith, harmony, and patience to allow the Universe to bring to you what you need at any given time, instead of feeling constrained by having to figure it all out with your limited rational mind. And, if you're really honest with yourself in looking back at your life, you'll probably find that, through all your trials and tribulations, you always have been taken care of in one way or another. There's no reason to believe it would be any different now.

Shifting Toward the Fifth Dimension

As you move toward 5D consciousness, you will find you need to let go of all your limited 3D strategies. If you are strongly attached to believing that things and people outside of you are responsible for your sense of safety, survival and happiness, you will probably be given the opportunity to find they are not. Many of these outer supports may disappear (either temporarily or permanently) to show you this.

If, for example, you lose your job, your life savings, your health, or an important relationship, remember that this learning dynamic may be what's operating. Instead of panicking, see if you can drop inside yourself and align with a trust that you will find the means of survival and stability in other ways – perhaps in ways that will bring you an even greater sense of joy, security and freedom.

Staying in the Present Moment

Remember that if you can stay in the present moment and not panic about what may happen in the future, you can usually find you are really okay *right now*. You have all the essential things you need to be reasonably comfortable and at peace.

And think about it: you really never know what's around the corner ahead of you – especially these days. Something very surprising can appear that will help you handle the hurdle, something that will "save" you. If you reflect for a moment, you have probably had many little miracles like this occur for you in the past. There are so many things you have no idea about that can happen, seemingly out of the blue.

Expect miracles – truly expect them – and they will happen. The higher fourth-dimensional energies now flooding the planet can create them for you with ease.

Surrendering to What-Is

Still, expecting miracles and looking within yourself for your security may be difficult at those times when you're in great fear. If all familiar supports are falling away, and who you've known yourself to be seems to be disappearing, it can feel terrifying.

What you need to do at such times is to simply surrender to what-is in the moment – fully accept all of the situation, along with all your emotional reactions to it – without judgment, struggle, or grasping. Allow yourself to let go and just be with yourself with all of it, while doing your best to consciously love yourself with compassion.

This doesn't mean falling into misery and wallowing in it. Stay conscious and be fully *with* yourself. Choose to surrender to what feels beyond you to fix. Trust that your Higher Self will step in to help resolve the situation.

Discovering Your Higher Self

If you look closely, you will realize that the disappearing parts of yourself, the parts that are leaving, are just aspects of your personality self, not your essential Self. You discover that there's a Higher YOU inside that never changes. It's the YOU that was the same when you were 3 years old, 15 and 35 years old. It is, and always has been, the YOU that is real. It is your Higher Self.

Your Higher Self is also the one that has always been leading you through life, whether you've been aware of it or not. In these current experiences of deep insecurity and loss of connection to outer supports, know that you are being called to trust your Higher Self. It is this Higher Self that has been guiding you through every challenge and helping you to awaken. You are not actually separate from it; it's the true, authentic YOU. But it can feel like an unfamiliar part of you until you are able to eventually merge with it on your ascension journey.

See if you can trust that this higher essence of who you are knows exactly what it's doing in bringing about changes in your life, including losses that initially seem painful. Know that the things you are losing are likely necessary for you to lose in developing 5D consciousness.

Trust Turns into Knowing

In 5D, there is no reliance on anything in the outer world for a sense of safety or survival. There is only reliance on trust – trust that life will bring you absolutely everything you need, when you need it. And, as you find that this happens over and over again, this trust is eventually replaced by a secure knowing, a certainty based on your own experience in seeing that you are always taken care of.

But until that knowing fully develops, trust is what you need to rely on. Trust that you are being guided and taken care of with the utmost compassion and wisdom. And, with trust as your guide, you will find synchronicities blooming all around you; little miracles will become commonplace in your life. And the more you live from this place of trust, the stronger your trust will become.

You'll see that there is nothing outside in the world that is permanent or totally dependable for your safety, survival or happiness. But with the trust you have inside, it won't matter. You'll have everything you need.

Learning to live fully from a place of trust is not always easy. But the relaxation and freedom from fear you experience when you begin to achieve this trust are monumental and will change your entire experience of life.

Chapter 23

Manifestation Difficulty

Much of what ascension is all about is learning the inherent power you have as a Creator Being and how to master this power – often after years and lifetimes of not even knowing you've had it.

It is possible to put too much emphasis on learning to create what you desire in life. If you get consumed by it, you may forget to appreciate and fully live the life you are currently living. However, learning to effectively create new experiences in your life is an important aspect of your evolving consciousness. It is especially valuable if you accomplish it with an intention to be aligned with Source in choosing what you'd like to create.

It's probable you have at some point attempted to manifest a better life for yourself through a particular method you learned. If you became discouraged in trying this, you're not alone. Perhaps you enthusiastically tried affirmations, visualizations and other methods that had been suggested by experts, but eventually gave up, because nothing much seemed to change. Or it felt like too much work.

Unfortunately, this is a common experience for many who are led to believe that manifestation is easy and fun and that anyone can be successful at it. Let's look at what is necessary to understand about manifestation in order for the techniques to truly work.

Law of Attraction

First, it's important to understand the universal Law of Attraction. Undoubtedly, you've heard of this law, and perhaps you believe you understand it. It's generally known these days in new age circles that it is through using the Law of Attraction that we create our lives. The law, in essence, states: *What we spend time thinking about, what we focus our attention on – especially with strong emotion – is what we create.* Or, more succinctly: *Energy flows where attention goes.*

In other words, you need to really become aware of the power of your thoughts and emotions, because they are what create your reality. How you think and feel broadcasts an electromagnetic signature that influences every area of your life. They also impact your biology – your cells, genes, immune system, hormones and the neurons in your brain.

In addition, it's important to be aware of the thinking/feeling loop that occurs within you: your thoughts create emotions; and these emotions, in turn, serve to reconfirm your thoughts. Together, they are a powerful force that creates your reality.

So, this is a start – to understand the power of your thoughts and emotions in affecting what comes into your life and how you respond to it. But how does this work exactly?

The Quantum Field

To understand, you need to be aware of the field of consciousness you are operating in when you're attempting to manifest something. It's been called the *Quantum Field*. It's what has been referred to in new age parlance as "the Universe". You send messages out to the Universe; the Universe responds to what you're sending out.

But this isn't just some vague concept. The Quantum Field is very real. It's a vast, endless field of consciousness that is beyond time and space and contains the energy of all of creation in it. It holds a huge array of energetic frequencies that make up an invisible, inter-connected field of information.

Furthermore, the Quantum Field is a field you live in at all times. You are constantly broadcasting signals into it and interacting with other energies within it. It's where all your thoughts and your emotions exist, where all of your energetic bodies reside. It's where creation of everything comes into form first, before manifesting in physical reality.

All possibilities exist in the Quantum Field. There are no limitations here. You can ask questions about anything and know your answers are available in this field. You can call anyone to you and have conversations with them – or you can receive or give remote healings here, because everything and everyone is connected through frequencies and vibrations they emanate. And, very importantly, this is where you go to attempt to bring something new into your life.

Entering Consciously into the Quantum Field

So you are always functioning within the Quantum Field. However, most of the time, you are likely unconscious about it and you inadvertently create things you don't consciously wish to. It's therefore important to learn how to work within it consciously, with purpose.

To begin, be aware that when your thoughts dwell constantly on your outer reality, there is no space for creating from your inner reality. Before consciously entering into the Quantum Field, you therefore need to call your energy back into yourself – all you've put out onto people and things in your environment – so you can use it internally to create your new future.

Then see if you can get into a deep meditative state, past all thought and words. Focus on entering into the immediate moment. You may begin to experience yourself simply as a spark of awareness – or become, as author Joe Dispenza says, "no body, no one, no thing – and be nowhere and in no time". Experience yourself as this pure awareness expanding out into space. Once you disconnect from your outer reality like this, you can consciously be aware of the Quantum Field, the field of infinite possibility.

Working in the Quantum Field

So, in understanding all this, the next thing to comprehend for effective manifesting is that it's not just a matter of spending a short time every day, focusing on what you want to create in this field through visualizations, affirmations or other techniques.

It's important to understand that the Quantum Field absorbs, records, and responds to *everything* you think, *everything* you feel, *everything* you do – and then reflects it all back to you. It's a composite of *all* energies you're expressing, not just what you do for a short time during your day.

If, after doing your manifestation work each day, you spend the rest of your time going in and out of focusing on what isn't working for you, or feeling sad or angry about your unrealized dreams, this is probably going to cancel out the positive affirmations you've said and the exciting visualizations you've focused on.

You have to become aware of all the unintentional signals you're giving out, as well as your intentional ones. Everything you think or feel, intentional or unintentional, emanates from you, creating electromagnetic ripples in the field – and attracting those things to you that are of a similar vibration. Therefore, it's a matter of becoming conscious of everything you're thinking and feeling, so you can be in charge of what you are creating.

Keys for Effective Manifesting

Manifesting a new future generally requires a reprogramming of yourself. Your mind and body have been programmed in 3D to live a good part of your time in the past and possible future. Through thoughts and emotions, you have formed certain neural pathways that have been engraved over and over again in your brain and have led you to the place you're in right now. In order to stop getting stuck in patterns you don't want, you need to form new neural pathways with new thoughts and emotions.

To do this, you need to change your electromagnetic field. Your thoughts are the electrical charge you're sending into the quantum field, and your emotions are the magnetic charge. So, to manifest something new and positive in your life, you need to change your thoughts and emotions.

Essentially three things are required:

1. Thoughts that carry a clear and detailed idea of what you'd like to create;

2. High-frequency emotions such as love, joy, excitement, inspiration and gratitude (experiencing an expansive love, in particular, can create a powerful current to carry your intention into the Quantum Field), as you visualize your creation;

3. Clear intention, which has an aspect of will and power in it.

If you simply use your own personal egoic will, you can be successful; but there may be side-effects to your creation that are not what you'd hoped for. It is therefore always helpful to align yourself with the will of Source first, before setting an intention. Not only does it make your intention stronger; it also helps you to align with what is for the highest good of all concerned – what the most benevolent outcome might be.

Experiencing and focusing on these three elements – clear thoughts, positive emotion, and strong intention – will create a new electromagnetic signal to draw what you desire to you. The new event, situation or relationship will find you.

It's helpful to write out your main visualization clearly with detail and to read it often, while feeling high-frequency emotions. Make your visualization as real as possible – as if you're already living the future.

Let go of trying to think of *how* your vision is going to come about. Your imagination is too limited. Allow the Quantum Field to come up with the best means for manifesting the experience you seek. What you have in mind is only one of the infinite number of possibilities that exist in the field.

Simply focus on the final outcome you're desiring and act as if it's already happening. It is essential to keep your visualizations going *all the time*, feeling a sense of well-being and gratitude, despite what might still be happening in your life. Meanwhile, make decisions in your present reality based on this new reality whenever you can. And do those things you can do *now* to start bringing it about, feeling positively expectant, knowing it's going to happen.

Take it Step by Step

At the same time, it's important to not try to create something so different from your current reality, that it seems impossible to attain it. Be realistic. Start with smaller steps, with something that seems possible and believable to you. Once you have success with smaller things, you are given the momentum and a new belief structure to go further in manifesting your larger dreams.

It all takes a lot of clear intention – as well as attention to your thoughts and emotions, and bringing them into conscious awareness. But this is so much of what ascension is all about: becoming aware of how your thoughts and emotions are impacting what you create. And then taking charge of these thoughts and emotions. Mastery of your mental and emotional processes is a necessary step for entering into the Fifth Dimension.

Affirmation and Response Technique

One technique that can help you gain mastery over your thoughts and emotions involves allowing the "countering" voice within you to speak and raise its objections and disbeliefs about what you're attempting to create – rather than trying to stifle it.

You begin by writing (or typing) the affirmation you wish to use. Then you pause and wait to see if some part of you might wish to counter the statement out of disbelief. When those words come up, you write them. You wait a bit and then, again, write the affirmation. Continue with this, back and forth. You will see that, in giving permission to the disbelieving aspect of yourself to speak its truth, you begin convincing it calmly, without argument, of the truth of what you are wishing to create.

As an example, let's say your affirmation is "I am feeling confident, worthy, and strong, able to speak my truth with conviction." Here's what you'd do:

1. **Write your affirmation.**

2. **Allow Countering Voice to speak:** After writing out your affirmation, wait and allow any countering voice to respond. Something like this might come up: "Bullshit! I don't feel confident at all. I cave all the time when my children criticize me. I always give in and do what they want in the end. And I can't stand up to my boss at all." You write this down after the affirmation.

3. **Again, write it out:** Pause, and then again calmly write out the affirmation and wait.

4. **Listen Again**: This time the response might be, "I am really scared. When my boss speaks to me tomorrow, I'm going to be so nervous. I'm afraid I'll start crying." You write this.

5. **Write affirmation again:** Again, after listening with compassion and respect, type the affirmation.

This back-and-forth process may go on for a number of iterations. But what you'll start seeing is that the part of you that is resisting the affirmation will eventually begin to wind down its opposition and instead start gaining hope. You'll find that it very much wants to believe the affirmation – it just needs to be listened to and understood before it will get on board with you.

You can discover a lot this way about the resistance you have to gaining what you're attempting to manifest. Change, even positive change, can sometimes be threatening to parts of you that are wounded and frightened. Other times, you might find there's a lot of anger about not ever getting what you need in life. Or despair that's never really been expressed or admitted to.

But if you, as the compassionate and strongly confident "parent" of these resisting parts within you, continue to affirm a positive belief, you will see their resistance to it eventually diminishes and disappears.

Fourth, Fifth and Sixth Rays of Creation

In the Mastering Alchemy course offered by Jim Self, there is a technique that can be helpful in shifting out of a failure mode and learning to manifest a more positive reality for yourself. Especially valuable when you wish to change an entire set of emotions, beliefs and experiences you're having around an issue, it involves using what are known as the Fourth, Fifth and Sixth Rays of Creation. These are rays that can assist you in creating what you desire. They include countless codes and frequencies of light, sound and color.

You don't need to understand the intricacies of how they work – you simply need to be aware of how to use them. The way to start is by reflecting on a difficult issue you're working with inside yourself, and becoming aware of all the negative emotions, beliefs and conditions the issue has created within you.

As an example, let's say you are having a difficult time with a co-worker. You are feeling angry, betrayed and hurt because she told your boss something you had told her in confidence. You also feel anxious about having to confront her about this. In addition, you realize this is something that seems to happen often to you; you can't seem to trust people you confide in.

Here's what you can do:

1. **Call in 4th, 5th & 6th Rays of Creation:** Move into a meditative state of mind. Then call in the Fourth, Fifth and Sixth Rays of Creation. There's no particular way in which these fields of consciousness will manifest to you; just call them in and know they're there.

2. **Release Emotions & Thoughts into the 4th Ray:** Become aware of all your uncomfortable emotions and thoughts about your issue. One at a time, allow the emotions of resentment, hurt, betrayal and anxiety, along with your

judgments about yourself, to be released into the Fourth Ray. Here they will be pulled apart into clear and separate components of the problem.

3. **Take them into the 5ᵗʰ Ray:** Now take all you've placed in the Fourth Ray up into the Fifth Ray, which is like a workbench. Here you can get a good look at each component and make sure you'd like to remove them. You may wish to retain some part of the issue that might be valuable to you in some way.

4. **Toss what you don't want into the 6ᵗʰ Ray:** But all the rest of it you can then "toss" up into the Sixth Ray, one at a time, and see each piece disappearing. The Sixth Ray is the repository of absolutely everything in creation, a grand cosmic "library". You can borrow anything from it and also return anything you no longer want. It's another term for the Quantum Field. You may feel a surprising relief in throwing unwanted emotions and patterns into the Sixth Ray. It can be amazing how a simple act within your imagination can so affect how you feel.

5. **Ask the 6ᵗʰ Ray for what You Want:** Now it's time for you to think of what you would like to be *given* in return from the Sixth Ray, what emotions, beliefs, and experiences you would prefer to have regarding your co-worker.

6. **Bring it all into 5th Ray, then the 4th – and into yourself:** You can ask for anything; but generally, what you focus on you will likely be the opposite kinds of things of what you've given away. You might choose such things as compassion, confidence, harmony, self-love, trust and strength. Feel and see these qualities flow from the Sixth Ray into your arms, and bring them all into the Fourth Ray to be brought together into a new integrated package of positive emotions and energies. Pull this into yourself.

This exercise may sound too simple, and you may doubt it could change a situation you have in mind. But remember the extraordinary power of the imagination. It's where you create your reality. This technique may greatly surprise you.

Limiting Beliefs

Another angle you can approach manifestation from is discovering what beliefs you may have that are limiting your ability to create what you wish for yourself. In a certain way, your beliefs are the foundation of your personality. For example, they may define you as either competent or incompetent, worthy or unworthy, self-reliant or dependent, loved or hated.

Your beliefs have profound consequences, both positive and negative, in your life. Aside from affecting your self-esteem, they also affect your moods, relationships, job performance, physical health, and spiritual outlook. It's therefore important to become aware of any beliefs you have that are limiting and self-sabotaging, so you can learn to change them into beliefs that support you.

These negative beliefs are generally drawn from past experiences, often in childhood, that are stored in your subconscious mind. They likely originated as a response to traumatic experiences. While you may be mostly unaware of their influence on you, in many ways, they direct your actions and behaviors. They create the perceptual filters through which you respond to life's challenges.

Your ability to perform effectively, both personally and professionally, is profoundly affected by such beliefs as "I am competent", "I am powerful", or "I am safe." With beliefs like these, you can undertake challenging projects with confidence and stay focused on whatever task you take on. But, if you have beliefs like, "I don't really trust myself to do a good job" or "How things turn out is not really in my control," you will feel hesitant and resistant, fearing mistakes, criticism, and failure.

Therefore, awareness of your subconscious limiting beliefs and learning how to shift them effectively is essential for successful manifesting. There are a number of programs offered for learning how to do this. *Psych-K* is one you might want to look into. This is a program that helps you to communicate directly with your subconscious mind; while using whole-brain integration techniques, you learn how to change old self-sabotaging beliefs into new positive ones that support you.

Another similar approach to revealing hidden, limiting beliefs and then creating new beliefs through changing the neural pathways in the brain is a therapy called *Coherence Therapy* or *Memory Reconsolidation Therapy*.

Sometimes the reason you may be unsuccessful in manifesting something in your life is that there is something important you need to learn about why you're having this difficulty. Perhaps you have a belief that needs to be discovered and changed. Or maybe what you're wanting to manifest really wouldn't serve you. It's important to ask these kinds of questions if you're feeling blocked in what you're attempting to create. Being unsuccessful in your manifestation may actually be a gift.

Demanifestation Process

Here is a final clue that may help you in manifesting:

Become aware that the process of manifesting is essentially saying YES to something – whereas, *demanifesting* is saying NO to something. Often, if you want to manifest something new, you may also need to demanifest something you *don't* want anymore.

An example of a demanifestation process might be saying NO to people who are habitually late for an important meeting you've both agreed to. You decide you will no longer accept the feeling of disrespect their behavior generates – and let them know, in a friendly but firm way, what you will do if they are late again, e.g. you will wait for 10 minutes and leave if they are not there by then. Then the next time they're late, you follow through.

In doing this, you let people know clearly that there are consequences to their disrespectful behavior. You do this without anger or resentment – simply with a firm conviction of respect for yourself. You can come up with a similar plan with any pattern like this in which you feel disrespected.

Be aware that you will inevitably be tested at first, especially if it's a long-standing pattern and people know they've been able to take advantage of you in the past and have always been forgiven. But if your decision is strong enough and you follow through with consequences, people will feel an energy shift and stop their disrespectful behavior. What you are doing is making a decision that this kind of behavior toward you is NOT part of your reality.

Another example might be you're wishing to manifest more friendships in an area you've just moved to. And yet, you typically find yourself isolating yourself, staying at home a lot, even when community events occur in which you might meet people you'd enjoy. Perhaps you feel shy or inadequate, and you dislike small talk, so you tend to make decisions that keep you away from meeting new people.

Of course, you would begin using all the manifestation techniques you know, strongly imagining yourself talking comfortably with new people, meeting certain ones you feel a strong connection to and planning further get-togethers with them. And you feel strong positive emotions with this. But you may also find you need to demanifest patterns in yourself that have kept you isolated, such as deciding at the last minute not to go to a gathering after all.

In deciding this, you become aware that you need to demanifest this usual last-minute decision to stay home: you decide that if the feeling comes up in you the next time, you will shift past that habitual pattern and get ready to go, anyway. You envision this action within yourself taking place easily, with a strong feeling of positive anticipation, and then picture yourself having a great time when you arrive at the gathering.

As you can see, the process of demanifestation is pretty much the same as the manifestation process (decide, imagine, and take action), but it focuses on what needs to be eliminated rather than created. It can be easier than manifestation; sometimes just making the decision is enough.

True Fulfillment

After all is said about manifesting what you'd like in your life, it's also important to keep in mind that if you are only focusing on fulfilling your desires, you could be falling into a trap in your spiritual development.

You may develop a belief that only through your specific personal desires can you feel fulfillment. This can create a tendency to chase after the fulfillment of one desire after another – not realizing that it is the constant pursuit of desire that can block your ability to receive fulfillment. You need to balance all the seeking with periods of gratitude and reflection.

You may come to realize that true fulfillment is not measured by how many personal desires you can realize. Rather, it is an ability and choice to receive and appreciate the gift that each miraculous moment offers. When you are only focused on your desires, you generally only look for evidence of things coming your way that point to the fulfillment of these desires. If you don't find this proof, you probably feel disappointed and miss out on what is happening in the present moment, which always offers a subtle, but powerful, sense of fulfillment – no matter what is happening.

As you learn to distinguish the reality of true fulfillment from the fantasy of having your personal desires met, you are then able to be nourished and rejuvenated simply by your own vibration of light throughout each moment. This doesn't mean you shouldn't attempt to create things different in your life that feel good to you; it's simply important that you not rely on these things as your only gateway to fulfillment.

Instead, it is your willingness to receive all that is given to you with acceptance and trust. If you can also begin to see the current things in your life from new and exciting perspectives, you may experience a depth of fulfillment beyond the one that your insatiable desires might ever give you.

Chapter 24

Negative Thinking

Perhaps one of the most important things you can do to shift out of a depressed or irritated mood is to really become aware of the thoughts you're thinking, as they are probably not very positive ones.

It's been said that we are not responsible for what thoughts come into our mind – but we are responsible for which ones we keep there. Thoughts that enter our mind are sometimes not even our own; we pick them up from other people and from the collective at large. But what we do with those thoughts, wherever they came from, is what is important.

If you're like most people, you may find you are not always conscious of what you're thinking, that you can get lost in a negative train of thought for long periods of time and not even realize it. But if you have the intention to become more conscious of what you're thinking in times you're feeling down, you will find you have a choice to begin shifting your thoughts to something more positive. And, in the process, you'll see that your emotions will automatically follow these new thoughts.

In a certain way, this is the key to changing everything happening in your life: what you think about, what you focus on, is what you are creating your future with. This is the Law of Attraction: What you focus your attention on, especially with strong emotion, is what the Universe is going to provide for you.

Another part of this universal law that is important to remember is that whatever you create, you must also experience. It's all part of being a Creator Being.

Cancel That Thought

Therefore, watching and managing your thoughts is essential. If you can become conscious of a negative thought while you're thinking it, you can then focus on ways to turn it around. Sometimes a thought is just habitual; although you have known the falseness of it and have tried to avoid thinking it, you tend to keep thinking it anyway.

With this kind of thought, one of the simplest, yet very effective, ways to counter it is to say "I cancel that thought." And then make a statement that affirms the opposite and feel how and where something shifts. If it's a long-time habit, you may need to do this a number of times. It's just a matter of retraining your mind to think differently about a certain subject.

The Power of Words

However, if you find yourself caught more deeply in negative thoughts and the emotions that accompany them, you may need to do more. Something you can become aware of is how words carry vibrations, and how some words have a great deal of power in affecting how you think and feel. These vibrations create an electromagnetic field that pulls things, people, situations and states of being toward you.

There are certain words in particular, called "living words" that can raise your vibration and create positive experiences fairly rapidly. For instance, words like *love* and *joy* and *peaceful* have an especially high vibration when thought or spoken aloud. So when you're feeling stuck in a sour mood, you can start by simply repeating one of these words to yourself. Or you can add the words "I am" before them.

As you do, you can become aware of the impact their frequency is having on you and feel a shift. You'll see that your body remembers the experience of feeling love or joy or peace; it's felt it before. And just repeating the word helps it to remember and activate the emotion in your body and mind.

Happy is another fun word to try. You'll find it's hard to prevent a smile coming onto your face by the third repetition or so. Other words, such as "powerful", "certain", "capable" or "confident" are also quite effective. As is "gratitude".

Sometimes you can decide on three powerful words that can be helpful for you in a given situation or at the beginning of a day. To remember them, you can see them in a triangle in your mind, and decide to either "wear" them as this triangle in some way – or to stand on the triangle as a platform.

Of course, you can also use affirmations to achieve this result. Especially important are simple ones that are easy to remember. One simple one if you're feeling anxious, for example, is: "I am calm, relaxed and peaceful." As you say each word, breathe into it, and feel the vibration of it in your body and then note how your mind also responds.

Another powerful affirmation is "All is well". Very simple, but something you might find yourself repeating often during a stressful day.

A rather interesting one to try is "I like me". Repeat this out loud to yourself a number of times, and again, watch the smile come on your face and feel a sense of confidence and inner strength arise within you.

Remember that, in creating affirmations, it's important to state them in positive ways, such as "I am happy", rather than "I am no longer sad". Avoid using negative words altogether.

Ask Yourself Questions

Another simple way to shift your thoughts out of negativity is to ask yourself questions, like:

- How am I not loving myself in this moment?

- Am I judging myself about something?

- Am I shaming myself for something?

- Am I not allowing myself to feel a certain emotion – or do something I want to do?

Asking and answering these kinds of questions can often get you immediately unstuck from an irritable or negative state of mind. It will also bring in a feeling of compassion and self-respect, as you allow yourself to be as you are, without judgment. This can be an important practice to develop when you are in the process of wanting to learn how to love yourself more.

Chapter 25

Powerless

There's nothing quite like falling into a state of feeling powerless in your life, in which you feel weak and unable to get your needs met. This feeling often drags in so many other negative states of mind and emotions that you can end up wanting to curl into a ball and just disappear.

Can't Get What You Need

Sometimes you may feel this way because something important you very much want to achieve doesn't occur. You keep making every effort to push for it to happen, but you are blocked, time and time again. You feel powerless.

If this struggle scenario is happening, realize you are using a 3D habit of pushing and struggling to make something happen. In a higher-dimensional mode, you would realize there might be an important reason this thing you're trying to accomplish isn't happening, even as right or important as it may seem to you. And to keep pushing for it will probably not be successful, no matter how hard you try.

Often it's wise to simply cease your struggling. Rather, do your best to just step back and shift your attention to something outside of the situation for a while. Take a few breaths, and maybe even get involved in something else entirely for a bit. Clear your mind. Once you've calmed down and centered yourself, you can then go back to it and see if anything else you try is going to work.

However, if at some point you're still struggling with no results, be aware you may be attempting to accomplish something that just isn't wanting to happen. It's not in the flow of what is right action for you, at least at this time. If you can let go and surrender to what *is* happening in the moment, you then have an opportunity to see what else may unfold for you that is going to be better for you in the long run.

You may initially feel that what's happening is not right, not what's "supposed" to be happening. But if you have trust and stay tuned to your inner knowing, you'll probably realize in time that it's actually been perfect. There have been things you weren't aware of or things you've needed to experience and learn. Or maybe there were other people involved in what you were attempting to do for whom your desired goal would not be best.

There are so many things we're not aware of in the moment when we're functioning from a 3D habitual stance and experiencing the negative emotions that come with it. It's hard to see the broader picture or to tune into what might be for a higher good. But when you're stymied by block after block in accomplishing what you want to create, it's time to surrender to what-is – and to trust that what is occurring is actually serving to lift you toward a higher consciousness.

Feeling Powerless with Other People

Another situation in which you may feel powerless is when you're with another person or in a group, and you're feeling unseen or unheard, unable to assert yourself. Perhaps you feel invisible or disrespected by other people; and when you speak, your voice is not as confident or authoritative as you'd like.

Alignment of Three Centers

One key to turn this around is to become aware of a particular energetic alignment you can create within yourself. This involves three different aspects of your energetic being.

Sacred Heart: The first is your Sacred Heart, which is different from your emotional heart, existing somewhat above that heart. It's a sacred space which has been called the "Seat of the Soul". It's where you experience unconditional, spiritual love and feel the presence of Source and your Soul. It's your inner sanctuary, and a very powerful place from which to function.

Center of Your Head: The second aspect is one pointed to by Jim Self in his Mastering Alchemy course: it's an area that is in the center of your head, behind your eyes. You can know you're in this space, when you can feel your attention inside your head behind your eyes, looking out through your eyes into the world. Because your emotional and mental bodies extend further out than your physical body, you probably often project your attention and sense of identification outside of your body into these fields.

Other times, when you're with other people and not feeling good about yourself – perhaps needing their approval – you may be reaching out to them and actually projecting yourself energetically into their fields. Not a place of personal power!

Doing this is natural for many people. But you can become aware that, when you're floating somewhere outside of your body like this, you are not experiencing your center of power. You are often lost in thought or feeling – and usually in the past or future. Whereas, if you bring your awareness into your body, behind your eyes, you'll suddenly feel strong and centered. You are present, here and now. You are owning your inner space and taking charge of it.

By coming into the center of your head, you are also bringing yourself fully into the present moment, which adds to your sense of empowerment, as it is only when you're in the present moment that you can create something new for yourself.

Higher Mind: The third center within you is what is often called the "Higher Mind". This may initially be experienced somewhat above your head. You likely know this space – it's the consciousness you're in when you're feeling free of the mind and emotions, somehow not identified with them. There's a sense of lightness, a neutrality and a freedom, and you're also very aware and empowered.

You may think you can't access this part of yourself by will; but, with some exploration and focus, you will likely find you can. You probably just haven't paid much attention to "where" you are when you're functioning from this higher consciousness. Try focusing somewhat above your head and relaxing into that space. Feel the consciousness that is there. See if you can merge with it.

When you have become familiar with all three of these power points within yourself, then it's time to practice being in all these three places at once. (If this is initially difficult, you can just center yourself in one of these centers to begin with.) Once these power centers are explored and experienced, you'll feel a sense of expansion and empowerment. And focusing on them will give you a sense of authority, strength and certainty that naturally demands respect and caring.

You realize you are not a weak or unempowered ego-personality self but a powerful, aware Spiritual Being.

Bless the Things that Hurt

Another way to empower yourself when you're feeling weak, unloved or disrespected is to bless the things that hurt you. This isn't just a sweet throw-away technique to contemplate, a kind to try once and then forget. It's a profound way to experience your inner power through being aligned with your Sacred Heart.

If you are feeling hurt by someone, you are at the effect of that person's actions, which creates a sense of powerlessness. With these feelings, it's natural to flip into blame and bad-mouthing the one who has been hurtful. But, as you may have realized, this only keeps you feeling like a victim, an angry one.

And, no matter how much you blame and how angry and resentful you may get, you never stop being a victim. Someone has done something to you that has been hurtful and you're feeling you can't do anything about it, except to strike back. Trying to hurt someone back doesn't, in the end, truly give you a sense of power or peace. It holds you in a contracted, conflicted 3D state of being.

However, if you can step out of the blaming mode (and the self-pity that is also usually present), you can discover that blessing the person who has been hurtful can actually bring a sense of empowerment and peace to you. You can say out loud, "I bless this person who has betrayed me."

In doing this sincerely from the Heart, you have stepped out of the victim role and into one in which you are following the dictates of love. In actually blessing the person, rather than blaming or essentially cursing them, you have aligned yourself with the spiritual truths of understanding and compassion. And, when done sincerely, this brings a profound sense of power and freedom.

You can also then ask yourself, "What is the hurt saying to me? What does it tell me about myself and about my life?" The answers to these questions can be extremely valuable to you. In the end you can see that the hurt – and the person who has been hurtful – have actually given you a gift.

Chapter 26

Relationship Difficulties

If you are deep into your ascension process at this point, you are probably realizing that one of the areas of your life that is undergoing a "dimensional remodel" is that of your relationships with other people. This can be a challenging process.

You may be realizing that in order to continue to rise in vibration, you are being compelled to take a good look at the relationships currently in your life and seeing what may no longer be resonating with the higher frequencies you are now embracing.

Old 3D Relationship Patterns

One thing you may be finding is that certain people you've related to for much of your life are people with whom you have little in common anymore. This can be confusing and unsettling. People who were once so important in your life might seem to be drifting away. You perhaps don't miss them, but there may not yet be anyone else replacing them in your life.

Even those relationships with people you are still feeling some resonance with could be presenting challenges you haven't encountered before. The ascension process tends to bring up all the unawakened patterns you are expressing with others, patterns that continue to cause you suffering and conflict.

In fact, you are probably being compelled to examine the dysfunctional ways in which you have managed relationship, in general, throughout your life. And what you see at this point is likely reflective of how you have related to people throughout your entire existence in the Third Dimension

– a dimension in which an inherent sense of fear, separation, and unworthiness have existed in your consciousness.

One thing you can probably note is that most of your unhealthy relationship patterns are ones you took on naturally as a child in this life, growing up in a world in which people were generally spiritually asleep and unaware of what actual love from a higher dimension might be like. These patterns are ones that tend to cause you disappointment, grief, anger and hurt in your relationships. They may include unhealthy dynamics that are generally recognized today as "co-dependent". There are many 3D labels given to people in this type of relationship, such as "narcissistic", "abusive", "caretaking", and "enabling".

If you're currently involved in relationships that might be labeled in this way, you are likely finding there's a new intensity lately that has arisen in them. The fifth-dimensional energies that are entering your relationship dynamics are intensifying painful emotions you may have until now been able to ignore – but no longer can.

3D Dependence in Relationships

It's probably easy enough these days to identify relationship patterns you have that you've always known to be somewhat dysfunctional. There are certainly plenty of books and webinars out there that can help you find solutions on how to shift these patterns into healthier ones. And unless you pay attention to these patterns, as you ascend into higher vibrations, you're going to get really uncomfortable.

However, from a fifth-dimensional point of view, there is one reason that is rarely, if ever, named in self-help books that in many ways has pretty much been the cause of *all* relationship difficulties. And that is the common 3D belief that the purpose of relationships with family, spouses, and good friends is to give us an essential sense through their love and approval that we are lovable, valuable, and important.

In the old third-dimensional paradigm you likely grew up in, you were probably taught that your loved ones were there to fulfill this emotional need. This belief can sound so right, so warm and cozy. It's familiar. And it's appropriate for children to feel; they need to feel protected, loved and valuable to grow up feeling good about themselves. But if, as an adult, you still carry this belief that it's other people's responsibility to fill your basic emotional needs, it may be what gets in your way to forming healthy intimate relationships.

To some degree, you may have managed to survive certain situations in life till now because you have felt your emotional needs to be at least mostly met by your relationships. But as you move forward on your ascension path, it can be valuable to question this belief. Is that really the purpose of relationship in adulthood? If you think about it, you can see how this assumption includes a belief that you are not inherently whole or able to experience your own value, lovableness, and inherent worth on your own.

And more importantly, it means you must continue to put up with all the grief and rage you can sometimes feel when your loved-ones don't give you the love and feeling of being valued and respect you feel they "should" give you.

How many conflicts throughout your life has this tacit agreed-upon arrangement that your loved-ones are there to fill your emotional needs created for you? How many times have the people you've assigned the task of meeting these needs fallen short in fulfilling them? And how many times have you fallen short in taking care of their emotional needs? How many times have you – or your loved one – painfully exclaimed: "You're not meeting my needs!"

So many power struggles steeped in feelings of hurt, betrayal and guilt arise out of this usually unconscious agreement between people that they are there to fill each other's emotional needs. Such a sense of helplessness can arise when you've given the power to someone else to be responsible for your own happiness.

If you look at this issue, you can see how it points back to your need, as you shift into fifth-dimensional consciousness, to truly develop a sense of love for yourself and to be able to rely on *that*, first and foremost, for your sense of feeling valuable, loved and respected.

You need to see that if you are going to truly find a freedom from hurt, blame and anger in your relationships, it is not the job of other people to give you a sense of emotional wholeness; it is up to you. Whatever love and validation others offer to you can simply serve to *enhance* this sense you already have within yourself.

Freedom in 5D Relationships

If you're used to having relationships based on the typical 3D model, it may sound as if a relationship without this agreement to take responsibility for each other's needs would be an unemotional and disconnected type of relationship. But until you experience one in which this is not the agreement, you can't know this.

When you move into fifth-dimensional consciousness, you can find that without these emotional types of demands, you can have warm, loving, and highly-fulfilling 5D relationships that run smoothly without a lot of conflict. You see that although you do receive a great deal of love, respect and support from your loved one, you are not dependent on their feelings for you to feel lovable, valuable and important.

The love you receive from others is a bonus, an overflow that is much appreciated and valued; but it is not needed at the core of your being, because you are able to provide the love you need from within yourself. There is therefore no emotional demand that the others you're in relationship with give you the love you need in order to feel good about yourself.

And, very importantly, your love for *them* springs solely from your true caring and compassion for them – not from a need that they provide you with something in return. It's an unconditional love, free of demands that a person act in a certain way or be something different from who they are, in order for you to love them.

Importance of Self-Love

To be able to feel and express this kind of unconditional love to someone, of course, demands first that you learn how to love yourself in that same unconditional manner. In a certain way, the task of learning self-love is at the core of all your ascension learning. Being cut off from the true knowing of yourself as a Spiritual Being, as you have been for so long in the Third Dimension, has made it next to impossible to know your true inherent lovableness and value.

But thankfully, your journey back into full consciousness at this point is likely awakening you once again to the incredible magnificence of who you are and how you truly don't need any outer reinforcement or reflection to let you know and experience your inherent value and beauty. It is becoming self-evident. And, among other things, this realization can make your relationships with others much more fulfilling and able to flow with greater ease and joy.

Meanwhile, as you find your way through this shift of awareness toward 5D relationships, it's very important to find compassion for yourself and to rest in this higher-dimensional embrace. It can be a huge transition, especially in relationships you've been in for a long time.

It can help to remind yourself that you are emerging from perhaps thousands of years of awkward, unawakened attempts to find love and safety through your relationships with other people, who themselves have not been awake or fulfilled. There are a lot of age-old beliefs and illusions you need to courageously shed in order to discover what truly free and awake relationships can be like.

But as you do let go of your old beliefs and habits around relationship and learn to truly give yourself the love you need, there is incredible freedom, richness and joy you can discover in your new 5D relationships.

Unconditional Love vs. Allowing Disrespect

As you begin to love yourself unconditionally, you learn to distinguish between unconditional love and allowing someone to do something that is inherently hurtful or disrespectful toward you. Some people believe that unconditional love means allowing and putting up with any kind of behavior toward them. This belief is indicative of a lack of self-love. Especially in an intimate relationship, it is important to find ways to behave in a sensitive and loving manner toward each other. If this can't be resolved, it may be necessary to cease being intimate.

For instance, if your partner insists on having an "open" relationship and this is not what will work for you, you would want to cease your intimate relationship with them. Your love for yourself would demand this. But even if this occurs, since your love is unconditional, that love for your partner would remain. You continue to love them, even if you choose not to be with them anymore. It's important to distinguish between unconditional love and unconditional allowance of hurtful behaviors toward you.

Chapter 27

Resistance

When there's something you don't feel comfortable entering into, it's natural to feel a sense of inner resistance. Sometimes this feeling of resistance can be a benevolent inner warning to not go in a particular direction; and therefore, listening to it can be important. However, other times the feeling of resistance can be an indication that you're avoiding meeting uncomfortable emotions arising within you which relate to something unresolved. And this can leave you feeling irritable and stuck.

Rather than moving into denial, avoidance, distraction or attempting to immediately fix this kind of resistance, it is generally wiser to explore it and see if you can get in touch with the uncomfortable emotions that have arisen.

Resistance to Healing

Interestingly, you might actually find yourself resisting the healing of the emotions causing the disturbance. It may not look that way; you may be outwardly very eager to heal the uncomfortable emotions. You may have an attitude that appears "spiritual", but is actually denial, a type of "spiritualized resistance".

What this entails is using spiritual healing methods as an excuse to "get rid of" certain feelings and experiences, rather than taking responsibility for their presence within you, and learning to process them so you can release them. You just want them gone.

You may ask, "What's wrong with trying to get rid of painful emotions?" There's nothing wrong with this – of course you do. Aside from the suffering you experience with them, you know you can't take these lower-vibrational emotions with you into 5D. So you must somehow get clear of them.

However, if you're not wanting to discover how these emotions developed in you to begin with so as to avoid creating them in the future, the results of any healing you do will eventually be only temporary. In the end, you can discover that trying to just get rid of negative emotions without doing your own deep inner work around them is simply a form of resistance. And this just keeps you hooked into anxiety, depression, and resentment.

For example, you might discover you feel resistant to the suggestions your partner gives to you about changing something about yourself or your life style. Resentment may immediately arise, even when you know the suggestions are good ones. You know that resentment is not a high-vibrational trait and you therefore want it gone so you can continue to think of yourself as a responsible and spiritually-aware person. You then may ask some higher power to remove it or to call in the Violet Ray to dissolve it. That could possibly work – but probably only for a short time. Since you haven't understood your resistance to suggestions, it will probably crop up again in the future. It might be better to focus on understanding why you might feel such resentment.

For instance, you might become aware of your father's attempts when you were a child to control or direct you against your will. The real healing of the resentment might very well depend on understanding this and revisiting and forgiving the feelings generated by your overly-directive father. Stopping with just spiritual dismissal of the unwanted emotion may actually be a way in which you are resisting the necessary deep healing of it.

You need to understand that *trying* to heal is not always based on truly *wanting* to heal. If you find yourself desperately trying to heal yourself, but are experiencing no real results, you may actually be preventing yourself from healing in this way.

Meeting Your Shadow

It is helpful to understand that true spiritual healing is about facing, exploring, and integrating *all* that you are experiencing. It's not about trying to escape it. It's about meeting your Shadow Self with understanding, compassion, and a true desire to heal all aspects of this hidden self so you can integrate it into your inherent wholeness.

Resisting these darker aspects of your ego-personality self – even in a "spiritual" way – will only serve to deepen your stuckness and suffering.

The only way out of the pain of your emotions is *through* them. It's necessary to get to the core of your issues in order to heal them.

Spiritual Bypass

Meeting your Shadow can be a very challenging exercise; and you may, after first attempting it, find yourself deciding it's unnecessary. If you've learned to meditate and have had success with certain other spiritual practices – or if you have received a spiritual teacher's grace – one of the pitfalls you may have encountered in your quest to heal yourself through "spiritual" means is the tendency to attempt the "spiritual bypass".

Many people on a spiritual path try to get around the healing that is necessary for their full awakening by acting as if they aren't experiencing anything "unspiritual", anything negative. Or they decide they don't want to "focus on negative things". This can look and feel really good for a time. Their speech is generally positive and they speak about spiritual ideas. They enjoy being of service to others. And they deny feeling anything much negative.

And yet, if you were to look more closely, you might find they are simply attempting the spiritual bypass – denying the existence of their Shadow Self, while trying to escape it. They're using spirituality to avoid, suppress and escape from the uncomfortable and unresolved issues in their lives. And, in the end, this never works.

No matter how many spiritual awakening experiences you have in which you feel light and free and filled with love – if there are still aspects of your Shadow Self you haven't explored and integrated, these higher fourth and fifth-dimensional experiences will not last. You will be subject to falling into 3D reactions again whenever a trigger comes along.

However, if you feel you may be doing the spiritual bypass, be careful not to judge yourself. The bypass is a common response to uncomfortable issues you wish to overcome. It's not that meditation and other spiritual practices are not at all effective in helping you overcome emotional issues; they definitely can be. It's just that spiritual examination requires persistence; and spending just a few hours a week focusing on these practices is not going to get you very far, very fast.

Trying to resolve your emotional challenges through the method of meditation can sometimes take years and years of a dedicated practice. Most people these days, especially in the West, do not have the time for devoting themselves to this, let alone the motivation.

There are faster ways to work through stuff if you can add working with therapists or healers, especially those who are savvy about the ascension process. However, beware, because these faster ways can also have their own pitfalls.

Perhaps you've attempted to resolve your suffering by going to a transpersonal psychotherapist, energy healer, psychic, or astrologer – or someone who helped to "activate your DNA", "rewire your brain", or any of the other techniques offered these days for those eager to ascend. And maybe you have felt helped by these methods.

But perhaps the help has been only temporary. Have you ever felt great after one of these new age healing sessions for a short while – only to realize later that nothing has actually shifted permanently? If so, the reason is likely that you just went to hopefully get "fixed", to have something taken out of you or something added so you could feel more comfortable and clear. And once that was accomplished, you figured you could just go on living your life as you always had been.

You didn't realize that, unless you understood how you created those painful patterns to begin with, you would likely create them again. The same old habits would reassert themselves. And then it would look as if you weren't healed after all – you'd assume that the healing didn't work.

Resolving your 3D habit patterns truly is up to you. You need to understand them and take responsibility for creating them – or you won't be empowered to change them. You cannot bypass the darker aspects of your ego-personality self and hope to just merge with your Higher Self by focusing only on the light.

Awakening Can be Painful

However, experiencing a lot of pain – and resistance to it – doesn't always mean you're attempting the spiritual bypass. Often the ascension process, because of so much loss and change, includes periods of time that are extremely painful. It can feel as if you're not advancing at all on your awakening journey. You're flailing around in negativity and depression and not knowing how to get out of it.

The angst you're experiencing can simply be part of the awakening process you're experiencing. Pursuing the light and deeply committing yourself to your ascension path may well bring up tremendous pain and negativity. At a certain point, it can feel as if all your false beliefs, illusions, identities and judgments are crowding your mind and it's hard to know what to do with them all.

At these times, you need to surrender to the collapse and destruction of all familiar aspects of your ego-personality self that are still rooted in 3D and 4D. Keep in mind that you're breaking through all limitations in how you've perceived yourself and you're learning how to let go of all judgment of yourself and others.

This is the "dark side" of healing and awakening. You sometimes have to get down in the dirt and grit of what you've created within the Third Dimension, in order to heal and release it. It can be terrifying at times to experience the destruction of closely-held beliefs and false memories. But as you do this work and begin to see these illusions diminishing in their power over you, you'll discover that your life is much clearer. You're feeling more connected to yourself and others, and you feel more joyful in your daily life.

You realize the stuck feeling of resistance is gone. You discover there's no need to resist anything anymore; you know you can survive the exploration, the experiencing of the pain, and the ultimate release of what you at the core of your being are not.

Pop Quizzes

All this said, it's also important when experiencing resistance to be aware of something else that can occur in your healing process. If you have already dived deeply and have thoroughly done your inner work with a negative pattern – fully feeling all the emotions involved – and yet the issue arises within you again, know that it may just be up for one last time. It may a type of "pop quiz", to make sure you've really learned what you needed from the pattern, a test to see if you are ready for the next level, the next experience, the next stage in your journey.

If this is the case, it's probably best to not get all involved in it again, analyzing it and feeling the emotions one more time. Instead, just focus on accepting and embracing it and then releasing it into the light. If you can feel it release and experience a sense of relief and completion – and no more resistance – you can probably just put it behind you.

But if a sense of deep pain is still there, it's likely time to go back into it again and do yet further healing. Many patterns have a number of layers to them, created by all the different times throughout your life, and possibly lifetimes, you have experienced the troubling situation and all the emotions you attached to it. It can take time and patience to get to the bottom of it.

Chapter 28

Shame, Guilt, Self-Judgment

If you've been on your ascension path for a while, you may be noticing that emotions such as shame, guilt and self-judgment are coming up more noticeably than ever before. Experiencing these emotions more often and more intensely seems to be a common ascension symptom.

These emotions might be arising due to challenges that keep happening in your life, no matter what you do. It may feel as if you never quite "pass the tests" that come up for you. In response, you may decide something must really be wrong with you. You can't seem to learn.

Or – perhaps you feel you've really failed when it comes to manifesting a new life for yourself. You just don't seem to be able to create the joy and abundance in your life you desire. With all these thoughts, up come the shame and guilt.

You may even judge yourself for not understanding the teachings out there that tell you that highly-evolved people only experience positive, uplifting emotions. If you're suffering, it probably means you're not very awake. And if you feel shame about this, it means you simply don't love yourself enough; so you've failed at this, as well.

It's exhausting to even contemplate all this. It can feel overwhelming: How can you possibly figure out how to heal yourself of the shame, guilt and self-judgment when it's so complicated and convoluted? You maybe ask yourself such questions as:

- How can I get past the self-judgments that seem to automatically arise, especially around certain actions or aspects of my personality?

- How can I move out of the self-doubt that constantly comes up whenever I attempt to do something new or difficult?

- How can I forgive myself and let go of guilt for certain things I've done?

- How can I neutralize the profound pain that occurs when shame shows up?

- How can I stop the fear that tends to arise around certain actions I know I need to take?

You've likely discovered that getting past any of these emotions is not easy. So often, shame, guilt, self-doubt – as well as fear – can arise so quickly, there seems no way to stop them.

When you're stuck in 3D consciousness, it can feel as if experiencing these emotions is just a natural part of who you are, and that it's appropriate for you to be feeling them. The emotions feel accurate; you automatically assume you "should" be feeling them, because you believe yourself to be an inherently flawed person, inadequate and inferior in certain ways. And that you somehow need to "earn" your way into okayness through hard work on yourself.

You probably understand intellectually this is not really so, but it's much more difficult to *know* this on the emotional level. It's as if your lack of feeling okay, just as you are, is such a deep programming inside you, you can never successfully eradicate it.

Mental Health professionals have generally ascribed this whole experience of shame, guilt and self-judgment to a phenomenon they call the "superego" or the "inner critic". They say it's just a part of your psyche, an aspect of yourself you need to accept and even embrace as an integral part of who you are.

Although it may sound daunting to try to achieve this, it does sound like a rational explanation for the programming of guilt, self-doubt and shame and a wise way to deal with it. And maybe you have done a lot of healing work around these issues, believing this encouragement of how to deal with the superego.

Never-Ending Healing Work

But, have you ever noticed that no matter how much healing work you do on yourself, there always seems more to work on? That no matter how much healing you've accomplished, no matter how much spiritual practice you've done over the years, there's always, always more to work on?

You may have times in which you feel happy, because you're finally feeling better, and positive things are at last happening in your life. But how long does that good feeling ever last? Doesn't some new challenge always seem to come along eventually to pull you down into self-doubt or fear again?

Perhaps you've learned through hard work and practice to meet life's constant challenges with greater ease, balance, neutrality and inner strength. And you feel good about this – which you definitely should, because this *is* truly an accomplishment.

But doesn't that sometimes really make you weary – dealing with all these challenges you have to constantly meet in a balanced way? All these things to learn and practice and heal and fix – it can feel never-ending.

Does it ever feel as if it's somehow not fair, that it doesn't make sense, that something's not right about this? If God/Spirit is all-loving, why is there so much suffering in the world?

You might even wonder why you, in particular, have experienced so much suffering in your life. You know you're basically a good, loving person, attempting to live a productive and ethical life, being kind and caring and sincere in your intentions. And that you have worked really hard to heal aspects of yourself that keep you in suffering. You have done spiritual practice and have awakened to higher states of consciousness. Why is it so difficult to fully heal yourself and wake up?

You might believe it's because you've got karma; you probably weren't so good and kind in past lives and you made poor choices. So now you're having to balance that; now you have to pay for what you've done, although you probably don't even remember what you did. There's always more to learn. With resignation, you simply decide you're not worthy enough yet to spiritually wake up or have a comfortable life.

The System is Stacked against You

Has it ever occurred to you that maybe – just maybe – the whole system that's set up here on Earth in the Third and Fourth Dimensions is stacked against you? Have you ever wondered if perhaps the whole karmic and reincarnation system has somehow been corrupted in order to keep you on the Karmic Wheel, experiencing negativity over and over again – so that it's next to impossible to ever get off it? That maybe your difficulty in waking up spiritually is actually not because you're not worthy? That perhaps it's not your fault that it's so hard?

If you have, you're right. It may sound like a radical idea, if you have studied and accepted teachings in Eastern spiritual traditions. What do I mean your karma is not your fault? Or the difficulties you've had in getting off the Karmic Wheel have to do with some sort of tampering with the whole system, itself? Before you dismiss this possibility, see if you can take in this information and maybe find something within you that resonates with it.

First of all, this isn't to say you don't have to balance the karma you've created. You *do*. This is your responsibility. And this doesn't mean you're not responsible for your spiritual awakening – you *are*. What I am suggesting is there is a different reason for your having to do these things than you might think.

It's not because you were a bad person in the past and you now have to pay for that. It's not because you're somehow flawed and you need to heal and fix yourself, because you're unworthy in some way, not evolved enough. And that you should be feeling shame and guilt for all this, to motivate you to "do better".

The reason you're responsible for balancing your karma is that this is part of the agreement you made in coming to Earth in the first place. As discussed earlier in this book, as an Ascension Lightworker, there's a high probability you're what's known as a *Starseed* – an old Soul who originally came to Earth to assist humanity in its evolution. And subjecting yourself to the Karmic Wheel was part of the deal when you came to incarnate into human form.

It was the only deal available at the time. If you were going to come to this planet – a planet known to be a "fallen planet", one that had fallen into the dark depths of third-dimensional reality – you had to fit into the plan here that all human beings were subject to.

Corrupted Reincarnation System

As mentioned in Chapter One, the whole reincarnation system that has been in place on Earth since the Fall of Consciousness – and especially since certain dark alien forces invaded the inner realms here – has been corrupted.

If you are new to the idea of dark aliens controlling the reincarnation system and are doubtful about the truth in this story, it probably continues to sound like science fiction or conspiracy theory. But, if so, try to keep an open mind and see if this idea makes some sense out of why it is so difficult to wake up and to heal challenging kinds of emotions, such as guilt and shame. In my book, *Triumph of the Light,* I go into detail about this alien interference with humanity's evolution. But for now, just see if what I describe briefly here is something that makes sense or resonates with you.

In coming to the Earth to assist humanity, you had to go with the program, so to speak. You had to do your best to keep the Light in view at all times and act from higher consciousness as best you could, given the system that was set up here. But if you failed, you knew you'd have to pay the consequences.

You understood all this before coming here; but it was a challenge that probably turned out to be much, much harder than you'd anticipated. The darkness in third-dimensional Earth was much more powerful than you could ever have imagined. Even the most powerful and evolved Souls coming here have ended up getting caught on the Karmic Wheel. It's purposely designed to do this.

Primary Implant

Another element these dark forces have employed to keep humanity in their control has been with what has been called, as discussed earlier in this book, the *superego* or *inner critic* – the part of you that sends constant thoughts that create guilt, shame, self-judgment, and a feeling of disempowerment in your life.

Most people aware of this part of the human make-up just assume it to be a natural part of the human psyche. However, according to certain ascension teachings, this inner critic mechanism is something that has been attached to your brain on the etheric level. Called the *primary implant*, it's a type of very sophisticated AI technology the negative alien forces have used to help keep control over humanity for thousands of years.

From their position within the inner realms of the lower Fourth Dimension, these beings have managed to insert the implant into every human at birth. Far more than just giving you negative messages about yourself, it also serves to keep you in a position of feeling *separate from Source* and is designed to keep you feeling weak, disempowered, and in fear. These dark beings thrive on the frequencies of all the negative emotions caused by this implant; to them the frequencies of your fear, shame, guilt and all such negative feelings are a form of energetic food.

It is important to contemplate this, as it can explain how you may often feel controlled by negative beliefs about yourself, as well as fearful about your survival – even when it's clear to you intellectually that none of this is real. It also explains why it seems to take inordinate intention, awareness, and practice to keep reminding yourself that you are one with Source.

Although your rational mind might still be dismissing this possibility, perhaps a deeper part of you is responding with a knowing or memory of a truth you once knew, long, long ago. Doesn't this answer a lot of questions that have never really been answered by any spiritual teachings you've studied?

The good news is that because humanity is waking up, the hold these negative forces have on humanity is now greatly weakening. As time goes on, you may begin to feel freer of negative emotions about yourself. And, at some point in your ascension process, this implant will likely begin to disintegrate altogether – especially once the Event has occurred.

Dealing with Attacks of Guilt, Shame and Fear

However, meanwhile, it is still with you now, so it's important to understand how it functions. You can then learn to catch those automatic "attacks" of guilt and shame and fear, and not give them a lot of energy. It's important to remember the critical voice attacking you is not *you*; it's not even a natural *part* of you. It is simply something *with* you, as part of the experience of being in a physical body on 3D Earth at this time.

So, when you hear or feel that inner voice telling you there's something wrong with you, catch yourself from automatically falling into guilt or shame. Don't defend yourself or try to convince it that you really aren't as bad as it's saying you are. Your defensiveness and resistance just strengthen its hold on you.

Instead, you can remind yourself that you are not inherently bad or flawed. You're a highly-evolved Soul that is simply caught in a human incarnation in 3D, attempting to wake up against tremendous odds, with the cards automatically stacked against you.

Then, once you've attained some distance and freedom from this implant's voice, you can spend some time focusing on the little self inside you who has been bullied by this internal programmed voice all your life and comfort it with love, understanding and compassion.

As you begin to do this, the hold the shame and guilt have on you will diminish greatly and you'll find yourself rising a lot more rapidly in vibration. And you'll be able to hold yourself there more easily. Self-love will come more naturally.

Of course, this isn't to say you'll never make what could be called "mistakes", or never do anything that's hurtful to others that needs to be corrected. Like all of us, you probably do make mistakes and act hurtfully toward others at times – it's just part of living in the Third Dimension. And it's part of your learning and evolution in consciousness.

But with clarity about the profound difficulty that exists in the current reality you're living in, it can be a lot easier to avoid falling into automatic shame or guilt about what you've done. You can simply see where a correction needs to be made and take care of it in a neutral and self-loving way. Self-forgiveness can then happen as a natural occurrence.

Learning to love yourself may still involve a lot of healing, but it can be done from a consciousness of greater compassion for yourself and therefore achieve results much more rapidly. And, as time goes on, you'll be able to watch all third-dimensional imperfections and distortions naturally falling away.

And, further, as you're reducing your reactivity to the programmed voice inside you, you'll also experience a knowing that, simply as a Soul, you naturally deserve comfort, love, and happiness. It is your birthright. With this, you can begin to experience a greater overall feeling of well-being and happiness.

Dissolving the Primary Implant

Something else you can do if you are interested in further diminishing the impact of the negative voice within your head is to focus on dissolving the Primary Implant. Cobra, the Pleiadian contactee who describes this implant, states that the use of the Violet Ray is helpful in achieving this.

Using this ray simply involves calling it in and seeing it penetrating the frontal lobes of your brain where the implant is located. Also call in St. Germaine, the keeper of the ray to assist you. You may or may not actually see the violet color; do not worry if you don't. Just have the intention to hold it there to essentially melt the implant.

You may become visually aware of what the implant looks like: it might appear as a dark object attached to your brain – or perhaps like something that penetrates in different ways into your brain. Or there may be an energetic feeling that begins to occur. Just keep with your intention to dissolve it with the Violet Ray.

Using the Violet Ray in this way might be something you feel drawn to focus on for a while, perhaps during a five-minute period of time during your daily meditation practice each day. As time goes on, you may wish to check within yourself to see if the same tendency toward self-judgment, guilt and shame are still there. You will likely realize that this has diminished, and that you are freer, feeling more empowered and loving toward yourself.

Experiencing Yourself as a Soul

In doing this, you can then also see that your human personality self, with all its third-dimensional distortions and struggles, really isn't who you are, anyway. In reality, you are a Soul, a multidimensional Being of Light. Your human personality is just "clothing" you've been wearing for a long time. You can take it off and decide to wear another higher-dimensional outfit for a change – one comprised of self-love, self-respect, joy, confidence and well-being.

Keep reminding yourself that you truly are already perfect, just as you are – because, in reality, you are. Your human 3D self, of course, is not perfect. It is perfectly imperfect; it's designed to be that way. You will never perfect it.

Indeed, if you can learn to actually love and honor your imperfections, this can produce a miracle for you, a release from self-hatred that will change your whole experience in life. If you find yourself in a mindset of needing to "fix" yourself, stop and realize you're in 3D consciousness. You're identifying with your imperfect human self.

If you can shift into higher 4D, you will become aware that there's nothing inherently wrong with you. You just need to wake up more; you need to discover and then step more fully into your true identity – your Soul. This is the aspect of you that is already completely perfect. You may not know exactly how to do this yet, but you can at least keep that annoying critical voice at bay by knowing that it doesn't speak truth about who you are.

Soul Essence Exercise

One key that can assist you in remembering you're a Soul – a multidimensional Being of Light – is discovering which particular Soul qualities you express the most powerfully. Start by considering for a moment how Spirit/Source has a great variety of expressions. It's like a diamond with many different facets, such as love, beauty, peace, harmony, and joy.

And, as a Soul, you are an aspect of Spirit/Source; you too embody and express these same facets of the diamond. However, there are probably two or three qualities you express more clearly than others. They make up what could be called your "Soul Essence", the particular flavor of energy you generally emanate or transmit. In becoming aware of what these qualities might be, you can keep them as a reference point to remind yourself of who you really are. Even by just thinking of them, you can be lifted into a higher vibration.

Contemplate for a moment: which words would best describe your Soul Essence? The words could be adjectives, nouns or even verbs or adverbs. They can be separate words, or you can put them together.

Some examples might be: Luminescence and Joy (or Luminescent Joy); Silence and Peace (or Silent Peace or Peaceful Silence); and Presence, Radiance and Compassion (or Compassionate, Radiant Presence).

If you have difficulty in finding the words that best describe your Soul's Essence, ask friends to tune in and see what they may come up with.

Developing Unconditional Self-Love

So, learning about the primary implant can be helpful in understanding the mechanism that creates shame, guilt and self-judgment in you. And coming up with words that describe your Soul Essence can help to remind you of who you are in your highest expression.

But, since these negative emotions are likely still programmed in you, you probably need to continue in your quest to develop deeper unconditional love for yourself. As indicated in earlier chapters, this is essential for your ascension into the Fifth Dimension. But it's not easy to simply start loving yourself in deeper ways than you've ever known how to do.

One way to begin is to attempt to see clearly the specific ways in which you may not be loving yourself. Pay attention to catching the negative thoughts you have about yourself and change them. Which specific self-criticisms are most prominent or frequent? Explore your deeper beliefs about yourself that may be limiting you and suppressing your ability to accept and love yourself. See how they are inaccurate.

Another way that can be surprisingly helpful is to watch carefully how other people treat you. Their attitudes and actions toward you are a mirror of what the Universe is reflecting back to you about *how you treat yourself*. Importantly, this does not mean that if people tend to be dismissive of you, for example, you are dismissive toward *them*. It is a mirror of how dismissive you are toward *yourself*. Very simply, people tend to treat you the way you treat yourself.

If you find that people do not treat you with kindness or respect, you can then know that this is how you are treating yourself. You can begin watching to see how you treat yourself in the same way and focus on changing this.

And as you start to heal yourself in this way – treating yourself with respect and kindness, for example – it becomes exciting to see how other people naturally start to treat you with more respect and kindness, as well.

Putting Yourself First

One of the things you may discover in this quest to heal your self-judgment, guilt, and shame is how you might tend to treat other people better than you treat yourself; you naturally put their needs first and ignore your own. This is likely something you learned to do, growing up. You may have been taught that it is selfish and wrong to think about yourself first and ignore what other people need. Or you may have discovered that if you didn't take care of the needs of others who were important to you, you would be emotionally abandoned. You learned to diminish your own needs.

If you were a rather unevolved individual, caught up in low-energy pursuits, learning about your selfishness might be a good lesson. But it's likely you already learned long ago in your Soul's journey how to be loving and of service to other people. You already feel a natural compassion for the suffering of others and are drawn to assisting them when you can. And this is an important aspect of higher spiritual consciousness.

However, if you tend to experience a lot of shame and guilt, what you may not be so good at is being of service to yourself – and knowing how to love yourself unconditionally. To learn this, it is important to "put yourself first". You need to learn how, in every situation, to make your own physical and emotional needs important, and to take responsibility for seeing them met – before you attempt to be of service to others.

Of course, if you are a parent of young children, you do need to make their needs important – and it may be hard in certain situations to put their needs second to your own. But even with children, it is important to find ways in which you are not constantly supressing your own needs in order to take care of theirs. This will eventually backfire on you; you will, among other things, be expressing an energy of resentment and martyrdom.

Not only will taking responsibility for your own needs bring about a greater sense of self-worth, it will also enable you to serve others more effectively. In addition, you will be modeling to others how to take responsibility for their own needs in every way they can.

Self-Forgiveness

Another approach to learning how to love yourself involves a focus on self-forgiveness. Forgiveness processes can be very helpful – especially if you're caught in 3D consciousness and are feeling especially ashamed or guilty about things you've done. Twelve Step programs, as well as a number of other programs, offer excellent tools around forgiveness.

However, at some point when you're in a higher vibration, you may realize that there is really nothing to forgive yourself for, after all: You realize you were always doing the very best you could – given the circumstances, and what you understood to be true. If you really had known better, you would have done better.

You might think you *did* know better, but it was likely only intellectually. You didn't *really* know; you didn't really understand the spiritual ramifications of what you were doing. If you had, you would have acted differently.

And what's really important to get is that this is true about *everyone*. Everyone really is doing the best they can, given the circumstances, and what they truly understand. When you truly know this, forgiveness becomes a natural response.

Judging Your Body

Perhaps one of the most painful kinds of self-judgments you might have is one you have about your physical body. Maybe you have never liked how your body has looked in certain ways. Or perhaps it's been more recently since you've been gaining weight or getting old, that your judgments have developed. Either way, this type of self-judgment can hold you firmly in 3D consciousness, in which you're identifying with your 3D body/mind self – a very limited and restricted identification.

As with self-forgiveness, there are a great number of tools available for learning to love your body. And these are important to use, if this is an area of self-judgment for you. You can either work to change how your body looks, or you can work on learning how to love your body, just as it is. Either approach can be helpful.

The Body Elemental

But there is another teaching that can assist you in actually learning to respect and care about your body in a whole new way. And that is to see it not simply as a form of physical flesh that has been born and will someday die. Yes, there is this aspect to it, but there is so much more.

What you may not know is that your body is actually a consciousness, known as the *Body Elemental*. This doesn't just mean your body has consciousness in it, something many people realize. It means that it is actually a particular, individual consciousness you have chosen to live this life with. Together, you comprise who you are in human form.

The Body Elemental is a consciousness that knows how to create and run a physical human body; and, as such, it is extraordinarily wise and skilled. It is what entered your mother's womb immediately as your father's sperm merged with your mother's egg and then began creating your physical body.

And it has served you graciously your entire life, keeping your body running the best it's been able to, considering the sometimes-difficult circumstances you've been in, both physically and emotionally. It continues to keep your body running, even when you don't seem to care about your health. And it's the one that hears your judgments about how you look.

Just realizing that a certain type of consciousness was originally created so that a Soul could physically incarnate into the human being species can help you to bring in greater respect for your physical form. But what can create a greater sense of love is realizing that this consciousness, just like you, is also in the process of evolving. It too leaves the physical body at death and then reincarnates again with a Soul to continue learning and evolving.

And further – you have likely chosen it as your Body Elemental for this lifetime because you have co-existed together in human form before in previous lifetimes. You know each other well and you've learned a lot in working together. As such, you can see your Body Elemental as a type of loyal companion you've had with you your whole life. You are in this together. You can appreciate all your Body Elemental is doing for you and may even wish to apologize to it for any judgments about not only how your body looks, but also how it functions.

As your relationship with your body grows healthier, you will find you'll be able to shift further and further into the vibrations of the higher Fourth Dimension and into the Fifth. In the end, you discover that loving yourself unconditionally has to include loving your body and the Body Elemental consciousness unconditionally.

Chapter 29

Spiritual Mission Challenges

As an Ascension Lightworker, you likely feel you have a spiritual mission to accomplish in this lifetime. You know you've specifically incarnated during these times of great transition to assist in humanity's leap of consciousness into the Fifth Dimension.

As time goes on, and more and more continues collapsing in the world around us, the demand for spiritual leadership will be increasing dramatically. There will be a greater need for people with a sincere sense of purpose who want to help heal, guide and raise consciousness among people in any way possible. Much will be needed to assist people through the tumultuous times ahead of us.

Soul Purpose and Spiritual Mission

It's sometimes helpful to clarify vocabulary around feelings of spiritual purpose. As I see it, it could be said that everyone incarnating on Earth has a "soul purpose". Before birth, we all drew up a soul contract which outlined, among other things, a personal purpose for this incarnation.

This purpose is often to learn something in particular or to balance karma from past lifetimes. It might be to learn about love, or experience empowerment, or maybe serve as a mother to many children, complete specific karma for the family lineage – or some combination of these things. Everyone has this kind of "soul purpose".

However, not everyone has what could be called a "spiritual mission". A spiritual mission is a very specific kind of purpose; certain mature souls have taken on a calling to accomplish in this incarnation, a goal of serving humanity and the earth in a particular way during these times of ascension.

This is more than just enjoying being of service. A lot of good-hearted people are drawn to helping people whenever they can. But if you have a mission, you know you're here to help heal, support and guide people in a certain way toward higher consciousness in the great Shift that's taking place – or to help restore the earth back it its pristine beauty. In other words, you're here in some way to help create a new Earth.

Challenges with Your Mission

Knowing you have a spiritual mission can be exciting. But there are often challenges that come with it. For instance, you may definitely know that you have a mission, but you're still trying to figure out exactly what it is and how you should be expressing it. Or perhaps you just can't seem to find a way to get it started. On the other hand, maybe you are already involved with your mission, but you're having trouble in trying to expand your role, to be more effective in it, or clearer in your expression of it.

Perhaps you're feeling challenged by fears and self-doubt, or by ineffective relationship patterns that get in your way. Somehow, you keep sabotaging yourself in some manner. All of these common experiences can be really frustrating for people waking up to their spiritual missions, sincerely eager to serve in the best way possible.

Discovering Your Unique Abilities, Skills and Gifts

Before tackling any of these challenges, it's helpful to understand certain things about having a spiritual mission. First is that you inherently have particular unique abilities, skills and gifts of consciousness you have to offer. Some of them you may not even be aware of yet, and this may be contributing to a sense of being stuck when it comes to knowing what your spiritual mission is.

However, whether you've been aware of it or not, you've probably been expressing many of your gifts in one way or another for most your life. Maybe you've not seen these qualities as part of your mission. You might be dismissing them, thinking they have nothing to do with it.

You may also not see certain experiences you've had as having any relevance to your mission. But if you were to look back on everything you've ever done, experienced and learned, you might be able to see that it's all had a purpose in preparing you for your spiritual mission and has helped you in actually doing it along the way. You can discover that nothing that has ever occurred in your life has been random. Even the most difficult, challenging experiences have offered great learning that can be put to use for your mission.

If it's not clear yet what your mission is, know that it's likely similar to what you have already been doing or learning. But it will probably be a step up, a way that's a more concrete, more effective, or more expansive an expression of it.

Frequency Holders

A second thing to understand is that not everyone with a spiritual mission is what could be called a *spiritual activist* – someone expressing as a healer, teacher, speaker or leader in some outer way. Not all Ascension lightworkers are spiritual activists. Some are what could be called *frequency holders.*

If you're a frequency holder, you're probably not drawn to being someone with an obvious outer expression of your mission. And yet, you know you can hold a high and powerful frequency of love and light, and you're aware of the power of this ability.

Frequency holders with this power are very important. Their energy helps to create a field for the collective at large. You can't see it, but it's very real and can be tapped into. And frequency holders also act as a type of battery of light for those spiritual activists who *are* out there acting in the world.

But whatever your spiritual mission is, know that it's important – and that it's needed now, more than ever before. So it's important for you to get as clear as possible as to what your mission is and to clear anything that stands in the way of accomplishing it in the highest, most effective consciousness possible.

Discovering the Reasons for Feeling Blocked

So, whether you're someone who is still not sure what your mission is – or you already know, but are feeling somewhat stuck in moving forward with it as quickly and effectively as you'd like – let's look at some reasons that can cause this kind of uncertainty and stuckness.

The first reason could be that you have certain karmic situations or patterns that still need to be resolved before you can step more fully into your mission. Or there may be relationships you're involved in that are not conducive to whatever you're here to do. Some people, for instance, are fearful of letting go of a marriage or partnership they've been in for years, although they're aware that they are being held back spiritually by staying in it.

Common Traps

If you think you are already expressing your mission, but it hasn't been working well for some reason, it may be helpful to also become aware of two common traps that can prevent you from being as successful or effective in your mission as you might like.

Attaching your Identity to your Role: The first one is when you begin attaching your sense of identity to your role in your mission: like thinking "I am a healer", "I am a teacher", "I am an akashic reader", a "reiki master" – or whatever. In other words, you tend to identify yourself with what you do, rather than with what you are.

This kind of identification with your role in your mission can bring on certain difficulties with performing it, such as hidden ego agendas you're not aware of. For instance, although you know you sincerely do wish to serve, perhaps you're not aware of a need you may have to feel special, important or successful. That need may well be getting in your way.

If you have this kind of need to feel special and important, you're probably attaching your sense of self-value and well-being onto the success you feel you're having in expressing your mission. If you feel your mission is going well, you feel good about yourself; but if not, you feel bad, maybe even that you're failing. And this, of course, brings an imbalance into your service, a type of neediness or insecurity, which weakens your effectiveness.

This need to feel important or special is a hard one to tackle, because it's usually unconscious. And sometimes if an awareness of this *does* come up, a feeling of shame can also arise – because "your ego is showing", so to speak.

If you ever experience this, just realize that, unless you're a fully-enlightened Being, it's natural to still have some hidden ego agendas. You need to be compassionate with yourself. It's just important to become aware of these agendas that can stubbornly hang on sometimes, and to do whatever you can to heal them. Generally, what is needed is a greater sense of love for yourself.

However, there is another difficulty that can arise when identifying with the role you're playing with your mission: it can prevent you from knowing who you really are as a Soul. You miss experiencing the fact that you are a Spiritual Being, who happens to be doing something in this physical world called a spiritual mission.

It's important to remember, whether you're involved in doing your mission or not, that you are always YOU, an extraordinary spiritual Being who really doesn't need to do anything in the way of outer service to be valuable. Just your being, your presence, can at times be all that's needed. What you're doing – your mission – is simply an added bonus you're offering.

Attaching Financial Stress to your Role: Another trap you can also fall into when you have a spiritual mission is attaching financial stress to it. This comes from the belief that, in order to feel successful in your mission, you need to make money from it and earn your living by doing it.

If you have this belief, and you're not financially successful, you may start judging yourself, doubting your mission, and sabotaging yourself with fear and stress. Do understand that it's fine to make money from your spiritual mission. There's no problem with this. But if there is stress attached to this process, it's not helpful.

Exploring your Experience with your Spiritual Mission

So, these are some common reasons people get stuck when attempting to bring their higher purpose into full expression. You may relate to these reasons, or you may have some that are more specific to you. Either way, it can be helpful to explore more deeply the reasons for the challenges you may be experiencing.

You can start by exploring what your spiritual mission may actually be. It could be helpful for a friend to read the following suggestions to you, so you might fully focus inwardly on receiving answers. But you can also simply try reading each step and then closing your eyes to see what appears. Either way, just follow these steps:

1. **Focus on what your mission might be:** Drop into meditation mode and ask for higher guidance. Then bring to mind what you believe your spiritual mission to be. If you're not sure what it is, just tune into what brings you a sense of passion and joy – or how you've served others so far in your life.

2. **Set Intention:** Set an intention to receive greater clarity about it. And also to understand how you can shift past any blocks you may have in your way.

3. **Explore Your Gifts:** Now begin to explore the gifts you bring to whatever work or service you've ever done. Don't be humble about this. Stand strong and honest within yourself and acknowledge the gifts and abilities you know you have. Perhaps focus first on your practical talents and skills which have shown up in whatever you've done over the years. Or even simply in your everyday personal life that you may take for granted. For example, maybe you have natural leadership qualities – or organizational abilities. Or perhaps mediation abilities; you naturally facilitate communication between people or when you're in a group. Or maybe you're good at math, science, learning languages, writing or teaching – or in solving puzzles, or making things with your hands. Perhaps you have a comprehensive understanding about what's happening in the world. Take a moment to be fully aware of what practical skills you have developed.

4. **Valuable Experiences:** Next, bring to mind the valuable experiences you've had in your life, ones in which you've learned a great deal. This would include any important awakening experiences you've had, or impactful relationship experiences. It would also include any major life challenges you've had and what you learned in making your way through them.

5. **Gifts of Consciousness:** And lastly, take a look at any gifts of consciousness you've either brought into this life or have developed as you've grown older. Perhaps it's a deep sense of empathy and compassion for others. Maybe you find that people find it easy to talk to you, confide their secrets in you. Or maybe you have healing abilities. Remember that you don't have to be trained in a certain profession to be a healer; there are many ways healing can be expressed. Or perhaps you have a deep love and understanding of children, or

animals, or plants. Perhaps you have psychic abilities. Do you ever experience telepathy with people, read their minds? Or maybe you have experiences of clairvoyance, clairaudience or clairsentience? Perhaps visions or powerful dreams? An ability to communicate with higher-dimensional beings? What are the most important gifts of consciousness you have to offer? Which ones bring you joy and a sense of passion?

6. **Ask again what your mission is:** And ask yourself again now, in contemplating all this: What is your spiritual mission? What are you here to offer to humanity and the earth during these challenging times of transition? It might be a little different from what you've thought it to be.

Experiences Blocking You

It can now be helpful to explore what generally happens when you have expressed your gifts and abilities.

1. **What are people's reactions to your gifts?** Ask yourself: Are people basically receptive to them? How were your abilities and gifts received when you were a child? Were you supported by your parents and teachers? Did they get who you were and encourage you to express yourself?

2. **Did you develop confidence?** Then ask: Did you develop confidence in who you were? Or were you afraid to attract attention or stand out in some way because you felt you were different? Did people ever make fun of you? Did any of your earlier abilities just close down at some point, because it didn't feel safe to express them? Or, maybe later on, there were important people in your life who didn't understand or value you – or perhaps they felt envious or competitive with you, or judgmental. Or maybe something uncomfortable, or even scary, happened

when you did express your gifts; and so, at some point, you made a decision to keep yourself small, invisible, or to hide parts of yourself.

3. **Have your earlier experiences stood in your way?** Contemplate now: Have any of these types of experiences stood in your way as you've attempted to activate your spiritual mission? Or to fully express it and expand further into it? Do you keep bumping into self-judgment and doubt?

4. **How to dissolve the blocks?** Ask: What could you do to begin dissolving any of these blocks to your full expression of your mission?

Exploring Past Life Blocks

At this point, it's important to explore further than the experiences you've had in this life. You have likely also brought in blocks from experiences in past lives when you attempted to express a spiritual mission you had in those lives. These are really important to be aware of and often hard to tune into because they're usually unconscious.

But you can ask for help in remembering what traumatic events may have happened in a past life that have brought on a decision to be wary about ever putting your head "above the radar" again.

1. **Drift back in time:** See if you can simply drift back in time, with the intention to find such an experience – a lifetime in which you were attempting to assist humanity into a higher consciousness. Or perhaps to create more compassionate circumstances for people.

2. **Allow information to flow in:** Just allow any information to flow to you in any form it may, and don't judge or dismiss anything you receive. You can always decide later whether you wish to believe it or not. For now, simply be open to anything that comes to you. See if you can become aware of a life in which you were perhaps in a leadership role, attempting to bring about greater justice for people. Or you were a healer, or someone involved in the esoteric

arts. Or just someone who dared to speak the truth. Tune into a time in which some kind of interference against you occurred, perhaps in the form of persecution, violence, or death. Or maybe it was deep humiliation and shame you experienced – a time in which you made a courageous attempt to bring more love, peace, healing and truth to the world – but somehow failed. And, due to the trauma and pain you suffered, you made a decision to never try it again. So, no matter how much you try now to fully express what you believe you're here to do, you keep getting stuck or finding you're sabotaging yourself. Somehow, it doesn't feel safe. Just allow this memory to come to you. It may come in images or flashes. Or it may be in words – or in sensations or emotions. Or it may just come as a knowing.

3. **Ask how to shift blocks:** And then, finally, ask what you can do to help shift any blocks or impediments due to these past experiences – so you can embark fully on accomplishing what you're here to do during these current times. One thing you can become aware of is that these times you're living in now are very different from those you've lived in, in past lives. Despite how stuck humanity still is in corruption, violence, and greed – it really is not as dangerous to attempt to assist humanity toward greater awakening and wholeness as it has been in the past. The forces of light truly are powerful now upon the earth, and humanity is waking up. You have every chance this time of accomplishing your mission.

Even if it's still not clear either what your spiritual mission is or what it is that's blocking your fullest expression of it, do not worry. In right timing, when you are ready and when the circumstances in the world are ready for you, you will be called to action, and it will be clear what you're here to do.

Keep remembering that if you have a knowing that you're here to serve during these times on the planet, there are divine plans for your contribution. Most of humanity is still deeply asleep and will increasingly be needing support, compassion, and awakened guidance. And the Earth, itself, is going to need healing, as well. Whatever it is you'll be doing, it will be greatly needed. Your skills and consciousness will not be wasted.

So for now, just continue to heal and clear blocks as you become aware of them. And know that your time will come.

Chapter 30

Vulnerable, Unsafe

During your ascension process, there are plenty of reasons you may start feeling vulnerable – and even, at times, actually unsafe. Sometimes it's for good reason, as there's something actually threatening you. If this is so, of course, you need to take yourself to safety.

But sometimes there may be nothing obvious threatening you, and yet you still feel as if you're being impacted energetically in some way that is unpleasant and destabilizing. Somehow, you're not feeling grounded and totally "here"; you're disoriented and mind-fogged.

This kind of sensation may happen during periods when you're receiving ascension "upgrades" in your body or your mind. During these times, it can be difficult to come completely present; part of you seems to be somewhere else, but you can't call it back. As a result, you feel vulnerable and somehow not safe outside your home.

This is usually a temporary experience which calls for slowing down and resting as much as you can. But it can feel scary, if you're not aware of what is occurring. You need to trust that it will eventually pass.

Grounding Yourself

Nonetheless, there are certain things you can do to alleviate some of the unpleasantness of this vulnerable sensation. The first thing is to ground yourself. There are many ways to do this. If you're outdoors and can take off your shoes to put your feet in the earth or grass somewhere, this will immediately connect you to the Earth and bring a sense of calm and stability. You can tune in and feel the electromagnetic connection that is flowing from the Earth into your body and your mind.

But if you're indoors, it's just as simple and effective to focus on visualizing a grounding cord extending from your perineum (between your legs), or your tail bone, and shooting it down into the middle of the earth. This is actually a good daily practice to keep you grounded and centered, no matter what you're experiencing.

Pulling Your Energy In

Once you've grounded yourself, you can then check to see where your consciousness is. Are you firmly inhabiting your physical body – or are you floating around somewhere outside of yourself?

You have a number of energetic bodies (etheric, mental, emotional, etc.) that extend outside your physical body, and it is easy and natural at times to leave this denser body and hang out in these higher bodies. There is nothing wrong with this, especially if you're consciously aware you're doing it.

However, when you're feeling weak and vulnerable, it may mean you'd do better to center yourself inside your physical body, where your power exists. If you're feeling that your boundaries are somewhat blurred, parts of your consciousness, rather than being inside yourself, may actually be inside the auric fields of other people you're with. And this can leave you feeling vulnerable and not in control of your own energy.

In order to feel at your most powerful and in charge of your energy and sense of safety, it's essential to be centered and aligned within your physical body. The best way to do this is to bring your awareness into the "center of your head" – the place behind your eyes. You may think you're always there in this space, but it's likely you're not. You'll see this clearly when you do bring your focus to this place behind your eyes – and then look out at the world through your eyes.

In doing this, you will find that something "clicks" – you are in your power center, feeling aligned and in charge – and in the moment. Here, you can consciously choose what you wish to do, think or feel. You'll feel a sense of authority and empowerment.

Cutting Cords

Next, think about the energetic cords you may have attached to you, connecting you emotionally and mentally to other people you've engaged with. If you have strong empathic tendencies, you are likely feeling impacted by their emotions and thoughts through these cords you naturally form with them. Cords generally attach between chakras. Sometimes they are healthy cords, but often not. It can feel as if you've picked up their "stuff" and it's impacting your sense of emotional or energetic balance.

If you suspect you may have cords connecting you to people you've recently engaged with, ask inwardly if this is so. Or just check energetically, especially at your lower four chakras. If the answer is yes, do your best to visualize scissors cutting these cords. You will feel an immediate sense of being freed from something impinging on your energetic field. This is also a good practice to do on a daily basis. You do not need to have other people invading your space and pulling on you energetically.

Clearing Your Field

Another way to do this is to simply feel into your auric field and see if you find anything dark or shadowy that doesn't belong there. Trust your intuition with this. If you stay centered and grounded when you're with other people, you will feel right away when something has moved into your field.

Here are some keys for keeping your field clear:

Assistance from Celestial Realms – Call in Divine Light and ask for assistance from the archangels or ascended masters to clear your field. You may see or feel a gentle energetic hand move into your body and scoop the energy out, and then release it into the Light. Call in more Divine Light to fill the space it's left.

Own Your Aura Space - It's important to own your personal aura space. If you don't, you are more vulnerable to foreign energy entering it. Become aware of your aura boundaries (around an arm's length away from your body all way round, above and below) as a way to own this personal space.

Create a Protective Shield around Yourself – Especially when you're around other people, it's important to keep a protection of Light around yourself. Again, if you're naturally empathic, you can absorb other people's energy into your field. Even if they are genuinely loving people, they still go through their stuff, just as you do yours. It's tough enough working on your own stuff; you don't need to take on theirs.

One way to create this shield is to call in the Holy Spirit – an aspect of Source – and ask it to surround, fill and protect you for the highest good of all concerned. This provides powerful protection that can keep you safe from unwanted energies. Another way is to envision a beautiful rose (a very high-vibrational flower) in front of you. Keep it there and see it creating a shield all around your body. With either of these methods, you will sense a feeling of safely keeping your own energies in your field, without the interference of energies from other people.

Non-Resistance - If you feel uncomfortable around a certain person or in a group, be careful not to go into resistance as an attempt to protect yourself. See if you can instead shift into a state of non-resistance. Remember: whatever you resist, persists. It only serves to keep foreign energy stuck in your field. See if you can consciously move into a state of non-resistance. If someone throws something unpleasant at you, you can just see it bouncing off the light shield you have around you. Or, you can imagine it passing right through you.

Call back your energy - Just as you can take other people's energies into your field, you can also leave your energy in theirs. It can be helpful at the end of the day to call back your energy. One effective technique is to create an image of a bright golden sun several feet above your head and let it be a magnet, attracting all of your energy back into it and purifying it in the gold energy. Then bring it down through the top of your aura and into your crown chakra, releasing your energy back into your personal space.

Psychic Attacks

Despite your every effort to keep your auric field clear, there are times when it may be too difficult to do so. A darkness may slip into your field and cause you more than just a feeling of being vulnerable. You might actually feel invaded. Intense anxiety, depression, despair – and even terror – can seem to appear out of nowhere and roll through you in great waves.

There may be different explanations for these intense episodes. One is simply that something traumatic you experienced at some point in your life (or perhaps in a past life) that you were unable to fully experience and integrate at the time is now suddenly coming up to be experienced and then released.

But another explanation is that it could be the result of what's known as a "psychic attack".

Discarnate Entities: There are different kinds of psychic attacks. One can occur if you've invited (usually unconsciously) disincarnate entities into your auric field. This is a surprisingly common occurrence for people. Many people with entities walk around with no idea there is anything at all in their auras.

But people who dwell in a lot in negative emotions or who have experienced traumatic experiences in their lives are often subject to the invasion of these entities – especially if they are empaths and very sensitive to energy. Those who indulge in alcohol and drug consumption are also vulnerable, as these substances weaken the aura, allowing entities free access to their fields. Many people in mental hospitals have entities with them, causing them to be diagnosed as "schizophrenic" or with a "multiple personality disorder".

Usually, the entities are human in form – "earthbound" Souls who have died but haven't found their way into the Light and are stuck in the in-between worlds. They're lost and want to be with Souls who are still incarnated in form for a feeling of comfort. Other times, the entities are not human and hold an especially low vibration.

Until recent times, entities who have joined with people have perhaps only caused a degree of disturbance to the people they're with. These people generally experience a level of depression, anger, or despair that may seem "normal."

But currently, as people are waking up and their vibrations are rising, the entities, who have felt a vibrational comfort up to this point with their "host", are starting to feel disturbed by this new higher frequency in the body they're attached to; and they are pulling on the person, attempting to bring their vibration down again. This can cause a great sense of emotional and physical disturbance for that person.

Negative Energies and Thought Forms: Another form of psychic attack, perhaps less disturbing but equally puzzling, is one of which we often have no awareness. This is an attack of negative energy or thought forms we receive on the mental and emotional level that someone may have sent to us. Although there are incidences in which this psychic energy is sent deliberately (yes, curses have actual power), often it is sent unconsciously.

If you are an empath, you are especially vulnerable to these energies – and they often find you if you are working conscientiously to raise your own vibration and that of the collective. Lightworkers can become particular targets.

Casual Attempts at Protection may not be Enough: You may believe that if you just keep your vibration high and call in protective Light when you're with other people, you will be safe from these kinds of dark energies and entities. But you may not be.

Releasing Psychic Attachments

If you are sensing you may have entities and/or negative energies and thought forms in your aura, here is a technique you can try to clear them along with implants and psychic bonds that may come with them:

1. **Call in Divine Light:** Call in and visualize divine Light entering your body and your aura.

2. **Call in Guides:** Call upon angels, specific ascended masters, or galactic guides you resonate with to be present and assist you to clear your energy.

3. **Healed and Forgiven:** Speak compassionately to the entities, telling them they are healed and forgiven. Ask that they be surrounded with the Christ light and the Christ love.

4. **Into the Light:** Ask your guides to take them to their perfect place in the Light. Visualize all dark energies being gently carried out of your aura into the Light.

5. **Implants & Thought Forms:** Request that all negative thought forms and implants left behind be dissolved and lifted in the light of truth.

6. **Psychic Bonds & Cords:** Ask that all psychic bonds and cords be severed, and to surround and protect your auric field from all but that which is of the highest vibration.

You may need to repeat this process until you feel clear. It can feel amazing to suddenly feel clear of something dark that felt like a part of you – but obviously wasn't.

However, if you don't feel successful at it, you may wish to seek assistance in this process from a practitioner who is skilled in doing it. There are a great number of practitioners who can be found online who can help to release these entities, often long-distance, from a person's aura. You can just type "entity release" into a search engine and find them. You can also read about particular symptoms of entity attachment on these sites.

However, just because the entities are released doesn't mean you are home-free. If you don't consciously work to keep your vibration high, stay as positive as possible, choose high-vibrational company, and hold protective Light around yourself – you may simply attract more entities back to your field.

In going through ascension, keep in mind the utmost importance of keeping your vibration high; in essence, ascension is all about raising your vibration. But those who have been susceptible to entity invasion especially need to be vigilant about this.

Remembering Yourself as a Soul

Chapter 31

Qualities of the Soul

As we have seen throughout this book, during these challenging times of ascension, it's important to compassionately meet, without resistance, the frequent and often inevitable low-dimensional mindsets that may arise within you. Learning how to heal yourself from all third-dimensional woundings and traumas is essential.

And yet, it is also important to focus on the positive progress you've made on your healing journey and to give attention, as well, to those aspects of yourself dwelling in higher dimensions. In particular, it's helpful to remember you are a powerful Soul, an identity you've often forgotten while living in the Third Dimension.

In reaching the Fifth Dimension, you will be identified fully with your Soul, completely free of all identification with your limited 3D personality-self. You will have left behind all tendencies to fall back into emotional suffering or thoughts of lack and limitation. You will know yourself, beyond a doubt, to be the glorious multidimensional Soul you've always essentially been.

What is the Soul?

So what is the Soul exactly? Probably every spiritual tradition has made an attempt to describe this divine Presence within us. Some descriptions are likely more accurate than others; and, depending on a person's beliefs and experience, one explanation may make more sense than others.

In this book, I have referred to the Soul as a creation of Source/God/Creator, an individual spark of that very same Essence. As such, it is the most primal, essential part of who you are. It also lives on many different dimensions, some of which you are currently aware, and many of which you probably are not.

In addition, the Soul has many facets to it, various qualities we can experience, such as love, light, joy, harmony, peace, and freedom. When we experience these qualities, we are in tune with our essential nature as a Soul. However, the Soul appears to have two primary qualities that comprise it as an entity. At the core of who we are, we are the essence of divine Light and Love: one essence, two somewhat different expressions of it.

Therefore, as you begin living more fully within 5D consciousness, you can expect increasing experiences of these qualities and gradually knowing yourself to actually *be* them. And, as this happens, you also begin to experience the Soul quality of transcendent Joy flowing into your life.

In the following chapters, I offer suggestions for learning how to more fully embody the essential qualities of Light and Love, as well as the Joy that naturally springs from this experience.

Chapter 32

Giving Up Your Story of Suffering

Like many serious Ascension Lightworkers, you have probably been deeply focused on healing the woundings and traumas you've experienced in the past. Despite how difficult this can be, you've also concentrated on waking up spiritually. It's likely been a long, arduous journey of overcoming obstacles, pushing past fears, and learning to live with loss and grief. It's a hero's story.

And yet, it's important to ask: Are you *identified* with this story of suffering you've been living?

Is this who you keep believing you are? Despite all you have experienced in waking up to the reality that you're a powerful spiritual Being, a Soul, do you on a daily basis continue to act as if this limited human being, living a challenging life on planet Earth, is who you are?

Are you still identifying with the problems in your relationships you need to heal, your painful or aging body, your inability to really manifest what you want in life? Are you still believing at times you are the sum of all your painful experiences from childhood, your financial challenges, or the failed marriages you've suffered through?

Secondary Gains

No matter how awake you are and how much healing you've done, it can still be difficult at times to let go of these sticky third-dimensional identifications. This is especially so, if you have, over the years, developed what's been called "secondary gains" attached to your painful experiences. Secondary gains are somewhat positive experiences you end up seeking when you can't seem to manifest the love, appreciation and compassion you really want in your life.

One of these secondary gains might be the compassion, attention or respect you receive from other people when you tell them about the kind of suffering you've endured – or the incredible things in life you have managed to accomplish, despite all you've suffered. If you're suffering and don't know how to stop, you might feel that at least you can have these empathic and awe-inspired responses that seem to help you go on.

But guess what? Those warm and fuzzy responses from others simply serve to strengthen your need to continue suffering. They help to bring on even more experiences of suffering, so you can continue to receive these responses. That's the way the Law of Attraction works. A focus on suffering – even on healing it – can attract continued suffering to you. It can be very tricky.

Identifying with your Story

But the main thing to realize is that if you are somehow still identifying with your story of suffering, you are keeping the story going. No matter how you may have forgiven your parents, your children, your friends and spouses who have betrayed you – and even forgiven yourself through years of healing – you may still be believing that this is who you are: someone who has suffered greatly, but is now healing or has been healed.

Perhaps you even believe you gave up your story of suffering long ago, realizing it's not who you are. But is that story still in your field? Do you still share it with people new in your life? Do you still feel a need to connect with people who understand suffering the way you do?

If so, you probably have not yet truly let go of this story of suffering. And to wake up to who you are on the most profound level of your being, this is necessary. It's not easy – especially if you're in the middle of a heart-wrenching situation or chronic physical pain.

Letting Go of the Story

And yet, even in facing and attempting to heal all the hardships you may be experiencing these days, you can still give up your identification with the one who is suffering through these experiences.

This doesn't mean abandoning this lower self; it doesn't mean discounting it. Just the opposite, in fact: it requires being totally *with* it, with great compassion, and a willingness to keep moving through whatever is arising.

And this is the key: you are *with* this suffering self – you are not identified *as* it. You are identified with a higher Self, a wiser, more awake Self, who is watching the suffering – and who is able to assist and compassionately guide the self in pain through the healing process.

There is love for this smaller self in your heart, and light and clarity in your mind. You understand that it's an opportunity to learn and develop your inner strength and power. And you keep in mind that whatever is occurring is temporary.

Even more important is that, if you can approach the current suffering without dragging the baggage of all the past suffering behind you, you will find that your current situation is not so difficult to navigate. You're looking at something that looks challenging because it always has been before, but maybe now no longer is. You are clear and new in the moment, and you're open to new ideas, new solutions.

How to Do It

But how to really do this, how to actually let go of the story of suffering? Just saying you'll do it, or thinking you can through intention, doesn't really accomplish it. You can start with this, but there must be constant attention to this resolution, constant attention to your thoughts and words and actions. Your sense of identification as the third-dimensional human being is profoundly embedded in your consciousness.

One way to approach this challenge is to begin by actually writing out your story of suffering – all the slings and arrows you've received, starting in childhood, all the way up to current day. You can do it in sentences or in bullet points. Take some time to develop this – remember the major hurts and injustices, especially those you have felt self-pity about. If shame or guilt or hatred arise, feel the feelings — and then go on. Write it all out. The story deserves to be told in full, this one last time.

Perhaps take a few days to read it over and maybe add some points you'd forgotten. Allow, without judgment, all emotions that arise. Make notes of certain woundings you perhaps still need to focus on healing, and put these notes aside for now.

At some point, when you feel you have gotten down on paper at least the highlights of all of it, it is time for some ritual to release it all, such as burning it or tearing it up in tiny pieces. Or, if you're really into rituals, you can create a more elaborate one that will impact you deeply. Do this with great love and compassion for yourself.

Experiencing the New You

If you are truly tired of your story of suffering and have a deep conviction to let go of it, these kinds of actions will be very powerful. You'll find that your suffering will ease. You'll feel free, like you've embarked on a whole new journey, with a fresh new perspective. When you wake up in the morning, you'll find you haven't dragged the problems you were facing yesterday, or any time in the past, into the new day. You'll see you have the opportunity to create an entirely different experience for yourself into which new possibilities for joy and fulfillment can enter.

You will probably find you still have to closely watch your thoughts and emotions – and even your sighs and grumbling – as you react to on-going challenges in life. Habits can hold on. And you'll have to watch for any lingering need to attain secondary gains, like sympathy you might receive from friends and family when sharing your suffering experiences. You can still share about what's going on, but beware of the old habit of identifying with these things that are occurring and as the one who is suffering.

You can decide, instead, to identify with the one who is healing and has wonderful stories of healing to tell. But in the end, do you even need to be identified with any story at all? Even a positive one?

Do you even need to be that person who no longer has a story?

Chapter 33

Experiencing Yourself as Light

"And God said, 'Let There be Light', and there was Light." Most people growing up in a western culture have at some point read or heard these words quoted from the Bible. Perhaps, as you've grown into what you might consider a more personally-resonant spiritual understanding, you have put aside any interest in what the Bible says. But, like most spiritual texts in traditions around the world, there are passages that do definitely ring of truth.

In fact, many of the metaphysical teachings in the last half-century or so also speak often of Light, stating that Source/Creator emanates this ethereal divine substance out onto all of creation; and that, in fact, all actually *is* Light. Certain scientists also understand this.

You have probably had experiences that have reflected this truth. Perhaps you've seen this divine Light with your inner eye or have felt yourself surrounded and infused by it. Or maybe you have had a profound awakening experience in which you actually realized that Light is your essential nature – or that Light is all there is, that everything is composed of Light. These kinds of experiences can be exhilarating and leave a profound impact on you, leading you into deeper exploration of the spiritual realms.

This is because one of your essential Soul qualities is Light. Thus, when you're experiencing Light, you feel more connected to your Soul. In this state of being, your Soul can enter your human form more fully and you can feel it shining though you.

The experience of being Light is generally a glorious and fulfilling one. But it can be difficult to experience when you're not feeling great; it becomes a distant concept you can't relate to. At those times, it can be helpful to be aware of certain steps you can take to experience this greater reality of yourself.

Experiencing Divine Light

1. **Call in Divine Light:** A first step might be to initially go into meditation and quiet your mind. And then call in divine Light from Source. It's helpful if you can visualize the Light as it enters you, but it's not necessary. You can probably more easily simply feel it as an energetic shift.

2. **Draw Light into your chakras:** Take time to draw this Light down into your chakras and feel it filling your entire being and then streaming out into your aura and into the world. Feel its soft, gentle presence being drawn ever more deeply within you.

3. **Call up memory of a past experience with Light:** Then see if you can call up a memory of an experience you've had in the past involving divine Light. It might be a profound experience, or it may be just a flash or glimpse, a feeling of light in your awareness or your body. If you can't remember a particular profound experience with Light, seek memories of feeling lighter, more positive – and perhaps more ethereal – an experience in which you clearly were not merely your dense mind/body personal self.

4. **Bring experience into present moment:** Take time to consciously bring back the experience of it into your present moment. You'll see that both your mind and your body do clearly remember it; it's just dropped into your subconscious as other experiences have taken its place.

5. **Feel the emotions:** As you bring this memory up, focus on it and feel into it. Summon the emotions you felt in this experience. In doing this, you'll realize how clear the feelings of joy, exhilaration and peace still are. And, very importantly, you'll be indicating to your mind that you want to continue remembering these experiences with Light that you've had in the past.

Tuning into your Etheric Body

At first, simply recalling past experiences with the Light can be enough to bring your awareness of it present. But you can take a next step by becoming aware of what's called your *etheric body*, one of your several energy bodies, the one closest to your physical body.

Your etheric body is a replica of your physical body, although it is perfect in form, as it still retains an energetic form of any organ or limb you may have had removed. It is also the body you leave your physical body in when you fall asleep to experience other realms of existence. It vibrates throughout your physical body and also extends somewhat outside of it.

To become aware of your etheric body:

1. **Feel into the more energetic form of your body:** Close your eyes and relax your body. Feel into a somewhat deeper place within yourself that is less dense and more energetic. You know you have found it when you begin feeling a subtle vibrating energy all through you. You can realize that this energy body also slightly extends as an ethereal form all around your body. It's you – but a lighter you – one that's not caught up in thought or heavy emotions.

2. **Feel the freedom and bliss:** As you tune into this more subtle aspect of yourself, you'll find you immediately feel a sense of greater freedom and even a quiet sense of bliss washing through you. You're automatically in a higher state of awareness.

3. **Have fun with it.** Try lifting your etheric arm, away from your physical arm. Try stepping outside of your physical body. Or focus your attention on the part of this energetic body above your head and feel yourself lifting up out of your physical body. Float or fly around the room.

4. **Shift into even subtler body:** At this point, as you bask in this experience of yourself as energy, you may be able to shift into a still subtler body in which you feel even more ethereal and less dense. Feel yourself becoming translucent.

5. **Become pure, luminous Light:** As you become ever quieter and deeper in your awareness, see if you can experience how you are now becoming pure luminous Light. You can feel as if you are glowing and that you extend out into space in a much larger form. This is when a feeling of exquisite ecstasy and profound peace can take hold. You find you don't want to move or think any thoughts that might bring you back into a denser experience of yourself.

Experiences of Samadhi

In different traditions, this experience of yourself as pure Light has been called by different names. *Samadhi* is perhaps one of the most common ones, as it has been described by numerous saints and mystics of Eastern traditions throughout the ages. It is usually explained that it is an experience you can only attain after many years of concentrated meditation.

However, it is my experience that this is no longer so. Even people who have not meditated for long are having experiences of this state of ecstatic being. It may be true that you cannot "bring it on" every time you attempt to, through steps such as those I've described above, but you can at least begin to come closer every time you try it.

However, it's important to understand that, even in the Fifth Dimension, *samadhi* is not a state of being that is constantly experienced. It is an intense state of being that appears and eventually disappears. But, as these experiences come and go, your whole consciousness becomes more and more flavored with them.

The main thing to realize is that the state of *samadhi* is not foreign to you; you are already familiar with it. It is one of your natural states of being. And you've consciously experienced it before, probably in many lifetimes, both on and off this planet. You've just forgotten this throughout your sojourn in the Third Dimension.

Chapter 34

Opening to 5D Love

There is perhaps no feeling quite like that of suddenly experiencing your heart bursting open to a Love that fills your entire being and streams out to everyone and everything around you. Your chest feels warm and expanded, pulsating with vibrant energy. And all mind-chatter ceases, as you continue experiencing this extraordinary transformation of your being.

If you've ever had this experience, you have likely found that the energy rushing through you is so powerful, tears fill your eyes. You may even dissolve into sobs of joy and gratitude. Such an experience can be so intense, you can feel as if you are made of nothing but Love. It doesn't matter for whom you feel the Love; it's the Love itself pouring through you that fills you with joy and exhilaration. And you experience the immense power of this Love; you recognize it as perhaps the most powerful force in the universe.

Spiritual Love vs. Emotional Love

It can sometimes be confusing that this kind of transcendent Love emanates from the same heart in which very harsh and painful emotions can also exist. How can this be?

As described in earlier chapters, we all actually have two energetic aspects of ourselves that have been called the "heart". The first is our emotional heart, the one most people recognize. It's the one that can experience emotional love, but also can feel *all* emotions, including those of a lower vibration, such as hatred, fear, jealousy, and grief. This heart, of course, is the one that needs healing.

The other heart – the one we could call the *Sacred Heart, the Spiritual Heart,* or *the Higher Heart* – is actually a center within your being that has little to do with dark emotions. Located just above your emotional heart, it is a complex configuration of higher energies and is where you experience spiritual Love, one of the primary qualities of your Soul. It has been called the "portal" to the Soul; and, once you become aware of it, it can indeed feel like a doorway to this higher aspect of yourself.

However, the kind of Love you experience in your Sacred Heart is not the ordinary kind of love that most people living in 3D consciousness know about. In the Third Dimension, *love* has many different meanings for people. But it is probably safe to say that the word refers to an emotion that generally feels really good; yet, depending on how emotionally and spiritually mature a person is, it is often mixed and confused with a sense of need, emotional desire, and/or lust. It is also an emotion that is conditional; at times, it can even switch instantly into hatred. The experience of being "in love" is especially fraught with sensations of desire, need and lust, and usually with a hope of finally feeling loved and desired.

Spiritual Love is quite different. Even aside from intense heart-opening experiences as described above, spiritual Love doesn't much resemble the feeling of an emotion. Although a powerful emotional element can accompany it, spiritual Love actually is not an emotion; it is a quality of the Soul that naturally appears as an expression of this higher aspect of you. As such, it is totally unconditional in its expression.

When you experience spiritual Love toward a person, it simply is. There is nothing the person can do or say that will ever change it, because you are relating to them as a Soul, rather than as a personality. You may not choose to allow them to express certain behaviors toward you, or even wish to spend time with them; but, no matter what they may do, you continue to love them, just as they are. You understand that, like everyone, they are doing their very best with how spiritually or psychologically awake they happen to be.

In the Fifth Dimension, this is the kind of Love you will be experiencing toward everyone and every living creature. It will be natural, with no conditions. No matter what is occurring, compassion, understanding and empathy will be present.

Accessing your Sacred Heart

Experiencing spiritual Love in your Sacred Heart is an important step in preparing you to enter the Fifth Dimension. But, if you're feeling closed down and separate, it can sometimes be very difficult to experience it.

In order to fully enter your Sacred Heart and experience the profound Love residing there, it is generally necessary to first pass through your emotional heart. But to do so, this heart needs to be free of low-dimensional energies. Your emotional heart cannot be closed and full of fear or anger, as these emotions will block you in trying to enter your Sacred Heart.

So, if you are experiencing heavy emotions, it's important to first learn how to open your emotional heart to love. This can be challenging, as it can be painful to fully meet scary emotions that create so much suffering. You feel a natural resistance, a fear of getting overwhelmed by them. You just want them gone.

Healing Your Emotional Heart

To heal your emotional heart of heavy emotions such as grief, sorrow, and hurt, you must be open to allowing them to rise to the surface in your awareness and meet them with compassion. Before attempting to immediately release or change them, you need to be willing to fully experience them and accept them without judgment. In essence, your heart first needs to break, before it can fully mend and heal.

You may have noticed at times that when a sensation of deep love begins to fill you for someone, you initially experience a sense of your heart painfully breaking. Before you begin feeling the love, you surprisingly feel overwhelming grief or sorrow arising. For this reason, you might immediately want to close down, not realizing this is a preliminary step for you to experience the opening of your emotional heart.

At the same time, when you do feel deep grief arising, it's important to not fall into the third-dimensional tendency of feeling self-pity. Instead, you can choose to just consciously allow the sensation of heartbreak and be with yourself compassionately, as waves of sorrow pass through you.

In doing this, you will discover that, right behind this sorrow, is the Love you have so desperately longed for, along with an enormous sense of relief and gratitude. You realize that the Love that Source has for you has always been there; you've just somehow blocked it. And you become aware of the pain you have caused yourself in holding back your own Love for yourself. As the painful energy that has been locked up in your emotional heart is released, you may find yourself alternately crying and laughing.

With this release can then come a profound opening into the Sacred Heart and a sense of spiritual ecstasy that is part of your spiritual nature. And, with the discharge of negative energy from your emotional heart, you will find that your Soul can then enter more fully into your body and be experienced.

Breathing the Pain Out

Facing and releasing pain from your emotional heart can be an intense process. If it feels too difficult to do alone, it may be helpful to seek professional help with this. However, there are simple techniques you can try on your own that can help you to gently release painful emotions.

One of those is a type of meditation that involves the breath. You begin by taking some continuous deep breaths, in and out, from your emotional heart. With each in-breath, draw in divine Love from Source; with each out-breath, breathe out the heavy emotions. Or, you can breathe in the Love and then visualize it circling back around and re-entering your heart.

This practice can greatly loosen and release heavy emotions. At some point, you can feel into your Sacred Heart and experience there the warmth of the abiding Love that has begun flowing into your entire being.

However you manage to clear heavy energies from your emotional heart, you will find you again have access to the profound mysteries of your Sacred Heart. If you maintain a conscious focus on this Heart, you begin to naturally radiate Love wherever you go, and eventually you experience yourself *as* Love, itself. And, with this consciousness, you become a healing Presence to all around you and to the world.

Chapter 35

Bringing Joy Back into your Life

During these intense times of ascension, perhaps you have been working hard to function in a balanced and centered way. And you may feel good about how well you've created a general sense of contentment for yourself; your life is okay, you're handling it.

Yet, at some point, you might feel as if you've put in a whole lot of work for not a whole lot of gain. You may feel generally okay and able to enjoy life, but you might ask yourself: "What about JOY? It's great I'm able to feel fine with my life – but how can I find something that makes me feel *joyful* to be alive?"

Perhaps you long to feel the passion and excitement you once felt before the challenges of your ascension process started. You miss the bright expansion of consciousness in which your whole being used to light up and your spirit soared.

It may seem to you that in the past there were circumstances, events or relationships that seemed to create this kind of joy in you, but these are now gone. Or perhaps joy still appears from time to time, but it doesn't last, and you're not certain you can create it anymore. Too much has changed.

It can be hard to continue on, if nothing much seems to change, even when you're dealing well with the old energies of wounding that are coming up. It may feel like one uncomfortable thing after another keeps occurring, and that a state of joy is an almost impossible emotion to attain.

If you are experiencing this, don't despair. No matter what's happening in your life, you *can* ignite the joy you once felt – and, with a strong intention and an understanding of what joy actually is, even a more lasting joy.

Understanding the Nature of Joy

It is helpful to understand the nature of joy and from where it springs. What you can discover is that joy is *already a part of you* – it is one of the aspects of who you are as a Soul. You've probably already realized that Light and Love are part of your Essential Self. What you may not realize is that joy is also one of the natural, inherent aspects of your Eternal Self that can spring from your deepening experiences of yourself as Light and Love.

Since you've inhabited the Third Dimension, you have been essentially cut off from truly knowing this truth; it's part of what happened in the Fall of Consciousness. Just as, in entering the Third Dimension, you were kept from remembering your natural, eternal connection to Source, you were also cut off from your nature as an inherently joyful Being.

As a result, no matter how spiritually evolved you may be, no matter how deep your understanding of spiritual truth, you may have continued to believe that joy can only really be experienced when certain positive outer events, circumstances or relationships come into your life.

As you may have found, when you have this belief, you are always waiting for something great to happen before you can experience joy. And this waiting may go on for a long, long time, before something finally arises in your life that helps you at last to feel joyful again.

If you find yourself waiting like this, what you haven't realized – or remembered – is that true joy is not dependent on outer conditions, which come and go. Outer conditions can certainly ignite the flame of joy within you, at least for a while. But what you can learn is that joy is truly accessible at any point, no matter what conditions may be occurring in your life.

Joy is an unconditional state of being that already exists inside of you. It is always there, always present, within you. Indeed, the experience of true joy is actually an indication that you have, at least temporarily, merged with your Soul.

Creating a New Neural Pathway

So, if this is true, how can you learn to access this free, unconditional joy, no matter what is happening in your life?

One simple, but powerful, practice is to create a new neural pathway that leads effortlessly to the joy that resides eternally within your Soul. Although there are a number of ways you can create this pathway, one way is to do the following:

1. **Remember times of joy:** Take the time while in meditation every day to clearly remember times in your life when you've felt intense joy – those times when your whole being has felt as if it's expanding with light and fullness, and your spirit has soared with a sense of ecstatic freedom. Perhaps this has been accompanied by unstoppable laughter for a time. Everything felt far more than okay – it was all perfect. These experiences may be hard to remember at first, but most people have had at least some taste of this kind of joy in their life. See if you can bring these experiences clearly into your awareness and fully feel the elation you once felt as the joy again surges through both your mind and your body. You'll see that really remembering these experiences can bring the joy back fully into your being, here and now.

2. **Remember experiences of spiritual joy:** If you can remember experiences of spiritual joy that erupted during an awakening experience, this is best. But if you can't remember any time like this, it doesn't matter; just bring any experience of joy to mind and fully feel the intensity of this emotion.

3. **Pay attention to your body's response:** Be aware of how your body responds to the joy – it knows this feeling, it's familiar. You may have simply not focused on it for a while; you've allowed other less positive circumstances and emotions to dominate your awareness. In doing this, over and over again for a while, you are creating a new neural pathway that your brain will remember.

4. **Rest in your experience:** When you've summoned this joy from your memory, rest in the experience of it; feel yourself smile and your spirits lift. Feel gratitude for this gift. Your mind and body will get the message that this is what you want to focus on and experience.

5. **Call forth joy in the here and now:** After doing this process on a daily basis for a while, see if you can forget trying to summon the memory of what was

happening in past times of joy and simply call forth the experience of joy itself into the here and now.

6. **Note how quickly joy appears:** Now that you've cleared a pathway for it into your current awareness, see clearly how quickly the joy begins to appear within you. You will see that the joy has never left; it's still alive in you. You had just relegated it to the background of your mind and let it drop into your subconscious.

7. **Slip into joy even outside meditation:** Gradually, as you do this consistently, you will find that you more naturally and easily slip into this joyful feeling at any time, even outside of meditation. You begin finding delight in the smallest things in your everyday life, even a quiet sense of bliss for no reason at all. This is because you have created a new neural pathway in your brain, leading you naturally and easily to the experience of joy. And you will see that the programming that tells you that you have to wait for outer circumstances to change in order to feel joy is slowly being erased. You will know you have the power to ignite joy within you, no matter what is happening.

Creating Joy in the Quantum Field

All this said, it doesn't mean you should cease any efforts you're making to bring new positive events, circumstances or relationships into your life that will help to further ignite the joy already present within you. Of course, do anything and everything you can to experience joy. Any experience of joy will assist you greatly in raising your vibration to ascend even more quickly, with fewer back-slides into 3D consciousness.

As discussed in earlier chapters, one of the best ways to successfully manifest something new in your life is to learn about the *Quantum Field*. This field is not some rare mystical energy field that only a few advanced people can access. Actually, it's a field that is within and around you all the time; you may not be that conscious of it.

Very importantly, this field is impacted by every thought, emotion, word, and action you experience. When you hear the statement that you are "creating your own reality", realize that this field is where you are creating it. Unfortunately, most people are unaware of this and continue to create what they've created in the past over and over again with their same repetitive negative thoughts and emotions.

Another way to state this is that the Quantum Field is where the Law of Attraction takes place. Whatever you focus your thoughts on, especially when experiencing strong emotion, is what the field will create for you. Your thoughts and emotions very effectively attract the circumstances that match them. The Quantum Field deeply respects you as a Creator Being and is faithful in bringing to you what you apparently want more of, since this is what you are focusing on.

So, in clearly understanding this, you can then take the time to fully and consciously immerse yourself in the Quantum Field in the following way:

1. **Shift into your etheric body:** Shift your awareness into your etheric body, that subtle energetic aspect of yourself that pulsates inside your physical body. Feel yourself as this lighter energetic duplicate of your physical body that vibrates throughout your being and extends slightly outside yourself physically.

2. **Think thoughts and feel the joy of already having what you are desiring:** Then, once in that awareness, begin thinking thoughts and feeling emotions that will attract what you are desiring in your life. Concentrate on certain circumstances you know will uplift you. Clearly imagine your life and that it is bringing joy to you. Feel gratitude NOW for all these wonderful experiences, as if they are already happening.

Overcoming Negative Programming

These kinds of manifestation teachings are available everywhere these days, and you've certainly been aware of them. And perhaps you've already been somewhat successful in bringing in new and positive experiences in this way.

But if you haven't, you may not realize how much intention and perseverance is necessary to overcome negative, victim programming. It can become disheartening if you don't quickly get the results you're hoping for. Become aware that, although you are practicing conscious positive thoughts, you may be completely unaware of deeply-ingrained unconscious negative thoughts which might be sabotaging your desired outcomes.

Take time to meditate on this and see what unconscious opposing thoughts may be hidden within you. When you become aware of them, don't resist them, and don't immediately try to change them. Just accept them and allow them to be there. They likely have good reason to be present, due to past traumas. Feel compassion for yourself. Then, at some point, you can begin to create a new neural pathway as I've described above and attain results much more quickly.

Outer Conditions Come and Go

At the same time, it's important to remember that even if you are successful in creating new experiences which bring joy into your life, you have perhaps still attached the joy to the new conditions you've created. You've forgotten that outer conditions generally come and go. And if your joy is dependent on those positive outer conditions, then your joy also comes and goes.

Again – it's important to realize that outer circumstances don't create joy; they simply call forward what is already there within you. True joy is not dependent on these circumstances. It is a natural, innate aspect of your True Nature. You don't have to create it – simply rediscover it within you and call it forth.

So, as you continue to create a more positive future for yourself in the Quantum Field, keep this in mind: Learn to simply access joy, itself, from within yourself. Feel it for no reason at all, knowing this is YOU. And discover, in doing this, YOU will begin showing up in your life more and more.

Chapter 36

Merging with Higher Aspects of Yourself

As you give up your story of suffering and make it a practice to consciously bring light, love and joy into your life, you will be traveling into higher and higher levels of the Fourth Dimension and dipping more frequently into the Fifth. In this process, you will find you are increasingly merging with your Higher Self, the aspect of you that is assisting you on your journey Home. Merging with this Self is generally a gradual process, eventually involving experiences of actually *being* your Higher Self, rather than *having* one.

As you begin to consciously live and function as this Self, your life becomes an open-ended adventure. You feel naturally optimistic and empowered to bring about what you need and want in your life. You expect new and exciting events to occur, along with warm exchanges with people, and for your life to unfold in positive ways on all levels. And you trust you are being guided by loving forces in the Universe, and feel yourself riding a wave of flowing energy, one moment to the next.

In merging more and more with your Higher Self, you therefore increasingly experience love, empowerment, joy, and peace in your life. You become aware that suffering and lack are actually illusions, and you begin to understand the true nature of Source/Spirit.

Living Life from a New Perspective

In addition, as you begin to identify with your Higher Self, your perspective is much broader; you've stepped back and begun regarding yourself and your life from a more detached point of view. From this vantage point, you can more easily see the perfect pattern of how your life is unfolding with divine purpose, and this brings a sense of freedom and gratitude.

Anything you considered in the past to be a problem becomes more a puzzle or a mystery to solve. There's no suffering due to the situation; you're detached, rather like a scientist approaching a question to solve, with confidence you will find the answer. You trust you'll have both inner and outer guidance to assist you.

When you wake up in the morning, you don't carry yesterday's problems and personal issues into the new day. You understand that this new day has endless possibilities for creating joy and fulfillment. Throughout the day, you take note of any positive things happening and you experience gratitude for them, knowing that appreciating them keeps such experiences coming in. You may also notice synchronicities appearing in your life, indicating you're on the right track in what you are doing.

When what you were expecting or hoping for does not happen, rather than feeling defeated or irritated, you know there may be a positive reason for this unexpected result. You wait to see what occurs, understanding your future has not yet been fully created and you cannot know what surprises Spirit may have planned for you.

Indeed, perhaps the delay or canceling of an event you wanted to happen will unexpectedly benefit you in some way. Or maybe going in a different direction will help you avoid an accident or resolve a perplexing issue. Or perhaps letting go of your idea altogether will help you to meet someone who will prove important in your life. You may end up being very relieved that what you hoped would happen did not.

When you live your life as your Higher Self, you never know what delightful surprises may await you. But mainly, you are simply unattached to outcome, an attitude that brings a sense of profound liberation.

Awakening to the Soul

As amazing and freeing as the sensation of being merged with your Higher Self may be, you will eventually realize it doesn't even compare with the experience of merging with your *Soul* – the profound Essence of who you are at the core of your being. You understand that your Higher Self, as wondrous as this aspect of your being is, has simply served as a transitional bridge to your Soul. And in finally reaching your Soul, there's a thrilling sensation that you've finally arrived "Home".

Although everyone's experience of waking up to Soul is unique, one of the best descriptions may be that it's like suddenly waking up from a rather long and unpleasant dream. You immediately realize you've been asleep, dreaming, and have been believing the dream to be real. You see you've been experiencing yourself merely as a human being – a small and limited form of life, living in an imperfect and sometimes cruel world. And you are now remembering yourself as you truly are and always have been for eons of time. You may find yourself dissolving in uproarious laughter at the enormous joke of it all.

Identified with Soul, you experience an expansiveness of consciousness that goes even beyond what you discovered in merging with your Higher Self. You see that creation is never-ending, and realize it is all YOU. You are a glorious, light-filled Being of Light – and, at the same time, you are pure Consciousness that exists in all of creation. It's not just that you are *connected* to everything, something you may have experienced when merged with your Higher Self; you know, really know, you *are* everything.

You may even feel somewhat puzzled that there's a dense body/mind form that continues to follow you around. You know you're somehow connected to it and that you still have a responsibility for taking care of it, but it is not the essential YOU. It's just an extension of yourself that you as a Soul have created in order to experience the lower dimensions of reality and accomplish a mission there.

Although no longer identified with this human being self, you nonetheless feel an enormous compassion and caring for it. An incredible tenderness can arise in fully realizing all the suffering this part of you has endured in having been cut off from YOU for so very long.

In initially waking up to yourself as a Soul and merging with it, you may experience an expansion so enormous and joy-filled, you are unable for a while to function well in your daily life. You find you need to take some time alone, simply to rest and explore all the wondrous aspects of what this experience has brought to you.

This initial experience of merging with your Soul may be all it takes for you to fully assume your new 5D identity. It's all that's needed for certain individuals. However, for most people, totally merging with the Soul is a gradual process, just as it is with the Higher Self. The experience comes and goes over time, often for no apparent reason. But as you continue to ascend, the moments of merging with your Soul and functioning in 5D consciousness become more frequent.

Fully Merging with the Soul

And, as time goes on and you become more totally merged with your Soul, you are able to function well in your everyday life in a balanced, optimistic and cheerful way. People may not even realize what has happened for you, except that they notice you carry a clearer energy, a gentle neutrality and lack of emotional reaction to anything negative that may be occurring. Challenges still arise, but there is an ease with which you meet them.

In a certain way, it's as if nothing has actually changed; you go on, continuing your life as before in all outer appearances. You're still "chopping wood and carrying water". And yet, everything has changed. You are no longer identified with the limited human body or mind. You are free, living in Fifth Dimension reality.

Chapter 37

Conclusion

As you are certainly discovering, the ascension journey is extremely complex for you as an Ascension Lightworker, inviting you to meet and negotiate innumerable challenges of change, loss and uncertainty. To compound things, there is truly no knowing what lies ahead of you on your path, as you are in uncharted territory. The outer world continues in its upheaval and unpredictability. And your own personal world may be just as chaotic from time to time.

Your journey therefore demands a great deal of trust, trust that you are being guided safely through new and sometimes frightening terrain. And it involves constantly raising your vibration and stabilizing it within the higher frequencies that are flooding the Earth through these transitional times.

The material in this book makes it clear there are a great many keys you can use to lift your consciousness out of third-dimensional habits into a higher vibration. There are likely many more you are discovering on your own as you continue on your ascension journey and increasingly listen to your inner guidance.

Some Final Reminders

In conclusion, here are some final brief reminders I'd like to offer, especially when you're feeling weary of all the changes and uncertainties you may be enduring:

Be Compassionate with Yourself: Keep in mind you are in the middle of experiencing a very rapid transformational process. It is enormous: shifting so quickly from 3D to 5D, especially while still in a physical body, has never been done before. So the experiences you're having and the issues arising aren't the "normal", run-of-the-mill stuff you're used to dealing with. Acknowledge this and be gentle, patient, and compassionate with yourself.

Avoid Resistance: When challenges arise, do your best to relax into what is occurring. Don't argue with it, resist it, or try to change it right away. Don't lose yourself in the suffering, either. Just gently allow whatever is happening to be there. When you're in a mode of allowing and accepting, you are able to more clearly receive inner assistance and guidance to know how to best handle the situation and your emotional pain.

Look for the Gift: It can also be helpful to ask yourself what it is you're being invited to see or learn from the situation. Is there something you're being encouraged to release? Is there something you're running from that, if embraced, would bring you an unexpected sense of relief and well-being? Look for the gift being offered to you, as there is always one hidden within all challenging situations.

Trust, Trust and More Trust: No matter what your journey brings up for you, remember that, before you incarnated this time around, you knew full well what would be happening on Earth during your sojourn here. You fully understood and gratefully signed up for all it would probably entail. You trusted that all would fall into place as you made your way along your journey into the Fifth Dimension.

You must trust that decision you made; you must trust you are being guided every step of the way – not only by your Higher Self, but also by your guides, spiritual masters, and celestial and galactic Beings. Whether you're yet aware of them or not, they're all here with you, specifically to assist in the ascension process. You are not alone.

So again, at its core, your journey from 3D to 5D involves learning to trust whatever is occurring for you in your life, as crazy or frightening as it might be at times. It's all about learning to trust yourself, your inner guidance, and your ascension process itself.

Remembering You are a Pioneer

In addition, it's important to remember that you are a pioneer on this path into the Fifth Dimension, an Ascension Lightworker, with a specific spiritual mission to accomplish. Trust that you, along with others like yourself, do have what it takes to help to create an "Island of Light" in this world during these times of disruption, loss and uncertainty. You have brought the gifts, talents, fortitude, and wisdom to do this.

At some point, you will look back at the self you are now and smile with tenderness, compassion, and gratitude. This is a monumental challenge you've taken on. But you are a magnificent, powerful Being of Light – and soon you will fully know and experience that.

Acknowledgements

My deepest gratitude goes to Hari Meyers, who so graciously offered to edit this book at a time when I was not feeling very enthusiastic or confident about what I had written. He was both rapid in his work and minutely-detailed with his suggestions, and I learned much from him.

I also extend my gratitude and love to my daughter, who originally came up with the idea for this book, even before I did. Her enthusiasm for it and belief in its importance continued throughout my entire process of writing it.

In addition, I wish to acknowledge that much of what I've written here I have learned from my clients over the years, most of whom have been heart-warmingly sincere and conscientious in doing their inner work of healing and awakening. And some of my ideas have also come from a number of friends – some therapists and healers, themselves – who have found their own solutions for assisting people through these times of rapid transformation on the planet.

About the Author

Vidya Frazier has studied spiritual teachings from both western and eastern traditions for over 45 years. In 1993, she felt called to India to visit the spiritual master Papaji. Upon returning, she wrote *The Art of Letting Go: A Pathway to Inner Freedom* and began offering individual sessions, groups and workshops based on this book.

In 2007, she was invited to attend the Oneness University in India and was initiated as a Oneness Blessing Facilitator. She returned and offered the blessing to hundreds of people. Since then, she has studied with quantum healer Dell Morris and author Jim Self.

In 2014, Vidya published her first book on the theme of Ascension, *Awakening to the Fifth Dimension—A Guide for Navigating the Global Shift* and has given a number of presentations and interviews on the subject. A year later, she published a second book, a more in-depth exploration on the same theme: *Ascension: Embracing the Transformation.* In 2017, she published a third book describing the Ascension process occurring on the global scale, entitled, *Triumph of the Light.*

Currently offering sessions of Ascension counseling and Quantum Healing, Vidya assists people to find their way with clarity and ease through the powerful energies of the Shift of consciousness that is now occurring across the planet. She also assists people in discovering their spiritual purpose in life and stepping more fully into expressing it.

Drawing on forty-five years as a licensed psychotherapist, hypnotherapist, and spiritual guide, as well as on her own spiritual awakening experiences, Vidya serves as a unique bridge between the worlds of psychology and spiritual awakening.

Contact Vidya at **www.vidyafrazier.com**.